BUDGETARY CONTROL AND COST REDUCTION
FOR RETAIL COMPANIES

Budgetary Control and Cost Reduction for Retail Companies

by

D. T. WELCH
M.A., F.C.I.S., F.S.S.

MACDONALD AND EVANS LTD

8 John Street, London, W.C.1

1969

First published March 1969

MACDONALD AND EVANS LTD

1969

S.B.N.: 7121 0213 2

A/658.154

Printed in Great Britain by
Billing & Sons Limited, Guildford and London

PREFACE

Countless books have been written about budgetary control for business organisations and every facet of the subject would seem to have been fully examined. The reader might therefore ask why anyone should wish to write yet another book on a topic so well covered. My excuse is threefold.

First, most books on budgetary control concentrate on manufacturing industry. This book specifically deals with the technique from the view point of retail companies, an area in which writers on budgeting and cost control have been surprisingly inactive. It tries to set out a coherent body of knowledge and expertise which particularly caters for the special problems of retail companies, from the smallest to the largest organisations.

Second, this book is a *practical* guide. Without exception the methods of forecasting, cost analysis and financial control described below have been tried and tested in practice. They do actually work, and properly applied bring significant increases in profitability. (Necessarily, of course, the figures used for illustrative purposes in charts and tables are hypothetical, unless otherwise indicated.)

Third, as well as being too theoretical, many books on budgetary control seem to place too little emphasis on cost *reduction*. Making up a budget for expenses is useful but is only half of the story. More relevant to profitability is the critical examination of all expenses, which alone leads to higher standards of efficiency. In no other trade than retailing can this be more important, when one considers the pressures of taxation and competition to which retailing has been subjected over the last few years.

It is my belief that retailing under these pressures is moving into a new dimension of management sophistication. I hope that this book may make a small contribution to that process.

I should like to thank the Directors of Dixons Photographic Ltd for permission to reproduce the form shown in Table XXXVIII and to illustrate examples from other practices of control in use by that company. I am also grateful to the British Radio Equipment Manufacturers' Association for allowing me to quote from their statistics of television set production. I should like to thank Miss Anne Frost, Miss Pamela Wilson and Mrs. Roberta Plaskow for typing my manuscript, and my wife for her patient co-operation.

December 1968   D. T. W.

CONTENTS

LIST OF ILLUSTRATIONS

A*   ix

LIST OF TABLES

CHAPTER I

INTRODUCTION

Changes in the Retail Trade

It would be an exaggeration to say that a "revolution" in retailing has taken place over the past decade. The essential function of retailing, the reselling of bulk production in small quantities to satisfy local demand, has and always will be the same. But it would be equally far from the truth to deny that very significant changes in the economic structure of retail business have occurred, which are increasingly affecting profitability in most areas of the trade. Of these changes three stand out as being especially important; the development of supermarkets and self-service stores; the break-down of resale price maintenance; and the imposition of the selective employment tax.

Each of the three changes listed above has had a profound effect on some or all sections of the retail trade and has necessitated a reappraisal of management attitudes. But the emphasis has in each case been somewhat different. The development of supermarkets and self-service stores has been prompted from the desire to reduce wage costs per pound of turnover and to expand the range of merchandise offered. This increases profitability, but it also involves heavy capital outlay, which must be justified in terms of an improved (or at least maintained) return on capital employed. Otherwise the long-term interests of shareholders are jeopardised. The development of "capital-intensive" retailing has therefore demanded a more sophisticated approach to capital investment decisions than that to which the retail trade has been traditionally accustomed. Larger amounts of money must be committed for longer periods: likely returns must be that much more carefully evaluated.

The break-down of resale price maintenance, which was already beginning before the passing of the 1964 Act and is now accelerating fast, has shown the need for strengthening another area in the financial and management control functions of many retail companies: product costing, selling price policy and control of margins. Under the maintained price system the retailer earned his net profit margin by keeping his selling expenses as low as possible and reducing his buying price by increasing sales volume. This had a restraining effect on expenses, but relieved the retailer of the responsibility of calculating what selling prices *ought* to be under free-price conditions. Consequently, the processes of absorbing over-head expenses by product, distinguishing between fixed and variable expenses, analysing margins, etc., which are so essential to correct price policy in manufacturing industry, are only just beginning to be introduced in the retail trade.

The third and most recent development to affect the economic structure of retail business has been the imposition of the selective employment tax. Designed to shift labour away from service and distributive trades, it has so far only had the effect of increasing operating costs. But it has forced retail companies to examine critically all expenses levels, especially wage costs, and has re-emphasised the need for tight control of expenses by means of task-setting budgets. Its long-term effect must be to stimulate further the growth of self-service retailing and to extend this practice into sectors of the trade so far untouched.

Modern Management Techniques

It will be seen, therefore, that each of these developments makes substantial demands on the technical competence of retailing management. To the determined, forward-looking retailer each holds the prospect of defeating less able competition and enlarging the market-share, so giving greater profitability and a higher return on capital employed. This cannot be achieved, however, without effective commercial and financial control. Management must have the right information at the right time if profitable decisions are to be taken.

The aim of this book is to show how retail companies of all sizes and types can equip themselves with the techniques essential for full managerial control: forecasting, budgeting and cost analysis. Worked examples and charts have been extensively used in the following chapters because this is above all a practical book, written from experience. The methods described have been tried, tested and proved in practice. It is hoped that they will be found useful not only to those in financial departments, but also to directors and executives in general management.

The contents of this book divide roughly into two parts. The first—Chapters 2 to 8—covers the whole scope of budgetary control from sales, stock and expense budgets through to summarised trading budget, capital expenditure and cash budgets. Emphasis is placed throughout on adequate, accurate and timely reporting, because so many business failures can be traced to management's unawareness of the true trading position. Effective budgetary control guards against such unawareness. The second part—Chapters 9 to 13—

deals with three subjects of special relevance to retail companies in present-day conditions: the formulation of correct selling price policy, methods of reducing costs (particularly wage costs) and the use of computers, either by purchase or on a bureau basis. By making price and cost consciousness part of management's "philosophy," budgetary control becomes doubly effective. Not only are standards set up, which are a form of control in themselves, but those standards are constantly reviewed to bring them to a higher level of efficiency. Likewise the successful application of electronic data processing (E.D.P.) greatly increases a company's competitive ability by giving management faster and more selective control information.

A brief word must be said in this introduction about the installation of budgetary control. No company, big or small, need fear that setting up an effective budgetary control system will be prohibitively expensive. Provided that there is an efficient financial department the installation of budgetary control is virtually completed once the "historical" accounting system is adapted to produce the required control information. The definition of logical cost-centres, merchandise groups and expense categories, which will be mutually convenient for both historical and budgetary accounting, is largely determined by the company's particular trade. Monthly accounting is a *sine qua non*, because without it reports on variances of actual from planned results are usually too late to be effectively acted upon.

As to the qualities of the budget manager or controller, he should obviously have a strong background of accounting principles and practice. But since his work is very much concerned with numerical analysis he should also have a grasp of elementary statistical methods. Perhaps the most necessary quality, in view of his function as an adviser on commercial policy, is a sound understanding of business economics, not from a theoretical standpoint, but from a practical, empirical point of view.

Finally, it must be stressed that no matter how good the accounting system or how able the budget manager, budgetary control will be largely vitiated unless it has the active participation of management. This means that departmental managers and directors must be personally involved in the construction of budgets (to see that proper task-setting elements are introduced) and in the comparison of actual with forecast results (to see that variances are fully and quickly explained, and corrective action taken). Budgetary control then becomes not just an accounting exercise, but a technique of management which cannot fail to increase efficiency and profitability.

CHAPTER 2

THE SALES FORECAST USING COMPANY RECORDS

Introduction

Of all the estimates used to control the activities of a company none is more important than the sales forecast. This is because it sets the level of business which the management foresees in the coming year or period. It is, therefore, the most critical forecast since nearly all other budgets stem from it: buying, cash flow, expenses and so on. Indeed, where actual sales begin to differ by more than acceptable limits from the forecast, it is better to scrap the original budget in its entirety and make a fresh one, since the interrelated estimates of cash, expenses and stock movement which link to the sales forecast will prove more dangerous than helpful. It is also the most difficult budget to make up, because it is influenced by a great number of factors, many of which are incapable of numerical evaluation. Intuition as well as experience plays a part in the construction of a realistic and useful sales forecast. So does a knowledge of current affairs and economics, particularly the state of one's own trade, its growth prospects and likely technological developments.

Fortunately, a critical examination of one's own company's historical sales data will by itself prove a most useful (and sometimes surprisingly accurate) guide to the future. Here, one is, or should be, on reasonably firm ground. This chapter deals with the statistical methods used in making this internal analysis; the next chapter discusses those external influences which can modify the forecast.

Comparability of Statistics

Before going on to develop the statistical methods which can be used to interpret sales data, it is as well to say a word about comparability of statistics.

If meaningful inferences are to be drawn from statistics, the figures used must be comparable. For example, we must be careful not to let exceptional and non-recurring events distort our interpretation of sales statistics. Two retail outlets may be close together in the same town, and if one is closed for repair, trade will be diverted to its neighbour. This shop may show exceptional sales for several weeks, but when we prepare its forecast for a subsequent period we should, of course, eliminate what we consider to be the exceptional element. This must be done by making appropriate notes in the sales records, otherwise such information tends to be forgotten. The effect of local bargain sales, enlargement of premises or selling areas in branches and, indeed, new shop management must also be considered.

At the company, rather than branch level, the differing number of Saturdays must be taken in account when comparing sales of the same month in different years. Saturday may produce a third or more of a week's turnover and whether last October had five Saturdays and this October only four is a material factor in forecasting. Difficulties caused by months of differing length are overcome by using a thirteen four-weekly calendar, rather than a twelve-monthly one, and this practice is strongly to be recommended, particularly in the retail trade. A similar problem occurs when Bank holidays fall in different weeks and months during consecutive years. Retail sales usually rise before Bank Holidays, and this makes comparisons between the same weeks and months in some years impossible. Methods are available for adjusting sales to remove the effect of Bank holidays and thus make inter-year comparisons possible, but they are time-consuming and require a considerable degree of statistical skill. The best method is to make appropriate notes in the sales records of movable Bank holidays.

Having made sure that the company's sales statistics are, as far as possible, comparable between years (or where they are not, that explanatory notes are made) it is now possible to study the data with a view to detecting the emergence of trends. This is the main purpose of sales forecasting: to see whether a trend in sales for a particular commodity or in a particular branch or company is appearing, and, if so, whether it is likely to continue during the period of the forecast. Numerous statistical methods are available for this purpose, some simple, some highly complex and mathematically involved. In this chapter, we will consider some of the well-tried techniques which have been developed, and which require only a grasp of elementary mathematics. Of these, the *moving annual total* is the simplest and most widely used in trend-seeking.

The Moving Annual Total

Nearly all retail businesses are subject to seasonality. That is to say, sales rise and fall during the year according to demand for the company's products and in a reasonably set pattern. In some trades the seasonal pattern is extreme, as in photographic goods, and in others it is less extreme, as in food retailing. The purpose of computing the moving annual total of sales (or M.A.T. as it is usually abbreviated) is to eliminate the seasonal element in sales and show the true upward or downward trend. For it will be clear that if we are considering a full year's sales all the time we are including the whole range of peaks and troughs which occur throughout the year, and the moving annual total will represent only the rising or falling trend.

TABLE I. BRANCH MONTHLY SALES AND MOVING ANNUAL TOTALS

	1965		1966		1967	
	Month	M.A.T.	Month	M.A.T.	Month	M.A.T.
	£	£	£	£	£	£
Jan.	6,428		11,504	194,759	14,639	247,988
Feb.	7,992		15,744	202,511	18,000	250,244
March	14,904		18,450	206,057	22,200	253,994
April	11,130		18,631	213,558	19,200	254,563
May	19,443		26,131	220,246	28,466	256,898
June	22,405		24,116	221,957	28,530	261,312
July	23,935		31,476	229,498	36,764	266,600
Aug.	20,775		26,398	235,121	31,826	272,028
Sept.	16,654		17,577	236,044	21,648	276,099
Oct.	11,890		14,865	239,019	20,727	281,961
Nov.	10,098		16,160	245,081	20,048	285,849
Dec.	24,029	189,683	23,801	244,853	31,628	293,676
Total £	189,683	—	244,853	—	293,676	—

Table I shows the sales history for three years of a large branch in a company selling consumer durables and having a high summer turnover. (In this and other similar examples, which purport to describe real situations, for reasons of confidence the figures shown are hypothetical but the relationships between them are based on actual data.) The same information is plotted graphically in Fig. 1. It is clear from the table that there is a marked upward trend in sales, but it is not easy from the monthly figures to determine the approximate annual rate of growth, which is the starting-point for a forward projection. The M.A.T. gives this information.

The computation of the M.A.T. is extremely simple. When the first year's sales have been recorded and totalled (as for 1965 in Table I) it is then only a question of picking up the new month and dropping the corresponding month in the previous year, so giving the new M.A.T. Thus the M.A.T. for January 1963 is the total for 1965 (£189,683) plus January 1966 (£11,504) less January 1965

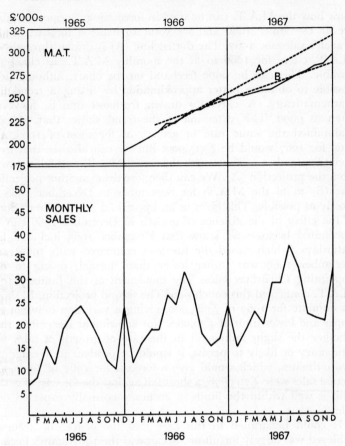

Fig. 1. Branch Sales Statistics (data from Table I).

(£6,428) which gives £194,759. This is much easier than adding up a full year's sales at the end of each month, which is the alternative method of computation. A check on the arithmetical accuracy of the first method is automatically provided at the end of each year when the M.A.T. should equal the total of the twelve individual months.

A glance at the M.A.T.s for 1966 and 1967 shows the constantly rising trend in sales. A clearer visual impression is obtained however by plotting the M.A.T.s on the same graph as the monthly figures but necessarily, of course, on a different scale. This is shown in Fig. 1, where a horizontal line separates the two scales. The steady upward trend in sales during most of 1966 was followed by a period of less rapid growth up to May 1967. This again was followed by a period of increased growth up to December 1967. The dotted lines show how the M.A.T. can be used in forecasting. Suppose that we are at December 1966 and we want to make a forecast of this branch's sales for 1967. The dotted line (A) is drawn through the M.A.T. curve for 1966 to fit the monthly M.A.T.s as closely as possible. This can be done freehand on the chart, although it is possible to obtain a better approximation by fitting a trend line mathematically. A carefully drawn freehand line is, however, often as good. This extension of the trend shows that, if sales maintained the same rate of growth as for most of 1966, the total for 1967 would be £315,000. But we can also see that from about September 1966 onwards the actual M.A.T. was falling away from the projection (A). We can therefore draw another projection line (B) to fit the M.A.Ts for September to December 1966 as closely as possible. This gives us an upper and a lower limit. Some of the effect of the absence of growth in December 1966 can be discounted because we know that December 1965 included five Saturdays (which raised the turnover compared with 1966) and December 1966 was rather lower than normal, owing to disappointing Christmas sales. The movement of the January 1967 M.A.T. confirmed this conclusion. The second projection, B, shows an estimate for 1967 of £285,000, giving a variation between the upper and lower limit of £30,000. Not knowing at December 1966 whether the slight falling off in the rate of growth of sales was temporary or likely to persist, it would be prudent to average the two estimates, which would give a forecast for 1967 of £300,000. Actual sales were £293,676, a short fall against the forecast of 2·1%. This is well within the limits of accuracy normally expected of a sales forecast.

It could be argued in this case that the degree of accuracy achieved was largely fortuitous, because as the 1967 figures became available they showed a trend lower than the lower projection B, and it was only the increased rate of growth from May 1967 onwards that brought the annual total above £285,000. This is partly true, and it would certainly have been prudent at May 1967 to have revised the forecast downwards to say £275,000, if an interim estimate had been called for. On the other hand, forecasts must be made, if businessmen are to act rationally, and they must be made in the light of all available and relevant facts and figures, of which the M.A.T. is one of the most useful.

However, by itself the M.A.T. is not enough. Other questions have to be asked and answered before the forecast can be said to be balanced and realistic. Imagining again that we are at December 1966 in our illustration, and we must make a forecast for 1967 of the branch's sales, these are the sort of questions we would ask. Is the slowing-down in the rate of growth from September 1966 onwards due to increased local competition—a new store just down the road? In this case, no. Is it due to a change of shop-management, resulting in lower sales aggressiveness? No. Is it typical of the sales experience at most of the company's other branches? No. Is our industry approaching a period of recession? No; it is, and has been for some years, one of the country's fastest growing industries and the rate of growth shows no sign of levelling off. Is the whole economy losing impetus and restricting the spending of money on consumer goods? This is less easy to answer, but the natural buoyancy of our own trade should persist through any slight national deflationary tendencies, and the answer on the whole is no.

By asking these sorts of questions in this sort of way, that is, by going from the particular and absolutely factual to the general and more abstract, we can modify the results of extending forward the M.A.T. In this case, we are led to the conclusion that the signs of slackening growth do not at this point justify a significant downward revision to the lower sales estimate (projection B on the graph) and that all other indications suggest that any present slackening is likely to be temporary rather than permanent. This conclusion, in fact, was largely borne out by subsequent events.

Many other factors would in practice be considered before the branch forecast was finalised and integrated into the overall company sales budget, *e.g.* the company's price policy, particularly if lower turnover and higher prices are likely to yield better profits than the converse; the supply and quality of merchandise and its promotion through national and local advertising and effective display media; the availability of suitable sales staff and shop managers; projected street alterations and traffic arrangements; planned refittings and resitings of branches, and so on.

Other Moving Totals and Averages

Sometimes the sales statistics we are attempting to "smooth" show patterns other than the one we have just considered: namely, a regular pattern over a rising trend. Table II shows the monthly sales data of another retail shop, over a period of six years. The same data are plotted graphically in Fig. 2. What is immediately clear both from the figures and the graph is the biennial cycle of sales superimposed on an annual seasonal pattern of high summer and Christmas turnover. Each good year is followed by a less good one, but the seasonal pattern within each year is roughly the same. In this case, the moving annual total would smooth out the annual seasonal cycle but it would not remove the two-year cycle. The M.A.T. would rise and fall roughly on a wave movement.

If, however, we use a two-year moving total, we will smooth out

TABLE II. BRANCH MONTHLY SALES AND MOVING TWO-YEAR TOTALS

	1962		1963		1964		1965		1966		1967	
	Month	Moving two-year total	Month	Moving two-year total	Month	Moving two-year total	Month	Moving two-year total	Month	Moving two-year total	Month	Moving two-year total
	£	£	£	£	£	£	£	£	£	£	£	£
Jan.	4,059		2,380		4,303	155,887	2,605	158,290	2,852	156,099	2,281	152,713
Feb.	6,000		3,964		7,700	157,587	5,100	159,426	4,446	152,845	3,426	151,039
March	5,800		3,428		6,500	158,287	4,700	160,698	6,026	152,371	3,402	149,741
April	6,100		4,080		7,000	159,187	5,200	161,818	5,449	150,820	4,386	148,927
May	8,254		7,502		9,373	160,306	6,501	160,817	9,271	150,718	4,988	147,414
June	9,431		6,914		8,519	159,394	6,147	160,050	11,714	153,913	5,997	147,264
July	9,408		9,117		11,075	161,061	7,317	158,250	10,674	153,512	6,755	146,702
Aug.	10,539		7,367		9,423	159,945	6,654	157,537	9,468	153,557	6,394	146,442
Sept.	7,175		4,856		6,209	158,979	5,164	157,845	8,204	155,552	4,828	146,106
Oct.	5,918		3,400		5,448	158,509	5,861	160,306	5,388	155,492	3,408	143,653
Nov.	5,694		4,108		7,178	159,993	3,582	159,780	5,100	153,414	4,661	144,732
Dec.	11,245		8,904		9,317	158,065	6,674	157,550	8,940	153,037	5,944	144,002
Total £	89,623		66,020		92,045		65,505		87,532		56,470	

both cycles, because we will always be including a low and a high year, each with a roughly constant annual pattern. Indeed, it can be stated as a principle that we use a moving total that covers the period of the cycle. The two-year moving totals from Table II are plotted in Fig. 2. The curve is by no means smooth, for two reasons. Firstly, there is a good deal of random movement in the sales: the summer of 1966 showed particularly good figures, which account for the hump in the moving two-year total in the later months of 1966. Secondly, the curve has been plotted on a comparatively large scale which magnifies the fluctuations in the two-year totals.

The latter drawback can be overcome by computing the moving two-year *average* rather than the *total*. This is simply a matter of dividing each moving two-year total by twenty-four, to give an

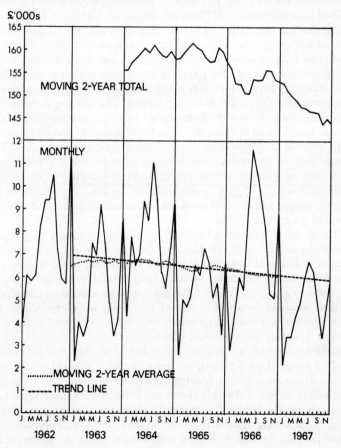

Fig. 2. Branch Sales Statistics (data from Table II).

average monthly figure. An M.A.T. is converted to a moving annual *average* by dividing by twelve, and so on. The use of an average has the additional advantage that it can be plotted within the monthly data, as in Fig. 2, thus dispensing with another scale and also enabling monthly deviations from the trend to be readily seen. To do this it is, of course, necessary to "centre" the average in the period covered. This means that the average for the two years January 1962 to December 1963 (£6,496) is centred at December 1962, because this is half-way in the two-year period. It can be seen that this shifts back the moving two-year average one whole year behind the moving two-year total.

The moving average can now be used for forecasting rather more easily than the moving total, since the fluctuations are so much dampened down. This is certainly true until experience has been gained in drawing lines of "best fit" freehand. Then, the larger scale of the moving total allows a greater degree of accuracy and is therefore an advantage. Assuming in Fig. 2 that we are at December 1966 and must make a sales forecast for 1967, we can draw a trend line to fit the moving averages for 1963, 1964 and 1965 as closely as possible. The moving average for 1966 is not available, of course, since it is computed from the 1966 and 1967 figures. The moving averages for 1964 and 1965 show a declining trend in sales, and we project this forward in our line of "best fit." The trend line crosses the December 1965 vertical at £6,300 and the December 1967 one at £5,800. This means that we expect average monthly sales for the two years 1966 and 1967 of £6,050, giving £145,200 in total. But we know that 1966 sales were £87,532, so our estimate for 1967 is £57,700 to the nearest round hundred. Actual sales turned out to be £56,470, an error of £1,230 or 2·1%.

There is, it will be admitted, nothing particularly impressive about the accuracy of this forecast, because even a cursory examination of Table II suggests that, if the alternating cycle of good and less good years continues, sales in 1967 should be in the order of £50,000 to £65,000. All we have done is to introduce an element of critical analysis into our study of the data, so as to show the emergence of a trend and moreover one that can be used to produce a more accurate forecast than without it.

Before we go on to consider the refinements that can be used to project trend lines forward, we may consider one other example which draws on a rather greater degree of statistical skill than that demanded so far. Table III shows the branch sales in another type of retail trade. When the monthly data are plotted graphically (Fig. 3) a strong quarterly cycle of sales appears. Following the principle that we take a moving total which covers the period of the cycle, we compute the moving three-monthly total, and this too is shown in Fig. 3. Also, for comparison purposes, we compute the M.A.T., which is again plotted in Fig. 3.

The computation of the moving three-monthly total, which attempts to smooth out the quarterly sales pattern, yields rather disappointing results, since the random element in the data is obviously pronounced. This is reflected in the uneven curve which appears when the three-monthly total is plotted. But it must be remembered that it covers a very short period and, unless sales follow a very constant pattern year by year, it will necessarily show marked fluctuations. The M.A.T., covering four times the period, dampens down these fluctuations. So, in order to facilitate trend fitting, we have plotted the three-monthly moving average as well.

TABLE III. BRANCH MONTHLY SALES AND MOVING THREE-MONTHLY TOTALS

	1965		1966			1967		
	Month	Moving three-monthly total	Month	Moving three-monthly total	M.A.T.	Month	Moving three-monthly total	M.A.T.
	£	£	£	£	£	£	£	£
Jan.	1,557		1,285	8,362	37,391	1,332	7,225	29,998
Feb.	1,346		1,292	7,740	37,337	1,476	6,666	30,182
March	5,354	8,257	4,014	6,591	35,997	3,541	6,349	29,709
April	2,283	8,983	1,728	7,034	35,442	1,691	6,708	29,672
May	1,110	8,747	1,462	7,204	35,794	1,465	6,697	29,675
June	4,179	7,572	4,391	7,581	36,006	3,040	6,196	28,324
July	3,875	9,164	2,498	8,351	34,629	2,380	6,885	28,206
Aug.	2,747	10,801	1,704	8,593	33,586	1,410	6,830	27,912
Sept.	4,313	10,935	2,787	6,989	32,060	3,202	6,992	28,327
Oct.	3.822	10,882	2,867	7,358	31,105	2,637	7,249	28,097
Nov.	1,914	10,049	2,065	7,719	31,256	1,519	7,358	27,551
Dec.	5,163	10,899	3,858	8,790	29,951	2,612	6,768	26,305
Total	37,663		29,951			26,305		

The question now is whether, for trend-seeking purposes, we should use the M.A.T. or the three-monthly moving average. Assuming that we are at December 1966 and must make a forecast for 1967, we can draw a line of best fit through both curves. These are shown in Fig. 3. The extension of the M.A.T. shows a forecast for 1967 of £23,500. The extension of the three-monthly average trend line crosses the December 1966 vertical at £2,400 and the December 1967 vertical at £2,000, giving estimated average monthly sales of £2,200, or £26,400 in total. Actual sales in 1967 were £26,305, so that it can be seen that the three-monthly average gives a better forecast than the M.A.T. This is because the M.A.T., covering a longer period, discounts the effect of the less rapid decline in sales which was appearing in the later months of 1966, whilst the three-monthly average, being of shorter duration, is more sensitive

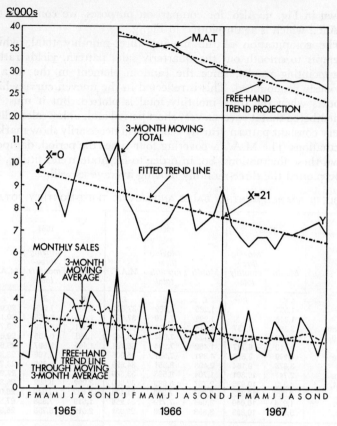

Fig. 3. Branch Sales Statistics (data from Table III).

and picks up this trend more quickly. The choice of the best moving total or average is, therefore, not always easy, but clearly careful selection of method will repay the time and analysis involved by enabling a more accurate forecast to be made.

Fitted Trend Lines

So far, we have projected trend lines forward freehand. As already stated, this can often give just as good results as fitting a trend line mathematically. But it must be realised that situations do sometimes occur when the freehand line is inadequate to the degree of accuracy required, and this is why a knowledge of the simpler methods of fitting trend lines statistically can be considered to be essential to anyone who wishes to take sales forecasting seriously.

In this section we describe only the fitting of a straight-line trend because this is the least difficult computationally. Reliable books on business statistics will give interested readers examples of how trend lines can be fitted to curves, *i.e.* to sales data that show a *varying* rate of growth, rather than a *fixed amount* , which is depicted by a straight-line trend. But it must be stressed again that, whatever the circumstances are, the extension of trend lines by mathematical methods should be done with the greatest degree of circumspection. We are, in fact, reading into the data a "law" of growth or decline, and the projection of this law into the future may not be justified, either because outside factors tell us that the trend observed is merely accidental or because the period we are covering is too short to defend confident extrapolation. It is more important to know *why* a trend in sales is appearing rather than the precise quantitative rate of growth or decline. But having satisfied ourselves from all points of view that the projection will give as good an estimate as possible, we can then go on to fit a trend line with confidence and an easy conscience.

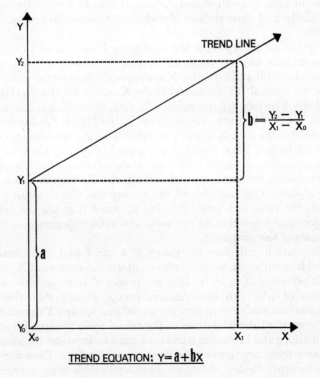

Fig. 4. Graphical expression of a straight-line equation.

Deriving a straight-line trend entails finding the values of the terms a and b in an equation of the form:

$$Y = a + bX.$$

This becomes clearer if we look at Fig. 4. The value a shows how far the trend line starts up the Y scale. The value b shows the *degree of slope* of the trend line. Clearly for any given value of $X_1 - X_0$, the larger $Y_2 - Y_1$ is, the greater will be the steepness of the slope, and thus the term b precisely measures the amount of growth. It can also be seen that if b is positive the trend shows an increase in growth, whilst if b is negative the trend shows a decrease in growth. Thus, by computing the value of these two terms a and b, we can determine the shape of any straight-line trend in any position on our sales graphs.

To illustrate the procedure involved in fitting a straight-line trend, we return to the example in Table III and Fig. 3 (*see* p. 14). The three-month moving totals plotted on the graph showed considerable fluctuation and to fit a trend line to this data freehand would be a difficult task. We will show how easy it is to fit a trend line mathematically and thus remove the chance element in freehand projection.

First of all we represent the months in Table III and the related three-month moving totals as X and Y respectively. It will be remembered that, in graphs, X is always the horizontal scale, whilst Y is the vertical. This means that the X-values are the *time* intervals and the Y-values are the *actual sales data*, or moving totals or averages. Table IV shows the data of Table III in this fashion. For simplicity, the first X-value is 0, against which we have a Y-value of 8·3 (the first three-month moving total of £8,257 rounded to the nearest hundred pounds, for ease of calculation). Each successive three-month moving total is shown against the next X-value, up to twenty-one. This includes all the twenty-two three-month moving totals for 1965 and 1966, it being assumed that we are going to project our trend line on the 1965 and 1966 experience to make a forecast of sales for 1967.

In order to calculate the values of a and b and thus obtain our trend line equation, we must also compute the squares of X, and the multiplication of X by Y. It is not proposed to go into the mathematics of why this is necessary, except to say that these two calculations enable us to find the line of *least squares*. This means that the sum of all the deviations of the actual from the trend line sales, both above and below the trend line, must be less than the sum of the squares from any other conceivable straight line. Thus our trend line becomes the line of best fit. The calculations of the squares of X can be found in any book of statistical tables, but the multiplication of X by Y must, of course, be done on a calculating machine or slide rule.

Having added up each of the four columns of figures in Table IV it is now possible to find the values of a and b by solving the following pair of simultaneous equations:

(1) Sum of Y $= Na + $(Sum of X)$b$
(2) Sum of XY $= $(Sum of X)$a + $(Sum of X²)$b$.

The summation sign is conventionally written as the Greek capital letter *sigma* (Σ) and this is how it is shown in Table IV. The value N is the number of X-values, which in our example is 22 (0 to 21 inclusive). When the two equations are set one above the other, it is possible to multiply one or other by a factor in order to be able to subtract them and thus determine the value for a or b. In the example in Table IV, multiplying the terms of equation 1 by 10·5 enables us to find the value of b, which is *minus* 0·096. This means that the

TABLE IV. COMPUTATION OF FITTED STRAIGHT-LINE TREND (data from Table III)

X	Y	X²	XY
0	8·3	0	0
1	9·0	1	9·0
2	8·7	4	17·4
3	7·6	9	22·8
4	9·2	16	36·8
5	10·8	25	54·0
6	10·9	36	65·4
7	10·9	49	76·3
8	10·0	64	80·0
9	10·9	81	98·1
10	8·4	100	84·0
11	7·7	121	84·7
12	6·6	144	79·2
13	7·0	169	91·0
14	7·2	196	100·8
15	7·6	225	114·0
16	8·4	256	134·4
17	8·6	289	146·2
18	7·0	324	126·0
19	7·4	361	140·6
20	7·7	400	154·0
21	8·8	441	184·8
231	188·7	3,311	1,899·5

(1) $\Sigma Y = Na + \Sigma Xb$
(2) $\Sigma XY = \Sigma Xa + \Sigma X^2b$
(1) 189 $= 22a + 231b$ (rounded)
(2) 1899 $= 231a + 3,311b$ (rounded)

Multiplying (1) × 10·5

$$1,984 = 231a + 2,425b$$

Subtracting $\quad \dfrac{1,899 = 231a + 3,311b}{85 = \qquad -886b}$

$$b = -0·096$$

Substituting b in (1) 189 $= 22a - 22$

$$a = 9·6$$

∴ Trend equation is Y $= 9·6 - 0·096$X
At March 1965 when X $= 0$, Y $= 9·6$
At Dec. 1966 when X $= 21$, Y $= 7·6$
At Dec. 1967 when X $= 33$, Y $= 6·4$
Average of three-month moving totals for 1967 $= 7·0$
∴ Sales estimate for 1967 $= £28,000$.

slope of the trend is downwards from left to right, which is what we expect. Having determined the value of b, we can now substitute it into either equation and thus derive the value of a, which in our example is 9·6. The trend equation thus is:

$$Y = 9·6 - 0·096X.$$

As the equation is of a straight line, we need only determine two values of X and Y on the graph to enable us to read off all other values of the trend line along its entire length, by connecting the two points. Thus when X=o, at March 1965, Y=9·6, and we can mark this point on the three-month moving graph in Fig. 3. Taking the other extreme value, when X=21, at December 1966, Y = 7·6 (9·6 less 2·0 approximately). We mark this point also on the graph and join the two, so giving us our trend line of best fit.

When this line is projected forward, it cuts the December 1967 vertical at 6·4, giving an average *three-month* total for 1967 of 7·0. The estimated sales for 1967 are, therefore:

$$\frac{12 \times 7·0}{3} = 28·0 = £28,000.$$

This compares with actual sales of £26,305 for 1967. Our freehand projection through the moving three-month *averages* gave a forecast of £27,400, so in fact it was rather more accurate than the fitted trend line. This was accidental, of course, and does not detract from the fitted line. Rather it shows the value of computing the fitted line, because, had the freehand line been absolutely accurate, it would have given the same forecast, and it was luck rather than good judgment which made the freehand line more accurate in the event.

TABLE V. ANNUAL SALES OF A RETAIL CHAIN

Year	Sales £ (nearest 000)
1955	30,000
1956	37,000
1957	36,000
1958	44,000
1959	40,000
1960	54,000
1961	52,000
1962	78,000
1963	70,000
1964	72,000
1965	92,000
1966	123,000
1967	114,000

Although we intend in this chapter to confine our examination of fitted trend lines to straight-line trends, we must mention the use of logarithms, since they sometimes enable the straight-line method to describe a trend which appears to have a *varying* rate of growth. Table V gives the sales statistics of a retail chain over a period of thirteen years. When plotted graphically, as in Fig. 5, the annual sales oscillate around a reasonably smooth curve, shown by the

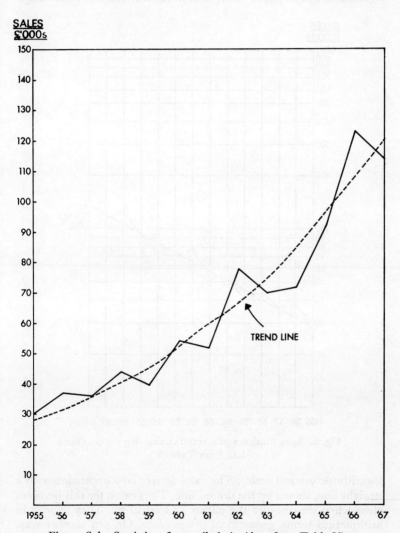

Fig. 5. Sales Statistics of a retail chain (data from Table V).

dotted line. This "trend" line appears to fit the data quite well. It is obvious that the upward trend of sales, year by year, has been at an increasing rate, rather than at a constant rate, and this is why a straight-line trend will not fit.

When sales or other statistics show a changing rate of growth or decline it is worth plotting them on semi-logarithmic graph paper. This is done for the sales of the retail chain in Fig. 6 (semi-logarithmic graph paper has a conventional horizontal scale, but a

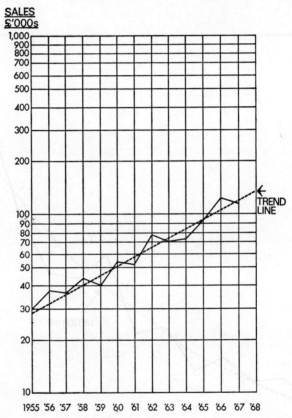

Fig. 6. Sales Statistics of a retail chain—log vertical scale
(data from Table V).

logarithmic vertical scale). The sales figures now approximate to a straight line, shown by the dotted line. The reason for this becomes clear when we consider the nature of logarithms. They express in arithmetical terms, geometrical progressions. Or, put another way, they show relative increases or decreases in the form of absolute changes. For most purposes, we use logarithms which are said to have a base of ten. This means that the

$$\log \text{ of } \quad 1 = 0 \text{ (because } 10^0 = 1)$$
$$\log \text{ of } \quad 10 = 1 \text{ (because } 10^1 = 10)$$
$$\log \text{ of } \quad 100 = 2 \text{ (because } 10^2 = 100)$$
$$\log \text{ of } \quad 1,000 = 3 \text{ (because } 10^3 = 1,000)$$
$$\log \text{ of } 10,000 = 4 \text{ (because } 10^4 = 10,000)$$

etc.

The equation of two identical *ratios*, such as

$$\frac{10}{1} = \frac{10,000}{1,000}$$

can be expressed *absolutely* in logarithmic terms as

$$1 - 0 = 4 - 3.$$

Therefore, when we plot on semi-logarithmic graph paper a series which has a constant *rate* of increase or decrease (rather than a constant absolute increase) it will appear as a straight line. This is because the effect of the logarithmic horizontal rulings is to reduce the constant rate of increase to a constant absolute increase. In our example, it can be seen that the trend of annual sales (notwithstanding considerable deviations around the trend) has been approximately an eleven per cent increase on the preceding year. As this constant rate of growth typifies the actual sales, it appears as a straight line in Fig. 6 and a smooth curved line in Fig. 5.

The fitted line in Fig. 6 was drawn freehand. If we wished to fit a trend line mathematically we would take the logarithms of the data and use the same form of equations as for a straight-line trend. The method would be exactly as described above, except that the Y-values would be the logarithms of the actual data. We would then convert the resulting equation back from logarithmic to normal form for forecasting purposes.

Although it is always worth while plotting a series which shows a changing rate of growth on semi-logarithmic paper, we must again emphasise the caution which must surround any prediction founded on the disclosure of a straight-line trend. It is not at all uncommon for a business in its early growth period to increase its turnover by a constant percentage year by year. But, sooner or later, a levelling-off will be experienced and must be anticipated, so that any projection forward must be carried out with the greatest discretion. What is important is to be alert always to the factors that might produce a levelling-off and modify one's estimates accordingly. As shown later, time series which have an increasing rate of growth over a certain

B

period are usually part of a long-term trend which rises slowly at first, then rapidly, then levels off, somewhat in the shape of an elongated "S."

Seasonal Percentages and Index Numbers

Up to now, we have considered ways of estimating future sales based on at least one whole year's previous experience. Most of the examples we have looked at cover several years, and, generally speaking, the longer the sales statistics go back into the past, the more accurate the forecast that can be made. But every expanding multiple retail group has the problem at some time that a forecast must be made for a new outlet for which little or no previous sales experience exists. In these cases, seasonal figures can be most helpful.

Seasonal Percentages

Table VI shows the average of three year's sales for the five outlets in a retail group, analysed over thirteen four-weekly periods. The lower part of the table gives each period's sales, by branch, as a percentage of the annual total. Thus, the sales of Branch A for period 1, £7,916, are 7·51% of £105,425. Sales for period 2 of £8,076 are 7·66% of £105,425 etc. It will be seen that although the five branches are in exactly the same type of business, the seasonal pattern shows significant variations between branches. Period 3 sales are 11·38% of the annual total for Branch E but only 8·72% for Branch D. Period 9 sales are 10·60% of the total for Branch A and 8·59% for Branch E.

These variations are, of course, to be expected. No two shops will have identical seasonal patterns, but in this example we have ensured that, as far as possible, the data are comparable. The use of four-weekly periods eliminates the distortions which occur owing to calendar months of differing length. The data have been adjusted for the different falling of Bank holidays in the three years covered. Further, the averaging of three years tends to dampen the effect of any exceptional year. So the variations that do occur are mostly random ones, which are due to such factors as local conditions, differing product appeal, shop-display effectiveness. It should be noted that no local press or other advertising was carried out, which might otherwise have influenced the figures.

The top half of Table VI gives the period totals of all five branches and shows them as percentages of the grand total, £569,140. Thus, average sales for period 1 were 8·35% for the five shops, 8·52% for period 2, and so on. The lower half of Table VI gives the period averages, calculated in the same way, of the *percentages*. The differing result is due to the fact that the former averages are *weighted*, and the latter are *unweighted*. This simply means that the period per-

TABLE VI. SEASONAL PATTERN OF THE FIVE BRANCHES IN A RETAIL GROUP

Period	Average %	Group total £	Average of three years' sales				
			Branch A £	Branch B £	Branch C £	Branch D £	Branch E £
1	8·35	47,533	7,916	5,303	3,909	17,414	12,991
2	8·52	48,473	8,076	6,366	4,225	18,122	11,684
3	9·76	55,534	10,415	7,543	3,919	18,907	14,750
4	10·42	59,328	11,665	7,403	4,824	21,453	13,983
5	9·38	53,407	10,442	6,414	4,638	19,253	12,660
6	7·50	42,699	7,421	4,887	3,871	17,555	8,965
7	5·96	33,941	6,564	4,246	2,131	14,173	6,827
8	6·97	39,665	6,938	5,260	3,193	15,429	8,845
9	9·87	56,150	11,175	7,960	4,300	21,588	11,127
10	5·26	29,918	5,683	3,684	1,781	12,573	6,197
11	5·22	29,721	5,282	2,766	2,487	12,749	6,437
12	6·44	36,657	6,957	5,575	2,612	14,397	7,116
13	6·35	36,114	6,891	5,218	2,771	13,247	7,987
Total	100·00	£569,140	£105,425	£72,625	£44,661	£216,860	£129,569

Period	Average %	Group total %	Branch A %	Branch B %	Branch C %	Branch D %	Branch E %
1	8·32	41·62	7·51	7·30	8·75	8·03	10·03
2	8·65	43·27	7·66	8·77	9·46	8·36	9·02
3	9·83	49·14	9·88	10·39	8·77	8·72	11·38
4	10·55	52·73	11·06	10·19	10·80	9·89	10·79
5	9·55	47·76	9·90	8·83	10·38	8·88	9·77
6	7·49	37·46	7·04	6·73	8·67	8·10	6·92
7	5·73	28·65	6·23	5·85	4·77	6·53	5·27
8	6·98	34·91	6·58	7·24	7·15	7·11	6·83
9	9·95	49·73	10·60	10·96	9·63	9·95	8·59
10	5·01	25·03	5·39	5·07	3·99	5·80	4·78
11	5·05	25·24	5·01	3·81	5·57	5·88	4·97
12	6·45	32·26	6·60	7·68	5·85	6·64	5·49
13	6·44	32·20	6·54	7·18	6·21	6·11	6·16
Total %	100·00	500·00	100·00	100·00	100·00	100·00	100·00

centages calculated from the values are influenced by the relative size of each value. If, for example, we had excluded Branch D from the table, total sales in period 1 for the remaining four branches would have been £30,119 out of an annual total of £352,280, *i.e.* 8·54%. But since Branch D is the biggest and its period 1 sales are below the average of the remaining four shops, it depresses the average of all five branches to 8·35% for period 1. Thus each branch influences the average according to its relative value, and we say that the average is weighted. The lower figures of Table VI, being percentages, are unweighted. Each branch, irrespective of its size, is exercising the same influence on the average.

In this example, which of the two averages to use is not very material, as the maximum difference between them (in period 10) is only 0·25%. But it could be an important choice if the weighted average differed significantly from the unweighted. Generally speaking, if we wished to obtain the seasonal pattern of the company as a whole, we would use the weighted average. If, however, we wanted to find the seasonal pattern of a *typical* shop, we would use the unweighted average. The choice, therefore, would depend on the use we had in mind for the figures.

The usefulness of these seasonal percentages can be illustrated by an example. Suppose that the retail group we are considering opens a new branch. The initial estimate of sales will have to be based on the size of the shop in relation to the others in the group, its relative position in the shopping area, the degree of competition relative to other shops in the group, and so on. When the shop has been running for a few months, we should be able to obtain a much more accurate guide to its likely potential. Assume that its first six four-weekly period sales are as follows:

Period 4	£3,714 (Part period)
Period 5	£8,756
Period 6	£6,973
Period 7	£5,196
Period 8	£6,447
Period 9	£9,146

We ignore period 4 sales, since the shop opened in this period and the full four-weeks' figures are therefore not available. Totalling the remaining five periods gives £36,518. The unweighted seasonal percentages for the five periods considered (we assume that the new shop's seasonal pattern will be typical of the other shops) are as follows:

	%
Period 5	9·55
Period 6	7·49
Period 7	5·73
Period 8	6·98
Period 9	9·95
Total	39·70%

Therefore, our estimate of sales for a full year from the start of period 5 is

$$\frac{100 \cdot 00}{39 \cdot 70} \times £36,518 = £92,000$$

and we can modify our original forecast accordingly. In practice, we would ignore more than the first part period. It takes perhaps three periods for a shop to settle into a normal trading pattern and we would eliminate the first three periods' sales from our calculation before "grossing-up" the remaining sales by the seasonal pattern figures to give a full or part-year forecast.

Although a simple seasonal pattern, as described above, is often adequate for many retail groups, there are circumstances when either several patterns have to be used or the single pattern has to be modified. It may be that the merchandise policy varies at different shops and attracts trade at different times. Or the provincial shops may show a markedly different seasonal pattern from the London ones. In these cases two or more seasonal patterns will be called for. But the extra work involved will ensure a greater degree of accuracy, since a new shop can be placed in a seasonal pattern according to its stock policy or locality, or other determining factor. Again, if there was a very marked upward or downward trend in sales at some or all of the branches when the seasonal pattern was computed, this will affect the pattern produced. If the trend was upwards, the earlier periods of the year will be a smaller proportion, and the later periods a greater proportion of the annual total than if the trend had been level. The reverse will apply for a downard trend. Indeed, if a new shop is likely to show a marked upward trend in sales from inception we should take account of this in the seasonal pattern by applying a trend factor.

Index Numbers

Frequently, it is useful to represent the seasonal percentage as index numbers. An index number measures the movements in a variable above or below a base value, which is represented as 100. Thus the percentage movement from the base value can be seen. To convert the weighted average seasonal percentages in Table VI to index numbers we divide the total of £569,140 by thirteen to give the average period sales and then multiply the result sequentially by each period's sales. This gives index numbers, with a base of 100 at the average annual sales level, as follows:

Period 1	108·5	Period 8	90·7
Period 2	110·8	Period 9	128·4
Period 3	126·8	Period 10	68·3
Period 4	135·5	Period 11	67·8
Period 5	122·0	Period 12	83·8
Period 6	97·5	Period 13	82·5
Period 7	77·4		
		Total	1300·0

The check on the accuracy of computation is to see that the total of the index numbers adds up to 100 times the number of values in the series, in this case thirteen. The usefulness of expressing the seasonal pattern in this way is that it enables the relationship of each period's sales to each other period and to the average to be immediately seen. For example, if the latest moving annual average sales for a branch are £5,000 at period 3, we can say that period 4 sales should be 35·5% above this figure, *i.e.* £6,770, or that period 10 sales should be 31·7% below £5,000, *i.e.* £3,410. If the moving averages show a marked upward or downward trend it will be necessary to project this trend forward by raising or lowering the moving average by the requisite amount and then applying the index number.

Seasonal index numbers can also be used among other things for stock replenishment. Suppose that the central warehouse replenishes branches so that each outlet has approximately two periods' stock at a time. Branch X has sold 300 units in periods 1 to 3 and has a closing stock of 50 units. What should be the stock replenishment to cover periods 4 and 5? The answer is to equate the 300 units to the seasonal index numbers for periods 1 to 3, to rate this down by using the seasonal index numbers for periods 4 and 5 (see page 25 for index numbers), and then to subtract the closing stock. Thus,

$$\frac{257 \cdot 5}{346 \cdot 1} \times 300 - 50 = 223 - 50 = 173 \text{ units.}$$

Summary

A reliable sales forecast is an essential basis for correct decision-taking and framing of company policy. Comparability of statistics is most important if correct inferences are to be drawn from sales data. Time spent on this aspect will be infinitely repaid in the quality of results achieved.

The careful application of elementary statistical methods, such as moving totals, freehand and fitted trend lines and index numbers, enables prediction to be based on an historical pattern of growth or decline which, *in the absence of reasons to the contrary*, can be used as a guide to the future. However, this is a very large qualifying clause. More important than the mechanics of fitting a trend line is finding out *why* the growth curve has this or that pattern. Knowing the conditions that have produced growth in the past, the likelihood of their continuing in the future can then be fairly assessed and a balanced forecast arrived at.

In the next chapter we deal with the modifying factors which must be considered before the estimates based on company records can be accepted as the final sales budget.

CHAPTER 3

THE SALES FORECAST AND MODIFYING FACTORS

Introduction

In the previous chapter, we limited our discussions of the sales forecast to statistical prediction based on a retail group's own internal branch or company statistics. This is clearly the most important part of sales forecasting and should determine the general framework of the overall sales budget. But in itself it is not enough. A realistic forecast must take account of all the external influences which may operate to increase or reduce the sales potential either of the group as a whole or any particular branch in it.

These external influences can be broadly divided into two categories: those that affect the particular trade of which the company is a part, and those that affect business generally, *i.e.* the economic and political situation in its widest context. Frequently, of course, this distinction is not valid, as, for example, when government action impinges directly on the activities of a particular trade. In many instances, however, it is a useful division to make, since it can introduce further refinements into sales forecasting, which otherwise might not be made. We deal first with factors affecting particular trades.

Factors Affecting Particular Trades

Most sections of industry and commerce have their own trade associations to which member firms submit statistics for analysis and collation, and eventual redistribution in summary form back to the individual companies. This information not only allows the company to see how its share of the affiliated trade is increasing or decreasing, but it also shows how the trade as a whole is faring, which may be just as important. Trade association reports are perhaps the most important source of information concerning a particular activity, but there are also many other non-government publications which contain useful statistics. The Economist Intelligence Unit produces *Retail Business* monthly, which gives special reports on selected trades with supporting statistics. The market research departments of the bigger advertising agencies and the research sections of many stockbroking firms also produce detailed reports on individual trades containing much valuable information.

Government statistics relating to distribution are mainly confined to the *Census of Distribution* and to the indices of retail trade published each month by the Board of Trade. The *Census of Distribution* is carried out only at intervals of several years and is largely concerned with detailed information about the structure and character of distribution, so that its value for forecasting is somewhat limited. Likewise, the monthly indices of changes in the volume and type of retail sales are of only broad interest, since their coverage is too wide to be of much use to many companies engaged in specialist or widely diversified retail trading. But in forecasting we are not solely concerned with the overall sales of the particular commodities which we are primarily engaged in retailing. Other statistics can be of great importance in estimating the likely level of activity. For example, classified population statistics will be of direct interest to companies manufacturing and selling baby-wear, prams, toys, etc. The level of disposable consumer income will influence expenditure on all products and services, particularly luxury and semi-luxury goods. This is why the more general government publications, such as the *Annual Abstract of Statistics* and the *Monthly Digest of Statistics*, can often be of use in assessing the effect of external influences.

An example of the use of such statistics in forecasting can be found in the television industry. Fig. 7 is a graph of the yearly production of black and white television sets from 1946 to 1967, compiled by the British Radio Equipment Manufacturers' Association. B.R.E.M.A.'s returns give 100% coverage of television production and their figures are subsequently published in the *Annual Abstract of Statistics*. The great growth in production of television sets is immediately apparent from the chart, as well as the falling away from the 1959 peak.

Four phases in production can be distinguished. Between 1946 and 1949 the growth of production was slow but steadily increasing as television became part of the social fabric. Between 1950 and 1957 production increased very rapidly as capital was heavily invested in the industry and manufacturing economies multiplied. From about 1957 production increased but at a declining rate, as the market became more and more saturated, with the notable exception of 1959. The fourth phase began in 1960 when production fell very rapidly because of overstocking by manufacturers and distributors, the inevitable result of the previous year's production boom. Since 1960 demand has been largely for replacement of "first" sets, apart from 1964 when the advent of BBC–2 caused an upsurge in production.

The dotted line in Fig. 7 shows a growth curve fitted to the

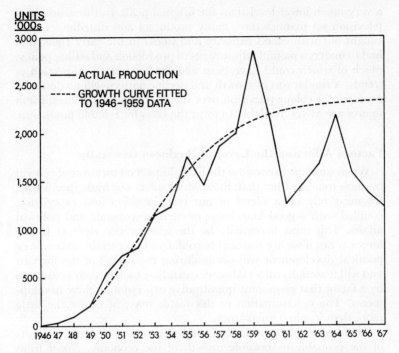

Fig. 7. Actual production of black and white television sets 1964–1967
(source: British Radio Equipment Manufacturers Association).

production data from 1946 to 1959 by mathematical methods. Its
purpose was to predict the likely pattern of demand for 1960 and
subsequent years. It can be seen that up to 1958 the curve described
the actual data quite well. In 1959, however, there was an exceptional production boom, when output climbed some 790,000 sets, or
38%, above the trend. Manufacturers and distributors who had
been following the growth trend of television sets closely were able
to detect two warning signals: first, that 1959 production was
excessive and must inevitably be followed by a cut-back in output
due to overstocking, and second, that the "first-set" market was
rapidly approaching saturation, which would lead to further con-
tractions in output. This is, in fact, what happened.

In other words, for goods such as expensive consumer durables, a
statistically fitted growth curve may prove very reliable up to the
point when it begins to become asymptotic to a horizontal line (the
top part of the elongated S curve), the point when "first-demand" is
becoming exhausted. After this, the fitted curve may be positively
misleading, since demand for replacement purposes only will be at

B*

a very much lower level than the original peak. In this example of television set manufacture, many producers and distributors were caught out with excess capacity and stocks in the early 1960s and had to undergo painful adjustments to production and selling policy, much of which could have been avoided by a closer inspection of trends. A similar sort of growth and decline pattern will no doubt be repeated for colour television over the next decade, but insufficient figures are as yet available to form the basis for reliable prediction.

Factors Affecting the Level of Business Generally

When we come to consider the likely impact on turnover of general business trends, rather than those which affect our trade specifically, we must rely on a blend of our own intuition and experience, coupled with a good knowledge of current economic and political affairs. This must necessarily be the least precise element in the forecast. But if we are reasonably confident that certain economic or political development will occur during the period of the forecast and will materially affect sales, we can adjust each branch's estimates by a factor that gives some quantitative expression to these developments. The determination of this factor may, of course, be little more than inspired guess-work.

There is certainly no lack of published material giving forecasts of the probable or possible growth of the economy. Apart from annual reviews of income and expenditure produced at Budget time by H.M. Government, White Papers are regularly issued which deal with the economic prospects of industry generally or with certain sectors of it. In addition, almost every management journal, the reviews of the major clearing banks and the investment departments of leading stockbrokers give informed commentary on economic affairs, often supported by a wealth of statistical information. This excludes the daily and weekly press, which furnish continuous economic and political commentary in the columns of the *Financial Times*, the *Economist*, the *Stock Exchange Gazette*, and many more journals.

The most ambitious forecast so far produced has been the National Plan, produced by the Department of Economic Affairs in 1965. The Plan gave estimates of the likely growth of the economy as a whole from 1965 to 1970, and detailed forecasts for all sectors of the economy, both private and public, over the same period. Much in the Plan was of general interest to companies in the retail and distributive trades: the proposals for regional planning and redeployment of labour, the proposed solutions to the problems of transport and traffic congestion, the estimates of consumer expenditure on various products, and so on. Unfortunately, the Plan was overtaken by events and quickly became obsolete for long-range planning purposes. Indeed, it would seem questionable whether any such comprehensive forecast covering a period of five years could be more than of general interest in a largely free enterprise economy.

The forecaster must therefore fall back on his own judgment of the likely out-turn of events. His judgment will be largely formed by selective and critical reading of published commentary and anticipation of the effect of general economic trends on his own business. The signs of overstrain in the economy can usually be detected by balance of payment figures, the level of unfilled vacancies, bankers' advances and similar types of indicators. The necessary remedial measures, such as higher Bank rate, hire-purchase restrictions and purchase tax increases, will undoubtedly affect trade generally and hit some business particularly severely. Large sections of the retail trade are especially vulnerable to the latter two regulators. It is only prudent to build into the forecast the anticipated effect of such restrictions, where experience shows that they have a direct relationship with sales volume.

In estimating the actual percentage factor to apply to sales to allow for spending curtailments, skilful use of all available information will help. Keeping notes of important influences on turnover, as described in the previous chapter, may enable the results of a previous credit squeeze to be used as a guide to the effect of present restrictions, actual or anticipated. Where a trade association or information body publishes statistics of total spending on a commodity or group of commodities, an estimate may be made of the downturn (or upturn) for the trade as a whole, resulting from government measures. This can be related to the share of the market which the company has, not necessarily in proportion to the market as a whole, since in adverse times a competitive company's share may increase, notwithstanding an overall trade contraction. Again, government measures may impinge directly on a particular industry: H.P. restrictions on motor-cars, for example. A retail chain with branches in the Midlands can then apply selective adjustments to the forecasts for these branches, perhaps using a smaller correction factor for other outlets to allow for the "wave" effect of local recession.

In assessing external influences on sales, account must also be taken of the likely effect of general government legislation, as distinct from the pure budgetary and economic controls referred to above. The forecaster should acquire the habit of examining all actual or proposed legislation to see if it may have an influence on his trade, and by how much. The virtual break-down of resale price maintenance, for example, which results from the passing of the 1964 Act, will hasten the growth of efficient retail groups at the expense of

TABLE VII. WORKING SHEET FOR SUMMARY SALES BUDGET

1	2	3	4	5	6	7		8	9		10
Branch	Actual sales 1966–67	Actual sales 1967–68	% 1967–68 up/down on 1966–67	Unadjusted forecast 1968–69	Basis used	Local factor adjustment		Reason	National (or trade) factor adjustment		Final budget 1968–69
	£000s	£000s	%	£000s		%	£000s		%	£000s	£000s
1	69·5	72·6	+4·5	75·0	Freehand trend	7·5	+5·6	Improved shop front and interior	1·0	−0·7	79·9
2	146·8	140·7	−4·2	135·0	Freehand trend	—	—		1·0	−1·4	133·6
3	44·1	52·4	+18·8	60·0	Fitted trend	5·0	−3·0	Unfavourable routing of traffic	1·0	−0·6	56·4
4	60·0	63·2	+5·3	65·0	Freehand trend	10·0	+6·5	Resiting of branch	1·0	−0·7	70·8
5	146·2	129·6	−11·4	120·0	Fitted trend	7·5	+9·0	Competing shop closed	1·0	−1·2	127·8
6	64·2	74·6	+16·2	75·0	Fitted trend	—	—		1·0	−0·7	74·3
7	P 36·2	136·4	—	130·0	Freehand trend	5·0	+6·5	Better management	1·0	−1·3	135·2
8	—	P 33·0	—	55·0	Seasonal index	—	—		1·0	−0·6	54·4
9	—	P 26·1	—	45·0	Seasonal index	—	—		1·0	−0·5	44·5
10	—	—	—	P 55·0	Estimate	—	—		1·0	−0·5	54·5
Total	567·0	728·6	+28·4	815·0		3·0	+24·6		1·0	−8·2	831·4

(Note: P = Part-year.)

smaller, less competitive ones. It would be unrealistic of a company not to include this sort of trend in its long-range sales target. (But we must be careful not to "doubt-count" these trend factors. If a retail group already reflects its increased competitiveness and growing market share in its branch sales, we must not apply a further trend factor, unless there is a good reason to expect an extra gain in turnover not already appearing in the branch trends.) However, apart from this sort of legislation, which specifically deals with the retail trade, it will be found that almost every new domestic law will have an effect on one or another sector of retail business. Anticipating such effects and planning accordingly is the art of successful management.

The Summarised Sales Budget

Having considered and evaluated the "external" as well as the "internal" influences affecting sales, we are now in a position to complete the final company sales budget.

As before, we take the period of the forecast to be a year, although similar methods of analysis apply for longer or shorter periods. Table VII shows a working sheet which can be used for summarising the branch forecasts into a total company sales budget. Ten branches are listed, but the same sort of working sheet can be used for companies with any number of retail outlets. Columns 2, 3, and 4 show the branch sales for the two most recent years and the percentage increases or decreases. This is useful information to have on the working sheet, although the percentage movements of the two preceding years cannot simply be projected forward into the forecast year without examining the shape of the branch trend lines. Columns 5 and 6 give the unadjusted forecasts and the method used to obtain them. As circumstances demand these will either be free-hand trend projections or mathematically fitted trends. Where a branch has insufficient sales history for a trend to be determined we use the seasonal percentages to arrive at the unadjusted forecast. For example, branches 8 and 9 opened for trading part-way through 1967–68. As we must now make a forecast for 1968–69, we "gross up" the 1967–68 sales by the seasonal percentages to obtain a full year's forecast sales. Branch 10 is planned to open during the period of the forecast, so we must make a pure estimate of its likely turnover based on, e.g. its location, size and position in the shopping area relative to other shops in the company.

Columns 7 to 9 are used to adjust the "internal" forecast of column 5 by any external factors that seem relevant. We have divided these factors into two categories—local and national (or trade) factors. The reasons for this division are obvious. In multiple retailing local conditions may significantly affect a shop's turnover and, with experience, the effects of these influences may be quite accurately assessed. (In local factors we also include the effect of improvements to the company's shops and the consequent stimulus to sales.) Factors affecting the trade as a whole or the overall economy are much more difficult to quantify, although their impact may be very real.

In our example, we have assumed that the slight slackening of growth in the trade and the general tightness of money and credit will reduce sales by 1% during the coming year in relation to the previous year. We therefore apply this factor to each branch's forecast to arrive at a final sales budget for each outlet and thence for the company as a whole. Probably it is better to adjust the trend forecast by the local factor and apply the national factor adjustment to the result, if either factor is very significant. In our example, the national factor adjustment is so small that we have applied it to the unadjusted forecast.

Columns 5, 7 and 9 thus add across to column 10. The final check is to compare columns 3 and 10 for each branch, *i.e.* to see whether the budget looks realistic compared with the sales for the year just completed, taking into account all the known factors. This comparison may indicate a badly drawn trend or an exaggerated assessment of the effects of local or national factors.

Testing for Accuracy

But no matter how careful our checks or sophisticated our analysis, actual sales will inevitably differ from the budget. The only relevant question is—by how much? It is impossible to lay down rules about acceptable variances in sales forecasting because some companies by the nature of their business, their size, their position in the trade, have an inherent stability which lends itself to accurate forecasting. Other companies, growing rapidly or exploiting a new product, may find it impossible to achieve acceptable limits of accuracy until their own expansion or the market settles down. Generally speaking, however, established companies in the retail trade should be able to forecast *total company sales* within limits of plus or minus five per cent. Variances larger than this will rob the rest of the budget, which is linked to the sales forecast, of much of its value.

We emphasise total company sales, because a retail chain or indeed any company with a multiplicity of outlets or products, has a self-correcting element in its forecasts which becomes stronger the larger the number of outlets or products. All this means is that for every branch or product forecast which is in excess of actual performance the chances are that there will be another one below, so that in total the "overs" and "unders" will tend to cancel out and the overall forecast will be much more accurate than any individual one. An example of this, based on actual data, is given in Table VIII. The realised and budgeted sales of the forty shops in a retail group are tabulated, together with the absolute variances, and the variances expressed as a percentage of the budget. Thus the annual sales of Branch 1 were 12·1% below the budget; for Branch 2 they

TABLE VIII. COMPARISON OF ACTUAL AND BUDGET SALES OF FORTY SHOPS IN A RETAIL CHAIN

Branch	Actual sales	Budget sales	Diff. £	Diff. %	Branch	Actual sales	Budget sales	Diff. £	Diff. %
	£000s	£000s	£000s			£000s	£000s	£000s	
1	105·4	120·0	−14·6	−12·1	21	74·4	84·0	−9·6	−11·4
2	89·2	79·0	+10·2	+12·9	22	56·4	55·0	+1·4	+2·5
3	86·7	86·0	+0·7	+8·1	23	52·4	50·0	+2·4	+4·8
4	89·0	91·0	−2·0	−2·2	24	51·6	50·0	+1·6	+3·2
5	140·7	138·0	+2·7	+2·0	25	73·0	78·0	−5·0	−6·4
6	73·6	72·0	+1·6	+2·2	26	63·1	64·0	−0·9	−1·4
7	72·6	72·0	+0·6	+0·8	27	78·2	86·0	−7·8	−9·0
8	106·1	110·0	−3·9	−3·5	28	81·4	75·0	+6·4	+8·5
9	95·7	100·0	−4·3	−4·3	29	104·1	140·0	−35·9	−25·6
10	113·7	138·0	−24·3	−17·6	30	74·6	65·0	+9·6	+14·8
11	288·7	264·0	+24·7	+9·4	31	48·4	50·0	−1·6	−3·2
12	73·6	75·0	−1·4	−1·9	32	95·2	85·0	+10·2	+12·0
13	103·1	96·0	+7·1	+7·4	33	56·1	65·0	−8·9	−13·7
14	44·7	48·0	−3·3	−6·9	34	50·3	60·0	−9·7	−16·1
15	129·6	144·0	−14·4	−10·0	35	75·4	72·0	+3·4	+4·7
16	216·9	200·0	+16·9	+8·4	36	57·9	50·0	+7·9	+15·8
17	63·2	65·0	−1·8	−2·8	37	43·6	50·0	−6·4	−12·8
18	70·1	76·0	−5·9	−7·8	38	76·9	75·0	+1·9	+2·5
19	58·0	55·0	+3·0	+5·5	39	70·3	80·0	−9·7	−12·1
20	92·5	101·0	−8·5	−8·4	40	136·4	138·0	−1·6	−1·2
					Total	3,532·8	3,602·0	−69·2	−1·9

Actual below budget sales	No. of branches	Actual above budget sales	No. of branches
0–5·0%	8	0–5·0%	8
5·1–10·0%	6	5·1–10·0%	6
10·1–15·0%	5	10·1–15·0%	3
15·1–20·0%	2	15·1–20·0%	1
20·1% and over	1	20·1% and over	—
	22		18

were 12·9% above the budget, and so on. It will be seen that although the percentage variances were as much as 25·6% one way and nearly 16% the other, the overall variation was only 1·9%—a very acceptable degree of inaccuracy.

The counterbalancing effect becomes more noticeable when we summarise the percentage errors into a frequency distribution. This is done at the bottom of Table VIII. For convenience we divide the maximum percentage error into class intervals of five per cent, both

for positive and negative errors, giving ten class intervals in all. Then
we go through the list of percentages summarising them into their
appropriate classes. Thus there are eight branches where actual
sales were up to five per cent below the budget, and eight where
actual sales exceeded the budget by up to five per cent. Likewise,
there are six branches where sales were between five and ten per
cent above and six between five and ten per cent below the budget,
and so on. The last class interval, 20·1% and over, is an open-ended
class which contains the one "freak" (Branch 29). The total number
of branches divides itself nearly equally into "overs" and "unders"
and accounts for the closeness of the total forecast to actuality.

Even more important, from a statistical point of view, is the way
the branches cluster symmetrically around the lower percentage
errors. This is shown more clearly in Fig. 8, where the frequency
distribution is expressed as a histogram. The number of shops in

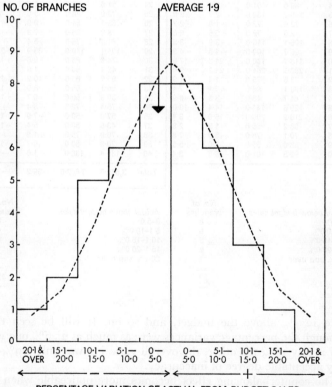

Fig. 8. Frequency Distribution of percentage variations of Actual from
Budget Sales and fitted "normal" curve (data from Table VIII).
The broken line indicates the "normal" curve of error.

each class is represented by a bar with the plus and minus classes arranged symmetrically on either side of zero. The *weighted* average variance is minus 1·9% and is the actual mean of the distribution. Had this figure been zero, the forecast would have been exactly in line with actuality, notwithstanding substantial, but completely self-balancing, branch variances round this mean.

The dotted line in Fig. 8 is a normal curve of error, fitted to the frequency distribution, to emphasise the *random* nature of the branch variances. The normal curve of error originated from games of chance because it describes the probability of wins and losses in these sorts of games. But its application nowadays is so wide (in quality control, sociology, medical statistics, public opinion polls, etc.) that it is the fundamental theorem in modern statistical methods. Its significance in this context is that, because the histogram of the branch variances fits the normal curve quite well, it suggests that little bias exists in the forecasts. In other words, the variances that do occur in forecasting the sales of the forty branches are distributed at random and can be expected if no particular bias is affecting the forecasts. Further, the greater the number of outlets, again assuming that no special bias exists, the more accurate the total forecast (in its percentage variation from actuality) is likely to be. A simple method of fitting a normal curve is given in most books on applied statistics. This type of post mortem into the accuracy of forecasting is well worth the time involved as it contributes to a deeper understanding of the principles involved and therefore to an enhanced degree of reliability.

The Special Problems of Department Stores

So far we have considered sales forecasting mainly in relation to multiple retail companies. We have seen that by the careful evaluation of past sales data and the use of elementary statistical methods a very worth-while degree of accuracy can be obtained. Essentially the same methods can be used to produce the sales forecast for department stores, but one or two modifications must be made in procedure to deal with the special problems of this type of retailing.

In multiple trading the sales performance of each branch as a whole is the most appropriate measure for estimating purposes. This is because site, locality, management and such factors are so important to the sales potential of a single shop. The merchandise budget is largely subsidiary to the overall sales forecast, as compiled from branch totals, and is developed from it. The total sales budget is then only amended by merchandise considerations if the competitive quality of merchandise is thought to be significantly different this (forecast) year from previous years.

For department stores the logical units of performance are the individual sales departments, but here there is an identity between sales department and merchandise group which does not exist in multiple retailing. To this extent the problems of forecasting for department stores are reduced: the merchandise sales budget does not have to be agreed back to the branch sales budget. Against this, however, is the fact that it is possible (and very often desirable) to alter the size and position of sales departments, which will obviously affect turnover, both actual and planned. To overcome this problem, department stores have evolved a number of statistical measures which are used as approximate guides to actual or expected performance: sales per square foot of total space, sales per square foot of direct selling space, sales per linear foot of counter space, and so on. Used in conjunction with the statistical methods of trend-seeking described earlier in this chapter, these ratios can provide a very reliable forecast.

The procedure is to eliminate the size and position factor in each department's sales, in the way that seasonal variations are smoothed out of a time series. This will leave the true trend, which should accurately reflect the long-term expansion or contraction of sales for the department whose activity we are budgeting. The following statistics of the sales of one of the departments in a large department store show the method which may be used.

Year	Sales	Average sq ft selling space	Sales per sq ft	Position index	Adjusted sales per sq ft
	£		£		£
1960	50,050	1,030	48·5	105	46·2
1961	51,670	1,095	47·2	105	45·0
1962	51,530	1,080	47·7	105	45·4
1963	53,480	1,140	47·0	105	44·8
1964	54,710	1,150	47·5	115	41·3
1965	55,390	1,200	46·2	115	40·2
1966	55,970	1,250	44·7	115	38·9
1967	56,240	1,270	44·3	115	38·5

Sales in absolute money terms show an upward trend, but at the same time the space occupied by the department has also increased in every year except one, and for the last four out of eight years the department has been sited in a more favourable selling position. This is denoted by the Position Index, departments in average positions being rated 100, those in better positions more than 100 and those in worse less than 100. The effect on sales of the amount of department selling space can be eliminated first, by merely dividing sales by average square footage of space occupied during the year. This gives average sales per square foot, and in the example under review a mainly declining trend is disclosed, especially from 1964 onwards. Secondly, we must eliminate the effect of position in the store on departmental sales. Here the position index can be used by reducing (or increasing) sales per square foot to a base of 100. Thus, in this example sales per square foot from 1960 to 1963 have been multiplied by a factor of 100/105, and from 1964 to 1967 by a factor of 100/115, so putting all years on a comparable basis.

Adjusted sales per square foot can now be inspected for trend in the ways described earlier in this chapter, *i.e.* by using either a fitted trend line or a freehand projection. A superficial examination of the adjusted figures suggests that the rate of decline in sales per square foot is slowing down and that a reasonable forecast for 1968 would be £38·0 per square foot. Thus, if the management decided to allot 1,200 square feet of selling space to this department in 1968 and to resite it in a position with an index of 110, forecast sales for 1968 would be calculated as follows:

$$1,200 \times 38{\cdot}0 \times \frac{110}{100} = £50{,}600.$$

Again it must be stressed how important it is to keep notes of all the other factors which may influence departmental sales besides size and positions: special promotions, exceptionally good or bad buys, advertising, management, display, local competition, and so on. As for multiple retailing, these factors are highly significant if forecasts are to be accurate and a real help to management.

When the sales of each department in the store have been forecast in the way described above they can be transferred to a summary sheet, as in Table VII. Adjustments can then be made for national and trade conditions likely to be encountered as deemed appropriate. The final test of acceptability of the forecast is that the summarised total of all departments gives a company sales budget which is consistent with the growth pattern experienced in previous years. It is again likely, as for the branches of a multiple company, that "overs" and "unders" per department will tend to cancel one another out, so contributing to the overall accuracy of the forecast.

Summary

The factors which may modify the "internally" generated sales forecast can be divided into two classes: those that affect business generally and those that impinge on specific trades or on specific locations only. Although difficult to quantify, an estimate must be made of their likely impact, otherwise the forecast may be seriously adrift. Close scrutiny and intelligent interpretation of government and trade statistics will reveal the emergence of trends which may be of great significance in long-range planning. Likewise all proposed legislation, fiscal or otherwise, should be weighed up in terms of its likely effect on trade.

Simple statistical methods can be used to check on the accuracy of forecasting, which should be regarded as an integral part of budgetary technique.

The statistical methods used for estimating sales in multiple retailing can be applied to department stores, after adjusting for the variable position factor of departments.

In this and the previous chapter, treatment of the more complex methods of sales forecasting, such as exponential smoothing, has been deliberately omitted; firstly, because it is inappropriate in a book of this sort, and secondly, because a very acceptable degree of accuracy can be achieved by using the simpler methods described. There is an immense body of knowledge on advanced forecasting techniques available to those readers who can draw on the requisite theoretical and practical (mainly computer) help. We have been more concerned to show how a straightforward empirical analysis of sales data, modified by common-sense considerations, can give a reliable overall sales forecast, which will be a satisfactory basis for financial planning and the broad outlines of merchandise policy.

CHAPTER 4

STOCK MOVEMENT AND
GROSS PROFIT ANALYSIS

Analysis of Sales into Product Groups

When the total company sales budget has been finally agreed by the management, the next step is to break it down into months (or four-weekly periods) and product groups. The analysis into periods can best be done by using the seasonal percentages, as shown in Table VI above, for the company as a whole, and also for individual branches, if budgetary control of branches is operated. The method is simply to multiply each period's seasonal percentage by the total sales *of all existing branches* and to add the estimated sales of the new branches as they are planned to open.

The breakdown of forecast sales into product groups and individual lines will require the same sort of statistical record keeping and projection that was used to produce the branch sales forecasts. The changing trends in demand for the company's merchandise can be detected from the product group sales records by inspection or by the statistical and mathematical techniques already described. A lesser degree of sophistication can be expected in the individual product analysis, however, since the buying department will constantly be searching for new lines to attract customers, which will necessitate considerable flexibility in the product group sales budget. In any company subject to the whims of fashion this flexibility will be more pronounced and more essential.

Table IX shows the breakdown of a company's total sales into thirteen four-weekly periods, further sub-divided into six major merchandise groups. Depending on the degree of control required, there could be a similar analysis of each branch's forecast sales into four-weekly periods, and also into main product groups, if necessary, which would total to the summary product group sales budget.

Stock Movement and Gross Profit

The stock movement and gross profit budget follows logically from the product group sales budget. For each main merchandise group a policy decision will be made in the budget whether to increase or reduce stocks during the coming year, and by how much.

41

TABLE IX. PRODUCT GROUP SALES BUDGET

Period	Total	Product group 1	Product group 2	Product group 3	Product group 4	Product group 5	Product group 6
	£000s	£000s	£000s	£000s	£000s	£000s	£000s
1	69·5	5·5	15·1	28·2	9·3	4·7	6·7
2	70·8	5·6	16·3	27·4	8·5	4·0	9·0
3	81·2	7·0	20·4	35·9	11·7	5·6	0·6
4	86·2	6·0	17·5	30·2	9·5	5·0	18·0
5	78·0	6·2	18·4	32·5	10·8	6·1	4·0
6	62·4	4·7	13·0	20·1	6·5	3·2	14·9
7	49·6	4·3	12·8	21·7	7·2	3·3	0·3
8	58·0	4·6	12·1	20·8	6·4	3·1	11·0
9	82·1	6·8	15·1	41·1	6·3	4·0	8·8
10	43·8	3·0	9·0	15·3	4·8	2·2	9·5
11	43·4	3·7	10·2	17·8	6·7	3·2	1·8
12	53·6	4·2	12·7	21·7	7·0	3·0	5·0
13	52·8	4·0	11·2	20·2	7·0	3·0	7·4
Total	831·4	65·6	183·8	332·9	101·7	50·4	97·0

Knowing the stock brought forward from the previous year at cost and the gross margin normally earned on this class of merchandise, budgeted sales at cost value can be calculated and hence purchases at cost. This fixes the buying budget for the particular product group. Decisions about the level of stock to be carried will be largely influenced by the company's liquid resources, and competing demands for stock between merchandise groups will have to be resolved before the stock movement budget can be finalised.

When the individual merchandise group stock movement and gross profit budgets have been agreed they will be summarised into a total budget, showing the breakdown into months or four-weekly periods. Table X gives an example of this budget. It will be seen that (since the company is on a rising sales trend) stock is planned

TABLE X. STOCK MOVEMENT AND GROSS PROFIT BUDGET

Period	Opening stock at cost	Pur- chases at cost	Total	Sales at cost	Sales at retail	Gross Profit		Closing stock at cost
	£000s	£000s	£000s	£000s	£000s	£000s	%	£000s
1	201·3	52·8	254·1	46·3	69·5	23·2	33·4	207·8
2	207·8	75·0	282·8	46·9	70·8	23·9	33·8	235·9
3	235·9	84·1	320·0	53·8	81·2	27·4	33·7	266·2
4	266·2	62·0	328·2	56·8	86·2	29·4	34·1	271·4
5	271·4	40·4	311·8	51·5	78·0	26·5	34·0	260·3
6	260·3	29·9	290·2	41·6	62·4	20·8	33·3	248·6
7	248·6	17·3	265·9	34·7	49·6	14·9	30·0	231·2
8	231·2	79·5	310·7	40·9	58·0	17·1	29·5	269·8
9	269·8	16·1	285·9	54·7	82·1	27·4	33·3	231·2
10	231·2	18·7	249·9	29·1	43·8	14·7	33·5	220·8
11	220·8	43·9	264·7	29·0	43·4	14·4	33·3	235·7
12	235·7	46·6	282·3	35·7	53·6	17·9	33·4	246·6
13	246·6	44·2	290·8	35·1	52·8	17·7	33·5	255·7
Total	201·3	610·5	811·8	556·1	831·4	275·3	33·1	255·7

to increase during the year. But it will also be seen that budgeted stocks rise and fall during the year roughly in sympathy with the seasonal pattern of sales, so that the stock investment is reduced in slack times and increased in busy periods, thus minimising the drain on the company's liquid resources. Gross profit is expected to vary from period to period since in the busy periods the company will sell proportionately more of its own "exclusive" lines (on which it makes a higher percentage margin) and therefore the gross profit ratio too will tend to follow the movement of the seasonal pattern. Periods 7 and 8 cover the annual bargain sale, which substantially reduces the margin, and this should be budgeted for.

In this example, we have assumed that a "true" costing of stock and stock movement is carried out. It is common practice in many retail companies for stock, both in the budget and in the actual financial accounts, to be valued at retail prices, from which the normal selling margin (say $33\frac{1}{3}\%$) is deducted to arrive at stock at cost value. This is a satisfactory system to operate when the buying of stock is almost entirely limited to items which are sold on a fixed mark-up basis. Thus, for example, stock at cost is marked up by 50% to a given retail value which earns a $33\frac{1}{3}\%$ gross profit. Where, however, a retail company markets its own special lines, on which it may earn a very much higher margin than normal, or where resale price maintenance is breaking down and a company is deliberately and selectively reducing selling prices, the need for a true costing of stock becomes paramount. For without it, the company cannot see the effect of its policies in its individual product group gross margins, which is vital control information. The amount of clerical work involved in costing each individual item sold at purchase value may, of course, be very considerable and the services of a computer may be required. In a later chapter, we consider the application of electronic data processing to the sales, stock movement and gross profit analysis of a medium-sized retail chain.

The Effect of Price-cutting on Gross Profit

If a retail company is to expand, gross profit in money terms must be increased, either by a greater sales volume, or by higher retail prices, or by better buying terms. From time to time, when old stock must be cleared or when the need to reduce stock is financially essential, a deliberate decision to cut prices is taken, which will certainly reduce the gross profit in percentage terms and also possibly in money terms, if the price reductions are severe enough. Table XI shows how the gross profit percentage is increasingly squeezed by successive stages in price reduction. Thus, a 5% reduction in selling price reduces gross profit from 20% to $15 \cdot 8\%$.

TABLE XI. GROSS PROFIT AND DISCOUNTS

Normal gross profit	Discount or price reduction				
	5%	10%	15%	20	25%
%	Gross profit after discount or price reduction (%)				
20·0	15·8	11·1	5·9	Nil	−6·7
25·0	21·1	16·7	11·8	6·2	Nil
30·0	26·3	22·2	17·6	12·5	6·7
33·3	29·8	25·9	21·5	16·6	11·1
35·0	31·6	27·8	23·5	18·7	13·3
40·0	36·8	33·3	29·4	25·0	20·0
	Percentage increase in sales quantities necessary to maintain gross profit in money terms (%)				
20·0	33·3	100·0	300·0	∞	Nil
25·0	25·0	66·7	150·0	400·0	∞
30·0	20·0	50·0	100·0	200·0	500·0
33·3	17·7	42·8	82·0	150·0	300·0
35·0	16·7	40·0	75·0	133·3	250·0
40·0	14·3	33·3	60·0	100·0	166·6

A 10% discount on a sale which normally earns 33⅓% reduces gross profit to 25·9%. Although retailers are aware that discounting will lower the percentage margin on trading, they are often unaware of the precise quantitative effect, and this must always be borne in mind. However, if a price reduction is possible and will result in a sufficient increase in unit sales for gross profit *in money terms to be increased*, then such a price reduction is in the company's interest.

When retailers embark on a deliberate policy of price cutting they are making assumptions about the *elasticity of demand*, a concept familiar to economists, but often not so well understood in its precise numerical significance by business management. Elasticity of demand is simply the relationship between the price at which an article is sold and the quantity demanded by the public. Thus, if a given decrease in price results in a less than proportional increase in the quantity sold, we say that demand is *inelastic*, and if the quantity sold is greater proportionately than the reduction in price, we say that demand is *elastic*. Where the price reduction produces an equivalent percentage increase in unit sales, elasticity of demand is said to be *unity*.

Although this concept is obviously of vital importance to all businessmen, its practical limitation is that it is often very difficult to measure. Without a costly experiment it may be impossible to judge how much sales will increase for a given price reduction, and there-

fore decisions about price-policy are often little more than acts of
faith. A small price reduction may not materially influence sales, so
that if elasticity of demand is to be truly tested, the price cut may
have to be quite substantial. Pilot surveys of price/demand conditions can be carried out by market research agencies on selected
sections of the buying public, and these can often be very helpful in
constructing price-policy. But they are expensive projects and
generally beyond the reach of the medium to small-sized companies.

In any event, so far as retailers are concerned, or indeed any
business organisation that buys at a fixed discount off selling price,
it is not merely a question of increasing total sales by price cutting.
Gross profit in money terms must at least be maintained and preferably increased. An example will make this clear. Suppose that a
retailer has a normal gross profit of 25% and sells 100 units at £1
each. His gross profit is £25. He now makes an assumption that a
10% cut in price will lead to a 50% increase in unit sales, which
proves to be correct. *Demand* is therefore very elastic. Sales revenue
is then 150 units at 18s. each, which is £135, and *cost* of sales is
150 units at 15s. each, which is £112 10s. 0d. Gross profit in money
terms has fallen from £25 to £22 10s. 0d. This means although
demand may be elastic and total sales revenue may be substantially
increased by a given price cut, it is not necessarily more profitable to
pursue this course. We need to consider a new concept, namely,
elasticity of gross profit.

This can be expressed as the percentage increase in sales quantities
necessary to maintain gross profit in money terms, for any given
percentage price reduction. More simply, a retailer will ask himself
—how much more must I sell to offset this price cut and maintain
my present profit? The answer depends not only on the elasticity of
demand for the product but also on the buying discount which the
retailer himself obtains. The greater the percentage buying margin,
the smaller the percentage increase in unit sales necessary to offset
a given price reduction, because the price reduction makes smaller
inroads into the margin. We can say that the elasticity of gross profit
is *smaller*, the *greater* the buying discount obtained.

Table XI shows how these factors operate for given discounts or
price reductions. Thus a retailer who buys at a 25% gross margin
must sell at least two-thirds more units if he gives a 10% discount,
whereas a retailer who buys at a 40% margin need only increase
sales quantities by a third for the same discount. What is evident
from Table XI is the very large increase in unit sales which must
take place to offset discounts and this is the usefulness of the table.
Although a retailer may not be able to judge in advance how
demand will respond to price cuts, he knows at least the *minimum*
increases in sales units which are necessary to maintain gross profit.

If he is fairly certain that the required expansion in sales is unlikely to be realised, then he should not reduce price.

The difference between elasticity of demand and elasticity of gross profit can perhaps be more easily seen from Fig. 9. Line (1) shows unitary elasticity of demand, *i.e.* the price and quantity relationships which maintain a constant *sales revenue*. Lines F to A show the corresponding relationships necessary to maintain *gross profit*, at

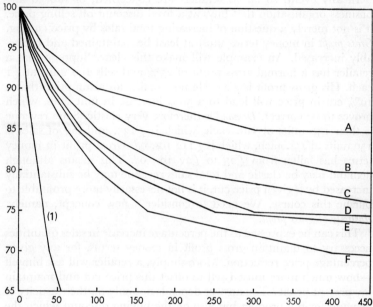

Fig. 9. Percentage increase in unit sales necessary to offset price reduction.
Horizontal axis = increase in unit sales

KEY: Line (1) Maintains Sales Revenue
	A	"	20%	Normal Gross Profit in Money Terms
"	B	"	25%	"	"	"	"	"	"
"	C	"	30%	"	"	"	"	"	"
"	D	"	33·3%	"	"	"	"	"	"
"	E	"	35·0%	"	"	"	"	"	"
"	F	"	40·0%	"	"	"	"	"	"

given buying discounts. The smaller the buying discount the more the line bends away from the unitary elasticity of demand curve, and therefore the greater the required expansion in sales. The lines would appear as continuous smooth curves if every possible discount at each buying margin had been computed. But we are concerned here only to clarify the principle involved rather than to cover every conceivable case.

In any particular example, the following formula can be used to determine the relationship between unit sales, buying margin, gross profit and discount:

Let the present retail price be 100. Then,

Percentage increase in unit sales necessary to maintain gross profit ($£$) $= \left\{ \dfrac{\text{Normal gross profit} \times 100}{\text{New selling price} - \text{Normal cost of sales}} \right\} - 100.$

As an example, let us assume that an article retails at $£13$ 10s. 0d., on which a 27·5% margin is normally made, i.e. cost of sales is 72·5%. What percentage increase in unit sales must be made to offset a 7·5% discount? Letting the normal retail price be 100 for the moment, and substituting into the formula, we have:

$$\text{Percentage increase} = \left\{ \frac{27 \cdot 5 \times 100}{92 \cdot 5 - 75 \cdot 2} \right\} - 100$$

$$= \frac{2750}{20} - 100$$

$$= 137 \cdot 5 - 100$$

$$= 37 \cdot 5\%$$

Therefore, if the retail price is reduced from $£13$ 10s. 0d. to $£12$ 9s. 9d. (i.e. 100·0 − 7·5 = 92·5) then unit sales must be increased by 37·5% to maintain gross profit in money terms.

The simplification in the analysis so far has been the assumption that the buying margin remains fixed. This is, of course, not true when the increase in unit sales envisaged is sufficiently big to justify larger purchases of stock, and therefore more favourable buying terms. Where the retailer is buying from a wholesaler, however, the extra quantity rebate may not be very significant for quite substantially increased orders, and it may be offset by the price reduction required to generate the necessary high sales turnover. In the case of direct deals with the manufacturer, it may be possible to negotiate terms which do enable a distributor to take advantage of lower prices and increased turnover. The manufacturer is reducing his unit costs by longer production runs and he may be happy to share this saving in order to secure larger orders.

Table XI shows the effect on the elasticity of gross profit of better purchase terms. A retailer who normally buys a line at a 25% margin must expect to increase sales by 25% to offset a 5% price reduction. However, if he is prepared to order in sufficient quantities to justify a 33⅓% margin, he need only increase unit sales by 17·7% to maintain gross profit.

The prerequisites to the latter course are quite obvious. First, the company must have sufficient liquidity to be able to finance the increased stock investment. Secondly, it must be reasonably sure of achieving the required turnover, otherwise not only may the gross profit in money terms be reduced but also a dangerous stock problem may build up necessitating further price cuts and inroads into the trading margin.

Buying and Stock Policy

These considerations lead logically on to the question of optimum stock levels and purchase quantities. In any buying decision there is this conflict: the larger quantity ordered may command a higher quantity discount, but it will necessitate more money tied up in stock and therefore not earning either trading or investment income. How much should we order at a time of any given line to give on balance the most profitable result, *i.e.* to have just the right amount in stock at a time?

This question has naturally attracted an immense amount of interest over the years from business analysts because it is so fundamental to profitability. Inventory theory is now a separate body of knowledge in the total mathematical and statistical approach to business problems which can loosely be called operational research. But, exhaustively as the subject has been covered theoretically, it is still in practice one of the most intransigent problems which confront businessmen. This is not merely because most businessmen cannot keep up with the higher mathematics involved (they should not have to—the theories should be susceptible of a non-technical explanation) but more because the factors which influence stock decisions are so numerous and so much subject to rapid change.

In a distributive company correct stock policy is even more important than in a manufacturing organisation, because stock is relatively a much larger proportion of total capital employed and will raise or depress the return of capital employed more strongly. Fortunately, the simplest analysis of optimum stock theory is more applicable to retail companies than to manufacturing ones (for reasons which will be apparent later) and therefore a very considerable improvement in any given stock situation can be achieved with little or no demands on sophisticated mathematical techniques.

The starting-point is the evaluation of those costs which rise as the quantity ordered is increased, and those which fall as the purchase quantity is increased. The costs which rise are insurance, depreciation, risk of obsolescence, storage and—biggest of all—interest, or profit forgone as a result of tying up liquid funds in stock. For a retail company, this "interest" cost may be a much larger figure than the return which the company makes as a whole on its invested capital, or can earn by putting money into outside securities. A sum of £10,000, say, "wasted" in excess stock would be enough to open a new branch, on which the company might

STOCK MOVEMENT AND GROSS PROFIT ANALYSIS 49

expect to earn, say, 30% per annum in pre-tax profit. The company's overall return or capital employed may be much lower than 30% because of the weight of head office and service department expenses and assets, but we should consider only the *branch* profit forgone, because the addition of one more outlet will not materially influence head office expenses. Therefore, the true cost of holding stock as against further expansion may be very considerable.

The costs which fall as the quantity ordered increases are ordering costs (a smaller volume of work in the buying office) and unit purchase costs, if quantity discounts are available. The most economic quantity to order will be that which balances these two sets of opposing costs. To take an oversimplified example, in order to make the principle clear, let us assume that an item sells at the rate of 1,000 units per year and that the company's policy is to run down stock completely before a fresh quantity is ordered. We also assume that each unit has a purchase price of £10 and that no quantity discounts are available. Ordering costs are calculated at ten shillings per order, taking into account all typing and checking time, associated record-keeping and filing. The final assumption is that profit forgone, insurance, depreciation, obsolescence and sundries can be lumped into one composite figure of 25%. The question now is: how often should orders be placed to satisfy the 1,000 units annual

TABLE XII. CALCULATION OF OPTIMUM ORDER SIZE

Purchase quantity	No. of times ordered	Order costs			Stock value			Average stock held			"Interest" at 25%			Total costs		
		£	s.	d.	£	s.	d.	£	s.	d.	£	s.	d.	£	s.	d.
5	200	100	0	0	50	0	0	25	0	0	6	5	0	106	5	0
10	100	50	0	0	100	0	0	50	0	0	12	10	0	62	10	0
15	67	32	10	0	150	0	0	75	0	0	18	15	0	52	5	0
20	50	25	0	0	200	0	0	100	0	0	25	0	0	50	0	0
25	40	20	0	0	250	0	0	125	0	0	31	5	0	51	5	0
30	33	16	10	0	300	0	0	150	0	0	37	10	0	54	0	0

Annual sales   1,000 units
Cost per unit   £10
Order cost   10s. per order
Return on capital   25% p.a.

$$\text{Economic order quantity} = \sqrt{\frac{2 \times \text{Sales} \times \text{Order costs}}{\text{Unit cost} \times \text{Interest}}}$$

$$= \sqrt{\frac{2 \times 1,000 \times \frac{1}{2} \times 100}{10 \times 25}}$$

$$= \sqrt{\frac{100,000}{250}}$$

$$= \sqrt{400}$$

$$= 20$$

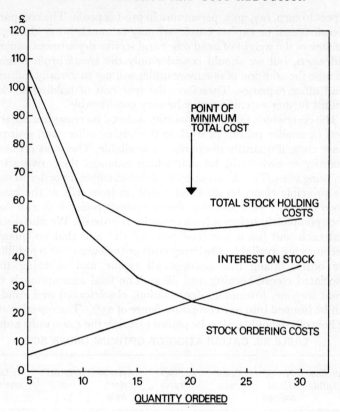

Fig. 10. Graphical representation of optimum order size.

demand and to balance the rising and falling costs, *i.e.* to minimise total costs?

Table XII shows the cost breakdown for various purchase quantities. Thus, if five are ordered at a time, 200 purchases will be made during the year and ordering costs will be £100. The stock value at cost of each order will be £50 and therefore, if stock is now run down completely before re-ordering, *average* stock held will be £25. "Interest" at 25% on this average stock investment will be £6 5s. 0d. and total costs will be £106 5s. 0d. Total costs for orders in multiples of 5 units are given up to 30 units. It will be seen that total costs are minimised at a purchase quantity of 20 units. For less than 20 units, total costs are still falling, and after 20 units costs rise again. Therefore, this item should be ordered 50 times per year to give the optimum stock-holding.

The cost analysis in Table XII is shown diagramatically in Fig. 10. The rising and falling costs intersect at the point of most economic order quantity, which is also the point, of course, where total costs are at a minimum. In practice it is not necessary to calculate the costs of a series of purchase quantities to find the one which minimises total costs. There is a simple formula which gives the answer for any set of conditions. This is given in Table XII, where it can be seen that the substitution of the data into the formula gives the required answer. Because of the need to find the square root in the calculation, it has become known as the "square-root formula."

The assumptions which have been made so far are that stock is run down completely before re-ordering takes place, no quantity discounts are available and that storage costs are fixed for all order quantities. The analysis can now be extended to take account of these factors. No company allows its stock to run down completely before re-ordering because this would leave it without a "buffer" stock. This buffer, or safety stock covers two eventualities: one, the time interval between placing an order and receipt of stock cannot always be precisely determined, and two, an unexpectedly large demand for the item may seriously deplete stocks and result in lost sales. Therefore, a higher stock than that given by the optimum order formula must be carried to cover variations in the "lead" time (replenishment interval) and the uncertainties of demand.

A great deal of statistical and mathematical analysis can, and has been devoted to the calculation of stock safety allowances, in many cases with considerable success. For example, by plotting sales data over a period of several years, a frequency distribution can be built up showing the variations around the average sales that may occur during each week, or other period of time. This histogram is analogous to the normal curve of error, which we considered in the previous chapter, and can be used to calculate the *probability* of demand being so high that the company would run out of stock of the particular line. Then, the cost of holding the extra stock necessary to provide for this possibility can be weighed against a monetary evaluation of the loss of goodwill which the company might suffer by being out of stock from time to time.

It will be apparent that this sort of detailed analysis can only be justified if the problem is very large and is worth the time and money devoted to it. For the great majority of retail companies an estimate of a suitable safety stock, based on current estimated and actual delivery dates and an intelligent scrutiny of past sales records, will be entirely adequate.

In order to include the safety stock in the economic purchase quantity calculation, we increase the annual sales by the required amount, rather than add an amount to the purchase order after calculating the optimum quantity. This gets the calculations in the

TABLE XIII. CALCULATION OF OPTIMUM ORDER SIZE WHEN QUANTITY
DISCOUNT IS AVAILABLE AND VARIABLE
STORAGE COSTS APPLY

Purchase quantity	No. of times ordered p.a.	Ordering costs			Unit purchase price			Stock value			Average stock held			"Interest" at 10%			Storage costs			Total costs		
		£	s.	d.	£	s.	d.	£	s.	d.	£	s.	d.	£	s.	d.	£	s.	d.	£	s.	d.
50	60	30	0	0	1	0	0	50	0	0	25	0	0	2	10	0	1	0	0	33	10	0
100	30	15	0	0	1	0	0	100	0	0	50	0	0	5	0	0	2	0	0	22	0	0
150	20	10	0	0	1	0	0	150	0	0	75	0	0	7	10	0	3	0	0	20	10	0
200	15	7	10	0	1	0	0	200	0	0	100	0	0	10	0	0	4	0	0	21	10	0
250	12	6	0	0		18	0	225	0	0	112	10	0	11	5	0	5	0	0	22	5	0
300	10	5	0	0		18	0	270	0	0	135	0	0	13	10	0	6	0	0	24	10	0
350	9	4	10	0		18	0	315	0	0	157	10	0	15	15	0	7	0	0	27	5	0
400	8	4	0	0		18	0	360	0	0	180	0	0	18	0	0	8	0	0	30	0	0

STEP 1: Calculate total costs at purchase quantity close to discount point. For purchase quantity of 200 total costs are £21 10s. 0d. p.a.

STEP 2: Calculate total costs at purchase quantity at or above discount point. For purchase quantity of 250 total costs are £22 5s. 0d. p.a.
Total costs *rise* when quantity discount is taken.
∴ optimum purchase quantity somewhere below 250.

STEP 3: Calculate optimum purchase quantity at unit cost of £1 by use of formula:

$$\text{Economic quantity} = \sqrt{\frac{2 \times 3{,}000 \times \frac{1}{2} \times 100}{1 \times 10}}$$

$$= \sqrt{\frac{300{,}000}{10}}$$

$$= \sqrt{30{,}000} = 173, \text{ or } 150 \text{ to nearest } 50.$$

right order. For example, if the annual sales are estimated to be 2,500 units, we may by experience increase this by 20% to cover variations in lead time and demand. This gives a revised sales estimate of 3,000 units. Table XIII shows stock carrying cost for annual sales of 3,000 units, with the following additional information:

(a) Ordering costs are 10s. per order.

(b) Unit costs are £1, except that a quantity discount of 10% is available for purchase quantities of 250 or more.

(c) "Interest" on stock is estimated to be 10%.

(d) Storage costs are variable with quantity purchased and are calculated at approximately 5d. per unit.

(e) Orders are for multiples of 50 units only.

This example takes account of two further conflicting cost elements: a *discount* which reduces unit purchase price beyond a certain quantity ordered, and therefore *encourages* larger stocks; and *storage costs*, which increase as stock is purchased and therefore *discourage* larger stocks. Is it worth while to order a large enough quantity to take advantage of the quantity discount, bearing in mind the other cost elements involved?

When quantity discounts are offered, the optimum purchase quantity cannot be found by simply solving into the formula. But very little extra work is involved. The procedure to use is shown in Table XIII. By computing total stock-holding costs on either side of the quantity discount level, it can be seen whether it is worth while to take advantage of the discount. In this example, the lower unit cost price, which results from the discount, does not compensate for the higher interest and storage costs. Therefore, the optimum purchase quantity lies somewhere below 250 units, *i.e.* at a unit cost price of £1. Then, we need only solve into the formula at a unit cost price of £1 to obtain the optimum order quantity. Table XIII shows the cost matrix for multiples of 50 units ordered up to 400 units, from which the most economic order is seen to be 150 units.

There is no doubt that this sort of analysis, intelligently applied, will result in a significant improvement in any stock situation, even if it serves only to bring home to management the measure of the costs involved. Ordering costs should be easy to calculate from the salaries and establishment expenses of the buying office and the number of orders placed per year. Interest costs will be largely estimated, but the measure is the return which could fairly be expected from putting liquid cash into some form of investment other than stock: for example, into a subsidiary company, or into new capital development, or into outside securities.

Where the square-root formula is inapplicable is in cases where the item is continuously coming into stock and being sold, *i.e.* where the stock held is merely a "transit" stock. This is why the formula is of no use to manufacturing companies who are producing and selling a line all the year round, because considerations of production runs, reducing unit costs and machine setting-up costs are important. But for a large part of the stock held by retail companies, who can switch intake off and on more or less at will, the analysis is relevant and useful.

Summary

In this chapter we have considered the interplay of forces which affect gross profit: selling-price policy, buying policy and rate of turnover of stock. The limits to which management can control these factors and guide them towards increased profitability will be different for every company, depending on such external factors as the degree of price maintenance on the goods sold and the available sources of merchandise; and on such internal factors as the financial strength of the company and its effectiveness as a marketing organisation. But, whatever these limits are, the aim should be the same: to achieve the maximum gross profit (in money terms) from the minimum stock investment. The analysis which we have described should promote these conditions.

C

Further, the gross profit and stock movement budget should take account of these aims. A useful budget should reflect not only what *may* happen, but also what *ought* to happen. Thus, by building into the budget target rates of stock turnover and gross profit, a task-setting element is introduced, which will raise efficiency and profitability, and highlight areas where slow-moving stock is accumulating. The follow-up stage is the continuous review of slow-moving stock, item by item, which alone gives effective stock control.

CHAPTER 5

CONTROL OF EXPENSES

Introduction

The techniques of budgetary control have probably been nowhere more successfully applied than in the field of expense control. This is because expenses are more largely determined by the internal factors in a business than other business variables such as sales and gross profit. They are inherently more controllable. Not only this, but they also exploit the task-setting element in budgeting more fully than the other variables. Departmental managers who are given a budget for salaries, overheads and direct selling expenses (such as advertising) can and should be called to account for the variations between actual and budgeted expenditure. This puts a direct restriction on wasteful expenditure and uneconomic use of resources, and leads to a closer realisation of desirable expense levels than would otherwise be the case. It need hardly be added that in retail companies where resale price maintenance imposes a fixed margin between cost and selling price the necessity for a strict control of expenses is paramount.

The achievement of this control depends largely on three conditions. First, there must be an adequate degree of analysis in the actual and budgeted expenses. This is largely a matter of common sense. The analysis should not be so detailed that the wood becomes hidden by the trees, but it must be sufficient to identify major cost-centres and expense-sources so that the reasons for expense variances can be given. It is important also that the actual and budgeted expense categories should be homogenous, in order to be able to compare like with like when reporting on variances. Secondly, the analysis of expenses must be done sufficiently frequently to enable the growing divergence of actual from budgeted figures to be detected. This means effectively a monthly or four-weekly analysis, resulting from a full extraction of the ledgers and preparation of the relevant trial balance and trading and profit and loss account. Without routine monthly accounting budgetary control is largely inoperable. Monthly accounting, of course, necessitates the breakdown of the budget figures into months also, so that period and cumulative variations can be seen. Thirdly, the explanation of the variations between actual and budget must be rapid, lucid and accurate. The management must be given the correct reasons for the divergences quickly and in a form which can be easily assimilated. In this way speedy corrective action can be taken and full control regained.

It is not proposed to be dogmatic about the costing system which should be used to obtain maximum control, because it will vary considerably from company to company depending on the precise nature of its business. Also, once budgetary control has been started the need for further sub-division of expense categories or amalgamation of groupings will become apparent when commenting on the

TABLE XIV. MOVEMENT OF MAJOR EXPENSE CATEGORIES, 1963–67

	1963	1964	1965	1966	1967	Budget 1968 (provisional)
	£000s	£000s	£000s	£000s	£000s	£000s
SALES	1,210·4	900·4	1,321·9	3,017·3	3,554·2	4,851·7
Advertising and display	47·2	61·2	87·2	113·0	84·3	127·1
Branch salaries	58·1	45·0	66·1	121·0	178·8	285·0
H. O. salaries	38·7	33·3	42·3	82·7	102·2	188·7
Establishment costs:						
Branches	54·5	45·0	63·5	117·0	217·1	346·7
H. O.	19·4	18·1	19·8	30·3	33·1	53·9
Overheads	20·5	16·2	22·5	52·4	102·2	161·8
Total expenses	238·4	218·8	301·4	516·4	717·7	1,163·2
	%	%	%	%	%	%
SALES	100·0	100·0	100·0	100·0	100·0	100·0
Advertising and display	3·9	6·8	6·6	3·8	2·4	2·6
Branch salaries	4·8	5·0	5·0	4·0	5·0	5·9
H. O. salaries	3·2	3·7	3·2	2·7	2·9	3·9
Establishment costs:						
Branches	4·5	5·0	4·8	3·9	6·1	7·2
H. O.	1·6	2·0	1·5	1·0	0·9	1·1
Overheads	1·7	1·8	1·7	1·7	2·9	3·3
Total expenses	19·7	24·3	22·8	17·1	20·2	24·0

variances, and thus a suitable costing system will emerge naturally out of the budgeting technique and the structure of the business. Whatever system is used, it is important to keep in view the historical movement of expenses, especially when the budget for the coming year or period is being prepared. This means that the expense forecast can be considered in relation to previous years' performance and any necessary adjustments can be made to it before it is integrated into the overall company trading budget.

Table XIV shows the sort of record which can be kept for a multiple retail group. Expenses are summarised into six major groupings and compared over a period of five years, both in money values and in percentage relation to sales. The latter figure is as important as the former because it shows how much of the gross margin is absorbed by expenses. Apart from 1964 when expenses as a percentage of sales were increased by depressed trading conditions, the expense rate averaged 19·5% of sales. This raises the query whether the provisional budget rate for 1968 of 24·0% can be accepted as it stands, and leads to a comprehensive review of all semi-fixed and variable expenses in the budget. The forecast increase in the expense rate over the preceding year for branch salaries and establishment costs may suggest, for example, that the new outlets to be opened in 1968 will have a higher expense rate in relation to turnover than the existing ones. This may be inevitable, as branch expansion increasingly covers the less profitable centres of business, but the reasons for the resultant *percentage* contraction of the net profit margin should be fully understood by the management.

The provisional expense budget shown in Table XIV is built up from more detailed individual expense budgets. In the remaining sections of this chapter we consider techniques of budgeting and analysis which can be used to control the expenses common to most retail and distributive companies. We make the assumption that branch accounting is confined mainly to keeping records of cash taken and product sales analysis, and that the responsibility for budgeting and forecasting is entirely in the hands of head office staff.

Advertising

The importance of the advertising budget depends on the type of distributive company under review. Some retail groups can come near to maximum possible sales with very little advertising, because their branch coverage is so wide that the shops themselves are their own advertisement. Others find that advertising sustains a much higher volume of turnover than would otherwise be the case, especially if a mail order activity is run in addition to the branch business. If advertising does form a significant part of total expenses it should be very carefully controlled, otherwise it may make severe inroads into the trading margin if the expected turnover does not materialise.

A typical advertising budget is shown in Table XV. Forecast expenditure is broken down into eight principal groups by four-weekly periods, and the actual expenses for the two previous years are also shown for comparison purposes. The extreme right-hand column gives the percentage amount of each type of medium. In this example more than 40% of the budget is allocated to advertising in national dailies (or weeklies) because the company operates an important mail order business. Other significant areas of expenditure

TABLE XV. ADVERTISING BUDGET

MEDIA	ACTUAL 1966	ACTUAL 1967	Four-weekly Periods														BUDGET 1968	% OF TOTAL
			1	2	3	4	5	6	7	8	9	10	11	12	13		
	£000s	£000s	£000s	£000s	£000s	£000s	£000s	£000s	£000s	£000s	£000s	£000s	£000s	£000s	£000s	£000s	
National papers	54·9	33·5	—	—	5·0	7·5	5·0	10·0	10·0	—	—	—	—	10·0	7·5	55·0	43·3
Local papers	3·8	1·7	—	—	—	0·3	0·3	0·3	0·3	—	—	—	0·3	0·3	0·3	2·1	1·6
Trade periodicals	16·4	15·6	1·0	1·0	1·0	1·0	1·5	1·5	1·5	1·5	1·0	1·0	1·0	2·5	1·5	17·0	13·4
TV/radio	—	—	—	—	—	—	—	—	—	—	—	—	—	—	3·0	3·0	2·4
Catalogues	19·7	20·0	—	—	—	—	—	10·0	—	—	—	—	—	10·0	—	20·0	15·7
Bulletins	4·7	2·3	—	—	—	2·0	—	—	—	—	2·0	—	—	1·0	—	5·0	3·9
Exhibitions	—	—	—	—	—	—	—	—	—	—	10·0	—	—	—	—	10·0	7·9
Shop display	13·5	11·2	—	1·0	1·0	2·0	1·0	1·0	1·0	1·0	1·0	1·0	1·0	2·0	2·0	15·0	11·8
Total	113·0	84·3	1·0	2·0	7·0	12·8	7·8	22·8	12·8	2·5	14·0	2·0	2·3	25·8	14·3	127·1	100·0

are advertising (throughout the year) in trade periodicals and a twice yearly catalogue.

One of the problems of the advertising budget is determining precisely the degree of success of the particular medium or insert. Where sales rise sharply after a product advertisement has been inserted in, say, a national daily, there is ample *prima facie* evidence to suggest that the advertisement caused the sales increase. But if sales rise only moderately there is the doubt that the sales increase may have been largely due to coincidental factors and the insert may not have paid for itself.

There is no easy answer to this, because once a fairly high level of advertising expenditure has been built up it cannot be suddenly switched off altogether. The "roll-on" (*i.e.* the momentum of the previous expenditure) will maintain sales for some time, but inevitably turnover will fall, and it will take a very heavy expenditure to build up sales again once advertising is resumed. Thus, adjustments to the budget must be done carefully and selectively. The essential factor is to maintain total advertising expense at or near the budgeted percentage of turnover and to devise the most appropriate and useful checks on success or failure of particular inserts.

Where a mail order business is coupled with retail outlets, the "coupon" response (*i.e.* the cut-out reply coupon on the advertisement) will be a certain guide to the effectiveness of the advertisement, at least so far as mail order business is concerned. Fig. 11 shows how mail order results from national advertising can be presented graphically to show degree of success or failure. The actual orders placed and the enquiries converted to orders for each advertisement can be accumulated to give total mail order sales for each insert. If the products advertised normally earn a gross profit of, say, $33\frac{1}{3}\%$ then each pound of advertising cost must produce three pounds of sales revenue to pay for itself, ignoring overheads. Two of the three pounds covers the cost of the product and one covers the cost of the advertisement. Therefore we divide total sales from each insert by the cost of the advertisement and draw a break-even line at £3. Any result above this figure means that the advertisement has shown a profit, on mail order sales alone. But some turnover must also have been produced at the shops, so it is reasonable to assume that a result near to, but below the break-even line (*e.g.* week 17 in Fig. 11) is marginally profitable.

The advantage of presenting the figures graphically is that the relative success of each insert can be seen easily. This method of control can also be adapted to a purely retail organisation, *i.e.* one without a mail order division. The shop sales in excess of the *seasonal average* can be totalled for a period covering the probable effectiveness of the advertisement and divided by the cost of the insert. The procedure is then as before. This gives a guide to the effectiveness of the advertisement, but without the coupon response an element of uncertainty is bound to be present.

Graphical presentation can be useful in highlighting the results on advertising by catalogue. This can be an extremely profitable form of advertising, if planned and controlled properly, particularly when it is run by a specialist mail order department of the company.

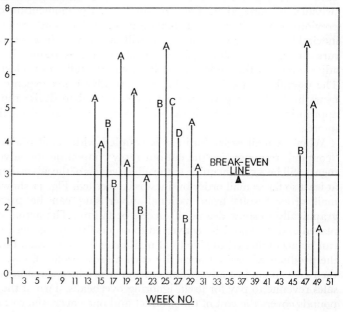

Fig. 11. Mail order results on National advertising (letter above each bar denotes national paper used).

A mailing-list is built up from all recorded and credit-worthy customers, both cash and hire-purchase, which may be supplemented by a list obtained from another company. For the catalogue to be profitable its revenue must cover all design, art-work and printing costs, as well as postage, mail-room costs and order department costs. A key factor determining the profitability of the catalogue will be the average value of orders received and this should be carefully recorded.

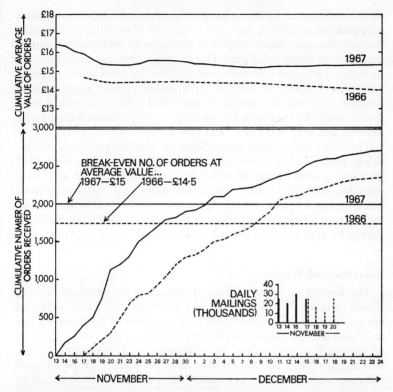

Fig. 12. Mail order results on Christmas catalogue orders 1966 and 1967.
(Sundays omitted on horizontal scale.)

Fig. 12 shows how the relevant information can be presented. The
top half of the graph gives the cumulative average value of orders
placed, and the lower half the cumulative number of orders placed
from the day of first mailing. The break-even line shows the number
of orders that must be received, at an estimated average value per
order, to make the catalogue just profitable, allowing for a certain
percentage of returned goods and cancelled orders. It can be seen
from the figure that in 1967 the catalogue passed the break-even
point earlier than in 1966 by a net difference of some three days,
after allowing for the fact that it was posted four days earlier. Also
the average value per order in 1967 exceeded the estimate by
approximately 8s. whereas in 1966 it fell below by 10s. The better
response of the 1967 catalogue and its higher average value made it
significantly more profitable than the 1966 catalogue.

Another relevant statistic is, of course, the number of orders
received per 1,000 catalogues mailed. This indicates the degree of
C*

customers' interest in the catalogue, but is not so important from a financial point of view, since the extra cost of printing and sending out another, say, 10,000 copies is not large in relation to the production cost of the catalogue. The *percentage* response may therefore be reduced by extra customer coverage, but the total orders received will almost certainly be increased, without necessarily a proportional increase in costs. We are now concerned with maximising total profits from the catalogue by selecting the optimum number to be mailed, and only experience will give a guide to this figure.

The other advertising expenditure in the budget—local advertising, inserts in trade periodicals, shop display—will be controlled in more general terms, as some degree of flexibility is obviously essential, and the rather piecemeal nature of the expenditure militates against tight control. Again the criterion will be that unless there are very compelling reasons to the contrary overall expenditure should be kept much in line with the budget.

Salaries and Wages

The budget for salaries, though important by virtue of its size, should present few technical problems. Care should be taken to ensure that existing head office departmental breakdowns are accurate, since an important element of control is that every member of the staff is responsible to a departmental manager, who is accountable both for his services and his salary. Proposed staff increases and reductions and salary increases should be notified to the budget department before the beginning of the new financial year on a form similar to that shown in Table XVI. The staff requisitions and salary proposals for all departments, together with their financial implications, can then be reviewed by the managing director, general manager or budget committee before the salaries budget is integrated into the total company trading forecast.

When any necessary amendments have been made to the staff proposals, the head office salaries budget can be prepared, as shown in Table XVII. The staff and salaries for each department for the preceding year are shown, and the planned increases (or reductions) in personnel and salary costs are effected in the appropriate four-weekly period according to the departmental requisitions (Table XVI). This means that when commenting on salary variances a full explanation can be given: number, type and salary of staff, and date of joining, compared with the budget. Associated expenses, such as employer's national insurance and pension contributions, or any casual labour, can either be allocated to each department or shown as a separate figure, both in the budget and the actual results. If the latter course is adopted an extra variance will be thrown up.

TABLE XVI. SUPPORTING SCHEDULE FOR HEAD OFFICE SALARIES BUDGET

Head Office Salaries Budget

Budgeted additional staff and salary increases   Department: Buying

Number	Job description	Budgeted annual salary	Period starting
		£	
1	Audio-typist	500	1
1	Filing clerk	400	1
1	Buying assistant	1,000	4
1	Comptometer operator	600	9
1	Part-time records clerk	300	9
5	Sub-total	2,800	
	Salary increases:		
	Assistant buyer £2 per week	100	1
	Copy-typist 10s. per week	50	1
	Filing clerk 10s. per week	50	1
5	*Annual increase in salaries* £	3,000	

Payments for overtime may be considerable at the height of the season and the salaries budget should provide for this in the departments affected.

The branch salaries budget should be approached in the same way as for head office salaries. The proposed increases in staff and salaries should be allocated to each period for all existing branches individually, after which will be added the staff and salaries of the new branches in the periods in which they are planned to open. If branch managers and sales staff are paid a commission on sales or profitability, or an annual bonus, care should be taken to give effect to this in the budget, otherwise the cash forecast as well as the branch salaries budget may be materially inaccurate. The correct method is to add up the basic salaries of all the staff in the branch, and then add total commissions (usually expressed as £x% of turnover) based on the forecast sales. This must be done for each four-weekly period, since branch salaries will tend to follow the seasonal sales pattern,

TABLE XVII. HEAD OFFICE SALARIES BUDGET
→ 13 four-weekly periods →

	ACTUAL 1967 £	No.	1 £	No.	11 £	No.	12 £	No.	13 £	No.	TOTAL BUDGET 1968 £	No.
Directors	26,000	6	2,000	6	2,000	6	2,000	6	2,000	6	26,000	6
Company secretary	6,200	4	500	4	600	5	600	5	600	5	7,400	5
Financial admin.	11,000	18	1,000	19	1,100	20	1,100	20	1,100	20	13,300	20
Internal audit	5,750	8	400	8	500	9	500	9	500	9	6,000	9
H.P. accounts	17,200	34	1,400	36	1,500	38	1,500	38	1,500	38	18,900	38
Personnel	3,600	3	300	3	300	3	300	3	300	3	3,900	3
Security	1,200	1	100	1	100	1	100	1	100	1	1,300	1
Advertising	6,000	5	500	5	500	5	500	5	500	5	6,500	5
Display	3,400	3	300	3	300	3	300	3	300	3	3,900	3
Sales promotion	—	—	—	—	200	2	200	2	200	2	2,000	2
Buying	5,000	7	500	9	700	12	700	12	700	12	8,000	12
Stock control	5,000	10	500	11	600	14	600	14	600	14	7,100	14
Data processing	4,800	6	400	7	900	15	900	15	900	15	7,900	15
Property and design	5,800	5	500	5	500	6	650	7	650	7	6,900	7
Maintenance	5,000	6	400	6	500	7	500	7	500	7	5,700	7
Records	1,300	3	100	3	100	3	100	3	100	3	1,300	3
Stores	15,000	32	1,400	33	1,700	38	1,800	39	1,800	40	20,000	40
Despatch	6,500	15	500	16	800	19	900	20	900	21	8,000	21
Transport	7,800	12	600	12	700	15	700	15	700	15	8,400	15
Repairs	22,700	40	1,800	40	2,800	50	2,800	50	2,800	50	27,000	50
Total	159,250	218	13,200	227	16,400	271	16,750	274	16,750	276	189,500	276

according to the relative amount of commission paid. If payment is made on profitability, the forecast branch profits before profit-sharing will have to be worked out before the branch salary budget can be completed. The remarks that apply here to bonuses and commissions apply equally to the head office salaries budget, if such payments are made to head office staff.

Complete control of salary and wage costs is not achieved by budgetary methods unless they are coupled with appropriate efficiency tests. This means that whenever possible, and without a disproportionate rise in administrative expense, the efficiency of staff utilisation should be measured and built into the salaries and wages budget as a task-setting factor. It is not possible, nor desirable, in a retail organisation to compute the detailed labour efficiency standards which are essential to control in a manufacturing business, but in certain areas some analysis of staff efficiency will be well rewarded, especially at the present time of selective employment tax in the distributive trades.

The key to this is to find a simple yet effective method of determining the required number of staff in a department or branch, given the volume of work to be done, and allowing for inevitable absence and seasonal influences. The latter is a very large qualifying factor in many trades and the problem may resolve itself to deciding how many permanent staff can be carried and how many temporary staff will be needed at peak periods. Also, some head office departments cannot be subjected to simple efficiency tests because their output is not measurable in quantitative terms, e.g. the company secretary's office, personnel department, security.

However the number of staff in other departments should be approximately variable with some form of output or load factor, which should be used to determine the optimum staff for budget purposes. Against this will be set the actual efficiency rates achieved during the ensuing year. For example, if the hire-purchase accounts department of 30 staff can maintain 60,000 accounts per annum without undue strain, then the output factor for budget purposes may be said to be 2,000 accounts per person per year. If the hire-purchase manager puts in a requisition for, say, five more staff, this suggests that he expects to take on approximately 10,000 new accounts, i.e. an expansion of about 17%. The relevance of this estimate should be tested against the sales budget (and the budgeted proportion of H.P. to total sales) before the requisition is accepted. Also, it is the responsibility of the budget department to check from time to time that the budget level of output is being maintained, and if it is seriously adrift, to find out and report on the reasons for the disparity.

Below are listed the output factors which can be used to test the staff-efficiency in the important departments of a retail organisation. The letter (A) denotes that staff are almost *directly* proportionate to the output factor and (B) denotes that staff are *approximately* proportionate to the output factor:

Department	Output factor governing no. of staff	
Financial Administration	Annual Sales Volume	(B)
Internal Audit/Stock Checking	No. of Branches	(B)
Hire-purchase Accounts	No. of H.P. Accounts	(A)
Advertising	Annual Advertising Budget	(B)
Display	No. of Branches	(A)
Buying	No. of Orders placed p.a.	(B)
Stock Control	No. of Branches	(A)
Data Processing	No. of Documents processed	(A)
Stores/Despatch	Annual Sales Volume	(A)
Transport	No. and "spread" of Branches	(A)
Branch Staff	Branch Sales Volume	(B)

Notwithstanding all the foregoing, where a company employs labour-saving devices such as office machines or a computer, there may, of course, be opposite trends of staff and output, and if this is the case the budget should be adjusted accordingly.

Establishment Costs

These cover the mainly fixed expenses of being established at head office and at the branches. Opinions will differ about the precise definition of this collective group of costs. We have chosen to include only the expenses that can be specifically and conveniently allocated to each separate establishment, *i.e.* rent, rates, light, heat, cleaning, telephone, depreciation and amortisation. Other expenses such as insurance, repairs and renewals may also be included if desired.

A typical establishment costs budget for a multiple retail group is shown in Table XVIII. There is a partly variable element in such expenses as light and heat, telephone and cleaning, and some forecasting must be done to budget for these in the year under review. The other expenses are fixed and come direct from the financial accounting records. It is useful to show the market rental of each establishment as this may differ substantially from the actual rental. The rental "profit" may then be seen, which enables fair comparisons to be made about the true profitability of each branch, assuming that each pays its market rent. Also, the capital profit which would arise on a revaluation of properties can quickly be calculated (by comparing columns 4 and 5 in Table XVIII).

TABLE XVIII. ESTABLISHMENT COSTS BUDGET

Branch	1 Total 1967 £	2 Rent Payable £	3 Rent receivable £	4 Net rent payable £	5 Market rental (net) £	6 General and water rates £	7 Light and heat £	8 Cleaning £	9 Telephone and telex £	10 Depreciation of fixtures and fittings £	11 Amortisation of lease premium £	12 Total Budget 1968 £
Head Office	33,158	31,000	9,000	22,000	25,000	8,250	5,660	2,700	5,000	8,000	2,290	53,900
Branch 1	5,237	4,500	350	3,150	3,500	590	520	150	230	900	—	5,540
Branch 2	3,359	2,000	—	2,000	3,000	380	310	120	80	400	180	3,470
Branch 3 etc.												
New Branches (part year only)												
Branch 40 (from period 3)	—	1,150	660	490	500	220	30	40	20	160	—	960
Branch 41 (from period 5)	—	1,000	—	1,000	1,000	230	40	50	40	170	100	1,630
Branch 42 (from period 6)	—	1,500	—	1,500	1,500	430	160	70	50	430	—	2,640
Total £	250,207	229,430	37,430	192,000	220,000	66,430	24,630	16,580	20,960	59,270	20,730	400,600

(*Note:* Column 5 is not included in cross-cast)

Since this budget covers mainly fixed expenses, there is no need to break it down into months or four-weekly periods. It will suffice merely to divide the total expenses of all *existing* establishments by 12 or 13, and then to add the expenses of the new establishments in the months or periods in which they are planned to open. The information in Table XVIII, therefore, is sufficient to enable the monthly establishment costs estimate to be put straight into the summarised trading budget, with possibly the use of an intermediate working-paper.

Overhead Expenses

These cover all the other expenses which do not fall into the categories previously considered. They can be summarised into four sections: financial, legal, distribution and other expenses, as shown in Table XIX. Some companies would treat distribution expenses as direct selling costs rather than as overheads, but we treat them in this way since they are not large enough to justify a separate budget. Many more expense headings could also be included as sub-classifications of those shown in Table XIX, but, as stated earlier, it is important not to present a confusing picture, which may well arise if the list of expenses is too long. When reporting on variances, it is always possible to make a more detailed analysis of invoices and vouchers and thus highlight exceptional items. Further, the break-down of expenses in the financial and cost accounts should be the same as in the budget to facilitate direct comparison; this itself precludes unnecessary sub-classification of expenses and resulting labour costs of coding invoices and vouchers.

Some of the items in the overheads budget cannot be entered until the cash budget has been made up: bank and loan interest, for example. The extent to which the company's trading activities will require financing by the bank and other sources must be estimated before the interest charges on such loans and advances can be computed. The other overhead expenses will either stem logically from the planned developments of the company or will be forecast on the most intelligent basis available. Legal expenses will be largely dominated by conveyancing costs, which will probably reflect the planned expansion of branches. Distribution expenses will be variable with both the expansion in branches and the concomitant expansion in sales volume. Repairs and renewals will likewise be based on a firm estimate of planned expenditure.

Other expenses, such as staff travelling, printing and stationery and sundry trade expenses, must be estimated in more general terms, usually on the basis of the growth experienced in previous years. The budget should in any event show the actual expenditure in the

TABLE XIX. OVERHEAD EXPENSE BUDGET

Four-weekly periods

	ACTUAL 1967		Period 1	Period 2	Period 3	Period 7	Period 8	Period 9	Period 10	Period 11	Period 12	Period 13	BUDGET 1968	
	£	% on T/O	£	£	£	£	£	£	£	£	£	£	£	% on T/O
Financial Expenses:														
Bank interest and charges	5,223	0·15	640	640	640								8,330	0·18
Loan interest	3,422	0·10	340	340	340								4,400	0·09
H.P. interest	1,240	0·03	200	200	200								2,600	0·05
Sub-total	9,885	0·28	1,180	1,180	1,180								15,330	0·32
Legal Expenses:														
Legal and professional	5,207	0·15	680	680	680								8,850	0·18
Audit	2,488	0·07	210	210	210								2,800	0·06
Share transfers	377	0·01	40	40	40								500	0·01
Patents and trade marks	417	0·01	30	30	30								420	0·01
Sub-total	8,489	0·24	960	960	960								12,570	0·26
Distribution Expenses:														
Postage	17,381	0·49	1,500	2,200	1,750								24,000	0·50
Packing	2,682	0·08	300	700	250								4,500	0·09
Motor and van	14,687	0·41	1,750	2,500	1,650								25,000	0·51
Losses on sale of M/V's	316	0·01	—	—	200								1,000	0·02
Sub-total	35,066	0·99	3,550	5,400	3,850								54,500	1·12
Other Expenses:														
Insurances	9,202	0·26	1,150	1,150	1,150								15,000	0·31
Repairs and renewals	18,105	0·51	2,400	1,000	3,000								30,220	0·62
Loss on sales of f/f	1,072	0·03	—	—	—								1,500	0·03
Directors' expenses	3,775	0·10	200	750	200								5,500	0·11
Staff travelling	1,007	0·03	110	120	130								2,000	0·04
Printing and stationery	11,472	0·32	1,300	2,000	750								16,000	0·33
Canteen	1,402	0·04	120	120	140								2,000	0·04
Sundry trade	2,736	0·08	500	700	600								7,180	0·15
Sub-total	48,771	1·37	5,780	5,840	5,970								79,400	1·63
Total	102,211	2·88	11,470	13,380	11,960								161,800	3·33

previous year, as in Table XIX, so that the financial implications of expansion can be seen and whether the forecast expenses look reasonable. Expenses should also be expressed as a percentage of sales turnover for the previous year and in the budget. This enables the management to see how much sales revenue is absorbed by each category of expense. In Table XIX the planned expansion of the company will lead to a greater *percentage* absorption of sales revenue by overheads (from 2·88% to 3·33%) particularly by distribution and other overheads.

A final point in constructing the overheads budget is to ensure that the analysis into months or periods is on the same basis as that which operates in the financial accounts. If, for example, the basis of charging legal expenses in the actual profit and loss account is to provide one thirteenth of the estimated annual charge each four-weekly period, this is the way the budgeted expense should be allocated. Whilst actual and budgeted expenses are running much in line, therefore, no variance will be shown on the monthly expense analysis. A number of small variances are thus eliminated. The overheads budget must, of course, be analysed into months or four-weekly periods, as some of the expenses (distribution particularly) are very much influenced by the seasonal pattern of sales, and others are known to occur in specific periods.

Monthly Reporting

Real control of expenses comes from the comparison of the actual with the budgeted figures, followed quickly by a concise and clear report on the variances. Monthly or four-weekly reporting is most useful, as it is neither too infrequent to impede effective corrective action nor too frequent to be an administrative burden. It is usually possible (if necessary by combining one or two of the smaller expense categories) to contain the monthly expense analysis on one sheet of paper, as shown in Table XX. The monthly and cumulative figures should be shown, as well as the percentage of actual expenses to actual sales turnover and the percentage of budgeted expenses to budgeted turnover. This enables the management to see which expenses are absorbing more revenue than budgeted and thus eroding the net profit return on sales.

The explanation for the variances between actual and budget should be set out on an accompanying sheet of paper and listed (by line number) in the same order as the expenses appear in the monthly analysis. Small variances should be ignored and larger ones should only be given enough commentary to explain briefly the reasons for the variance and what action has been taken, or is proposed, to correct the situation. Where no correcting action is possible, the

TABLE XX. PERIOD EXPENSE ANALYSIS

Period No.:
W/E:

| | Four-week period | | | Cumulative | | |
	Actual	Budget	Vari-ance	Actual	Budget	Vari-ance
	£ | % of T/O	£ | % of T/O	£	£ | % of T/O	£ | % of T/O	£
Advertising:						
1. National/local	— | —	— | —	—			
2. Trade	930 | 0·25	1,000 | 0·26	−70			
3. Catalogues/bulletins	— | —	— | —	—			
4. Display	130 | 0·03	— | —	+130			
5. Others	— | —	— | —	—			
Sub-total	1,060 | 0·28	1,000 | 0·26	+60			
Salaries:						
6. Head Office	11,347 | 3·03	11,900 | 3·06	−553			
7. Branches	16,221 | 4·33	17,600 | 4·54	−1,379			
Sub-total	27,568 | 7·36	29,500 | 7·60	−1,932			
Establishment costs:						
8. Net rent payable	13,750 | 3·67	14,760 | 3·80	−1,010			
9. General and water rate	4,927 | 1·31	5,100 | 1·31	−173			
10. Light and heat	1,747 | 0·47	1,890 | 0·49	−143			
11. Cleaning	1,047 | 0·28	1,270 | 0·33	−223			
12. Telephone and Telex	1,653 | 0·44	1,610 | 0·42	+43			
13. Depreciation of f/f	4,223 | 1·13	4,550 | 1·17	−327			
14. Amortisation	1,575 | 0·42	1,590 | 0·41	−15			
Sub-total	28,922 | 7·72	30,770 | 7·93	−1,848			
Overheads:						
15. Bank interest and charges	640 | 0·17	640 | 0·17	—			
16. Loan interest	340 | 0·09	340 | 0·09	—			
17. H. P. interest	200 | 0·05	200 | 0·05	—			
18. Legal and professional	680 | 0·18	680 | 0·17	—			
11. Audit	210 | 0·06	210 | 0·05	—			
20. Share transfers	40 | 0·01	40 | 0·01	—			
21. Patents and trade marks	30 | 0·01	30 | 0·01	—			
22. Postage	1,377 | 0·37	1,500 | 0·39	−123			
23. Packing	310 | 0·08	300 | 0·08	+10			
24. Motor van	1,685 | 0·45	1,750 | 0·45	−65			
25. Loss on sale of motor vehicles	— | —	— | —	—			
26. Insurances	1,150 | 0·31	1,150 | 0·30	—			
27. Repairs and renewals	2,746 | 0·73	2,400 | 0·62	+346			
28. Loss on sale of f/f	— | —	— | —	—			
29. Directors' expenses	15 | —	200 | 0·05	−185			
30. Staff travelling	136 | 0·04	110 | 0·03	+26			
31. Printing and stationery	1,215 | 0·32	1,300 | 0·33	−85			
32. Canteen	125 | 0·03	120 | 0·03	+5			
33. Sundry trade	774 | 0·21	500 | 0·13	+274			
Sub-total	11,673 | 3·11	11,470 | 2·96	+203			
Total	69,223 | 18·47	72,740 | 18·75	−3,517			

variance will be carried forward in the cumulative column each month, and instead of making the same explanatory comment each month attention should be paid to the *monthly* variance. The management accountant, budget controller or whoever is reporting on variances can speed up the production of his report by keeping in close touch throughout the month with the financial accountant or book-keeper and so be forewarned of any exceptional expense items that have occurred.

Salaries and wages should be the subject of a separate report so that the departmental and branch analysis is shown. This is only a matter of listing the salaries and wages straight from the payroll sheets and comparing them with the budgeted salaries and staff as in Table XVII. A brief report on departmental and branch variances can then be made, as for the total expense summary.

Allocation of Expenses to Departments and Branches

In our treatment of expenses so far we have considered them under their broad generic headings, *e.g.* advertising, salaries, overheads. This is both logical, because related costs can be viewed together, and convenient, because no cross-allocation of expenses among departments is involved. There may be circumstances, however, when it is desirable to know the cost of a department *in total*, not just the salary expenses and direct overheads, for example. Many accountants would not consider that a proper cost accounting system had been installed unless it provided for the absorption of all expenses by departments and by sales outlets. The argument in favour of this point of view is that only in this way does the management see the true cost of each department and how much must be recovered by each sales outlet to pay for head office expenses.

The arguments against this are threefold. One, cross-allocation of expenses among departments and branches entails a considerable amount of administrative work. Two, many of the expenses that are "charged" to each department are not under the control of the departmental manager and thus the rule of accountability is broken. Three, arbitrary methods of allocation are inevitable by the very nature of some of the expenses.

These points can perhaps be made clearer from Table XXI. The departments and branches are listed down the left-hand side and the major expense groupings across the top. Every expense is then allocated to a branch or department so that the vertical total at the extreme right equals the horizontal total at the bottom. Instead of filling in some specimen figures we have coded each column to show the method of allocation: either *directly allocated* (*e.g.* salaries), or *apportioned* on a reasonable basis (*e.g.* departmental rent and rates on

TABLE XXI. ABSORPTION OF EXPENSES BY DEPARTMENTS AND SALES OUTLETS

Department/Branch	Advertising	Salaries	Establishment costs	Financial overheads	Legal overheads	Distributive overheads	Other overheads	Total £
Directors	—	D	A	E	E	—	E/A	
Company Secretary	—	D	A	E	E/A	—	E/A	
Financial admin.	—	D	A	E	E/A	—	E/A	
Internal audit	—	D	A	E	E/A	—	E/A	
H. P. accounts	—	D	A	E	E/A	—	E/A	
Personnel	—	D	A	E	E	—	E/A	
Security	—	D	A	E	E	—	E/A	
Advertising	—	D	A	E	E	—	E/A	
Display	—	D	A	E	E	—	E/A	
Sales promotion	—	D	A	E	E	—	E/A	
Buying	—	D	A	E	E	—	E/A	
Stock control	—	D	A	E	E/A	—	E/A	
Data processing	—	D	A	E	E/A	—	E/A	
Property & design	—	D	A	E	E A	—	E/A	
Maintenance	—	D	A	E	E	—	E/A	
Records	—	D	A	E	E	—	E/A	
Stores	—	D	A	E	E	E/A	E/A	
Despatch	—	D	A	E	E	D	E/A	
Transport	—	D	A	E	E	D	E/A	
Service dept.	—	D	A	E	E	—	E/A	
Sub-total H. O.	—	D	D	E	E A			
Branch 1	E A	D	D	E	E A	E	D/A	
Branch 2	E/A	D	D	E	E/A	E	D/A	
Branch 3	E/A	D	D	E	E/A	E	D/A	
Branch 4	E/A	D	D	E	E/A	E	D/A	
Branch 5	E/A	D	D	E	E/A	E	D/A	
Branch 6	E/A	D	D	E	E/A	E	D/A	
Branch 7 etc.	E/A	D	D	E	E/A	E	D/A	
Total £	127,100	473,700	400,600	15,330	12,570	54,500	79,400	1,163,200

D = Directly allocated.
A = Apportioned on reasonable basis, e.g. floor area occupied.
E = Estimated on arbitrary basis.

the basis of floor area occupied), or *estimated* on an arbitrary basis (*e.g.* financial overheads on the basis of floor area or annual salaries bill).

Table XXI shows that a considerable proportion of the expense items must be apportioned or allocated arbitrarily to head office departments and this raises the question whether the end product is worth the work involved. It is true that some of the expenses can be allocated to specific departments, *e.g.* audit fees to the financial and administration departments, printing and stationery to the departments with greatest usage. It is also true that some benefit can be obtained from a departmental manager seeing the *value* of the services which he receives from other departments and expenses. But, if he has no control over these externally charged expenses, there is very little that he can do about them. Therefore, unless there are very good reasons to the contrary, the principle of accountability should not be departed from, *i.e.* every expense should be under someone's control and that person should be accountable only for the expenses actually under his control.

The circumstances which make the breaking of this rule unavoidable are when we consider the sales outlets by themselves. Allocation of head office expenses (in total, rather than individually) enables the manager of each branch usefully to see the value of the services he is obtaining from head office—advertising, centralised buying, accounting—and also enables him to calculate his break-even sales by adding his own branch expenses to this allocation, thus giving total branch costs. He knows that he must produce a certain weekly or annual turnover, whose gross profit covers his total expenses. Below this turnover, his branch runs at a loss and above it the gross profit earned is almost wholly net profit.

There is no simple, yet entirely satisfactory, method of allocating head office expenses to branches, and resort is almost inevitably made to an arbitrary basis. Nevertheless, it is important that the allocation is made, because *all* expenses must be recovered from the revenue-earning departments, *i.e.* the branches and mail order outlet, if any. In a later chapter on branch profitability (Chapter 9) we consider ways and means of achieving a useful and equitable apportionment of head office expenses.

Summary

Properly constructed budgets are an invaluable method of controlling expenses, provided that they are coupled with managerial accountability for variances. Wherever possible, task-setting factors should be built into the budgets to strengthen profit-consciousness. The value of inter-departmental recovery of costs is dubious, because the principle of complete managerial accountability becomes confused and the administrative cost involved may outweigh the benefits accruing. The important exception is that all expenses must be recovered from the revenue-earning outlets. All variable and semi-fixed expenses should be the subject of continuous scrutiny to see where reductions can be made. This entails adequate statistical analysis of costs and expenses in absolute terms and related to sales-revenue.

In the next chapter we consider further the relationships between fixed and variable expenses and their effect on profitability.

CHAPTER 6

THE TRADING AND
PROFIT AND LOSS BUDGET

Summary of Forecast Results

Having finalised the budgets for sales, gross profit and expenses, it is now possible to put them together and produce the budgeted trading and profit and loss account—the chief purpose of the whole budgeting and forecasting exercise. It must be stressed that up till this stage the "budgets" are still provisional, since if the forecast trading results are unacceptable there may have to be a further review of sales, gross profit and expenses. For a distributive company this review will particularly concern the estimated expenses of the planned new outlets, as these may be escapable costs if the forecast expansion yields a less than desirable net return. The pressure on liquidity which the proposed capital development will impose must also be considered before the trading budget can be finalised.

Table XXII shows the summary trading and profit and loss budget, analysed by four-weekly periods. As in the supporting budgets, the previous year's actual results are shown for comparison purposes and expenses and profits are expressed as percentages of sales. Ignoring for the moment the profit (or loss) arising from the financing of any hire-purchase business transacted, total expenses are simply deducted from gross profit to give net profit before tax. A further column could be added at the bottom of the table to give net profit carried forward cumulatively, which would cross-cast to the total column on the extreme right. In companies with a highly seasonal sales pattern there may be low-turnover months when net losses are unavoidable. These may be points of particular financial strain, owing to low cash income, and this makes the construction of a detailed monthly cash budget more than ever necessary. Gross profit in Table XXII is taken straight from the gross profit budget, so that it is not necessary in the trading and profit and loss budget to give the monthly purchases and stock balances. When reporting on the variance between actual and budgeted gross profit a separate analysis will be made of sales, purchases and stock movements by product groups to the extent available and required.

TABLE XXII. TRADING AND PROFIT AND LOSS BUDGET

←——————— Four-weekly periods ———————→

	Actual 1967 £	Actual 1967 %	Period 1 £	Period 1 %	Period 2 £	Period 2 %	Period 12 £	Period 12 %	Period 13 £	Period 13 %	Budget 1968 £	Budget 1968 %
SALES	3,554,207	100·0	388,000	100·0	402,000	100·0					4,851,700	100·0
Gross profit	1,137,104	32·0	128,400	33·1	135,500	33·7					1,666,000	34·3
Expenses:												
Advertising	84,319	2·4	1,000	0·3	2,000	0·5					127,100	2·6
Branch salaries	178,835	5·0	17,600	4·5	18,390	4·6					285,000	5·9
Head office salaries	102,223	2·9	11,900	3·1	11,900	3·0					188,700	3·9
Establishment costs	250,207	7·0	30,770	7·9	30,930	7·6					400,600	8·3
Overheads:												
Financial	9,885	0·3	1,180	0·3	1,180	0·3					15,330	0·3
Legal	8,489	0·2	960	0·2	960	0·2					12,570	0·3
Distribution	35,066	1·0	3,550	0·9	5,400	1·3					54,500	1·1
Others	48,771	1·4	5,780	1·6	5,840	1·6					79,400	1·6
Total expenses	717,795	20·2	72,740	18·8	76,600	19·1					1,163,200	24·0
NET PROFIT BEFORE TAX	419,309	11·8	55,660	14·3	58,900	14·6					502,800	10·3

TABLE XXIII. APPROXIMATE CASH FORECAST

	£	£
Net profit before tax (per trading summary)		503,000
Add		
Depreciation of fixtures and fittings	59,270	
Amortisation of leases	20,730	80,000
Net profit before tax and depreciation		583,000
Add		
Estimated increase in trade creditors	22,000	
Estimated proceeds of sale of leases	47,000	
Estimated proceeds of sale of investments	25,000	94,000
		677,000
Less		
Estimated increase in trade debtors	17,000	
Budgeted increase in stock at cost	210,000	
Estimated taxation payable	158,000	
Estimated dividends payable	63,000	
Estimated capital expenditure	186,000	634,000
Increase in cash in budget year		43,000
Estimated overdraft at beginning of budget year		137,000
Estimated overdraft at end of budget year		94,000

Approximate Cash Forecast

In order that the overall implications of the budget can be studied before it is finalised, an approximation must be made of the effect of the budget proposals on the cash position. This is not intended to replace the detailed cash forecast, but merely to enable amendments to be made to the budget, if required, before preparing the detailed monthly cash forecast and projected balance sheet. Table **XXIII** shows the sort of statement that can be prepared. Since we are concerned at this stage only to see the total cash movement, we short-circuit the detailed receipts and payments calculations by making an estimate of the balance sheet at the beginning and end of the budget period and adjusting it by estimated net profit and appropriations thus giving net cash flow. The balance sheet and cash position must be estimated at the *beginning* of the period since the budgets will normally be prepared before the start of the budget year.

The forecast cash movement made in this way should be reasonably accurate, provided that care is taken in estimating debtor and creditor changes. Study of previous years' balance sheets will be a good guide. Depreciation and amortisation charges, which must be added back to budgeted net profit before tax, are taken straight from the establishment costs budget. The stock change over the budget year is likewise taken from the stock movement budget. It then only remains to make an estimate of tax and dividend charges in the year, which should be quite accurate, and planned capital expenditure. The latter figure will reflect the branch and head office development programme, refitting and resiting of units, purchases of office machinery, and so on, and will be based on firm proposals. In Table XXIII it will be seen that, although a substantial capital expenditure programme is envisaged, there will nevertheless be a net increase in cash during the budget year. On the basis, therefore, that working capital will be adequate the budget is accepted.

Volume and Profit Relationships

The acceptance of the budget does not end the consideration of possible sales and profit levels. It is a statement of what results are likely to be achieved given reasonable conformity of actual to forecast events and decisions. But in times of rapid change, both technically and economically, actuality may defy even the most carefully conceived forecast, and thought must be given to likely levels of profit if sales, margins and expenses do differ significantly from the budget.

Table XXIV shows the type of table that should accompany the budget to give the management a survey of probable profitability levels at differing sales volumes. The key to a study of this nature is a precise differentiation between fixed and variable expenses, since the relationship of one to the other and to sales governs *marginal* profitability, *i.e.* the extra profit which results from extra sales turnover. In Table XXIV, establishment costs are assumed to be constant for all sales volumes, an assumption which is not entirely true because falling sales would exert a downward pressure on telephone and light and heat costs and any other semi-fixed expenses in this category. This would be due to management taking a more critical view of the abuse of telephone, light and heat costs and petty cash expenditure, which tends to go unnoticed in good times. However, the economies would be minimal and the assumption of fixed establishment costs simplifies the analysis. Semi-fixed costs are taken to include branch basic salaries, head office salaries and all overheads except distribution overheads. Branch basic salaries (*i.e.* excluding commissions and bonuses directly variable with sales) will tend to rise with rising turnover as more staff are engaged, but the rise will not be *proportional* to turnover. The same applies to head office salaries where, on the one hand, a fall in sales volume will not permit a large reduction in staff and, on the other, an increase in sales will not require further recruitment.

Obviously, consideration must be given to the likely permanency of the rise or fall in turnover, but this inflexibility of salary costs will

TABLE XXIV. SALES AND PROFIT RELATIONSHIPS

	Budget Sales less 38%		Budget Sales less 10%		Budget Sales less 5%		BUDGET		Budget Sales plus 5%		Budget Sales plus 10%	
	£000s	%	£000s	%	£000s	%	£000s	%	£000s	%	£000s	%
SALES	3,000·0	100·0	4,366·8	100·0	4,609·4	100·0	4,852·0	100·0	5,094·6	100·0	5,337·2	100·0
Gross Profit	930·0	31·0	1,445·0	33·1	1,558·0	33·8	1,666·0	34·3	1,772·0	34·8	1,867·0	35·0
Fixed Expenses:												
Establishment Costs (1)	400·6	13·3	400·6	9·2	400·6	8·7	400·6	8·3	400·6	7·9	400·6	7·5
Semi-Fixed Expenses:												
Branch basic salaries	150·0	5·0	170·0	3·9	185·0	4·0	203·0	4·2	215·0	4·2	230·0	4·3
Head Office salaries	160·0	5·3	170·0	3·9	175·0	3·8	188·7	3·9	200·0	3·9	210·0	3·9
Financial overheads	12·0	0·4	13·0	0·3	14·0	0·3	15·3	0·3	16·0	0·3	16·5	0·3
Legal overheads	11·0	0·4	11·5	0·3	12·0	0·3	12·6	0·3	13·0	0·3	13·4	0·3
Other overheads	65·0	2·2	70·0	1·6	75·0	1·6	79·4	1·6	83·0	1·6	88·0	1·7
Total Semi-fixed Expenses (2)	398·0	13·3	434·5	10·0	461·0	10·0	499·0	10·3	527·0	10·3	557·9	10·5
Variable Expenses:												
Advertising	78·0	2·6	113·5	2·6	120·0	2·6	127·1	2·6	132·3	2·6	138·8	2·6
Branch commissions, etc.	51·0	1·7	74·2	1·7	78·3	1·7	82·0	1·7	86·5	1·7	90·7	1·7
Distribution overheads	43·0	1·4	48·1	1·1	50·7	1·1	54·5	1·1	56·1	1·1	58·7	1·1
Total Variable Expenses (3)	172·0	5·7	235·8	5·4	249·0	5·4	263·6	5·4	274·9	5·4	288·2	5·4
Total Expenses (1)+(2)+(3)	970·6	32·3	1,070·9	24·6	1,110·6	24·1	1,163·2	24·0	1,202·5	23·6	1,246·7	23·4
Net Profit	−40·6	1·3	374·1	8·5	447·4	9·7	502·8	10·3	569·5	11·2	620·3	11·6

tend to persist through normal cycles of economic activity. All overhead costs, with the exception of distribution expenses, will likewise vary much less than proportionately to sales. Indeed, some expenses, such as bank and loan interest, may rise in times of falling turnover if day-to-day cash requirements must be met more and more from external sources. Other expenses are assumed to be more or less completely variable with sales. In Table XXIV advertising is held at the budget rate of 2·6% of sales at all levels of turnover—an arbitrary assumption. Branch commissions will certainly vary proportionately to turnover, and distribution expenses will be mainly variable, higher sales turnover necessitating more frequent deliveries to branches and postage of goods to customers.

Having made the classification into fixed, semi-fixed and variable expenses, the next step is to estimate the level of expenses at various sales volumes. This only involves the semi-fixed expenses, since the fixed expenses are constant at all turnover levels and the variable expenses are a fixed *percentage* of sales—5·4% in this example. The likely movement of semi-fixed expenses in relation to turnover may pose some difficult theoretical questions but it should be possible to arrive at a logically based progression.

Table XXIV shows expenses at the budget level of sales (heavily outlined) and at levels of 5% and 10% above and below the budget. A further assumption is that, as sales volume increases, gross profit as a percentage of sales increases, because the company can command better buying terms, *e.g.* in the form of quantity discounts. What is immediately clear from Table XXIV is the rapid increase in profit as sales turnover increases. This is because fixed and semi-fixed expenses absorb a smaller and smaller proportion of gross profit, which itself is increasing in percentage terms, as sales volume expands. The aim of all profit-earning organisations, both manufacturing and distributive, is to "spread" fixed costs over a larger and larger turnover and so reduce their incidence, but in the case of retail companies (especially multiple retailers) it is particularly important because of the high proportion of fixed costs (rents, rates, depreciation) in the total expense bill. Thus, in Table XXIV a 5% increase in sales volume gives a 13% increase in profits (from £503,000 to £570,000) and a 10% increase in sales gives a 23% increase in profits. The fall in profit is equally progressive when sales volume contracts.

This sensitiveness of profits to sales in "high fixed cost" companies makes the accuracy of the sales forecast doubly important if the profit forecast is to be even in the region of actuality, and imposes a considerable burden on the person ultimately responsible for the forecast. But, as stated earlier, in rapidly changing conditions the best forecast can be appreciably adrift and this is why it is important to acquaint the management with likely profit levels should actual sales turn out to be different from the forecast. Then, not only is the significance of the relationship between fixed and variable costs brought home to the management, but also an additional task-setting element is introduced in the form of a substantial profit incentive if the sales forecast is exceeded. Further, the evaluation of sales/profit relationships at various turnover levels is of considerable help when making interim forecasts, as we explain later in this chapter.

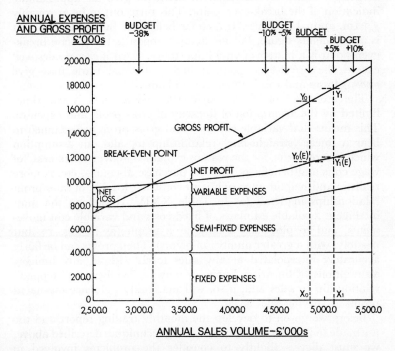

Fig. 13. Break-even chart (data from Table XXIV).

These relationships are frequently illustrated graphically by means of the so-called "break-even" chart, which is nothing more than a graphical representation of the sort of information shown in Table XXIV. It has the advantage, however, that profit (or loss) can be estimated at all conceivable turnover levels. Fig. 13 shows the data of Table XXIV converted into a break-even chart. Annual sales volumes are plotted on the horizontal axis and expenses and gross profit on the vertical axis. Fixed expenses are constant for all sales volumes, to which are added semi-fixed expenses at each sales level and then variable expenses. Having plotted gross profit at various sales levels, net profit can be read off the chart.

In Table XXIV profits at five sales levels are estimated between minus ten per cent and plus ten per cent of budget, and these are plotted in Fig. 13. Thus budget profit is represented by the distance X_0,Y_0 minus X_0,Y_0 (E), *i.e.* gross profit less expenses at budgeted sales level. Net profit when sales are 5% ahead of budget is shown by the distance Y_1,Y_1 (E). This is £570,000, or 13% up on the budget level. Also shown in Table XXIV and plotted in Fig. 13 is the profit at budget turnover less 38%, in order to give an approximate indication of the break-even point. This turns out to be at roughly £3·1m. annual turnover. It is so far below the budget level that it is an academic figure, but for many companies the precise break-even point is a matter of vital importance. Even if *annual* sales well exceed the break-even point a highly seasonal trade may give *monthly* losses and this is important to know.

The usefulness of break-even charts and analysis is sometimes limited by the assumption of linearity of gross profit and expenses. This means that variable expenses and gross profit are assumed to bear a linear (straight-line) relationship to sales, an assumption which is rarely true, for the reasons explained above: "stickiness" of wage costs and benefits of variable purchase discounts, etc. A more realistic and helpful approach is to construct a table of sales/profit relationships in detail (as in Table XXIV), based on the most intelligent available estimates of fixed costs and variable cost movements, and to plot such a table as a graph (as in Fig. 13, but possibly, with a greater number of points). Then profits can be fairly accurately interpolated at any sales level, without any limiting assumptions of linearity. Expenses may in fact bear a "stepped" relationship to sales and, if so, will materially influence estimated profits at varying sales levels.

Before we go on to develop the monthly trading report and the use made in it of the variable forecasting techniques described above, we must digress slightly to consider the problems involved in budgeting for hire-purchase profits and losses, since this method of sale may form a large part of the company's business.

The Hire-Purchase Profit and Loss Budget

How much work is entailed in making up the hire-purchase budget depends on the method of financing and administering the debt. At the one extreme there are the numerous small retailers who effect the H.P. transaction but then pass the whole responsibility for collection and control of the debt to a finance house, the retailer usually remaining liable under a recourse agreement for all or part of any bad debts arising. In this case no budgeting problems are involved other than making a suitable provision for recourse and discounting charges. At the other extreme are the big companies who finance the whole of their H.P. debt themselves and who cover administration expenses and bad debt provisions by the interest charged to customers. Here, a full-scale H.P. expense and finance budget is clearly required. Many medium-sized companies take the middle course, *i.e.* they administer and collect the debt themselves but fund it through a finance house, either under a block-discounting scheme or a debenture secured on the overall debt. Under this arrangement the interest charged to customers must cover collection costs and bad debt provisions, as well as interest charged by the finance house, before a profit is shown. Thus, a detailed budget is very necessary.

Table XXV shows how the hire-purchase profit and loss budget is made up for a company administering the H.P. debt itself, but financing it by an overall debenture. A breakdown into months or four-weekly periods is essential, since the profit or loss will differ substantially from period to period. The starting-point is the estimate of the proportion of H.P. to total sales for each period or month. Normally this ratio will tend to follow the seasonal sales pattern, *i.e.* as sales rise during the season the *percentage* of H.P. business increases, thus giving a double boost to H.P. turnover in absolute terms. This ratio can be accurately estimated by plotting monthly statistics of H.P. and total sales over a period of years and any trend element in the moving percentages can be introduced into the budget. There is usually an association between the general economic climate and the volume of credit business transacted.

The next step is to estimate the average expected rate of interest which will be earned on the credit business. This will not, of course, be the normal interest charge calculated on the cash price, since H.P. interest is charged *flat* on a *reducing* debt, so that the *effective* rate of interest is nearly double the quoted rate. The length of the agreement will determine the effective rate of interest on the total H.P. sales and therefore statistics of typical agreement durations must be maintained and referred to in the budget exercise. Statistics of returned and repossessed goods must also be kept to budget for short-falls in interest and capital repayments. In Table XXV the effective rate of interest is assumed to be $12 \cdot 5\%$ in each period of the year. An estimate must be made of interest carried forward, since it cannot all be assumed to be earned at the point of sale. Actuarial tables can be consulted to give the amount of interest which should be carried forward, based on the length of the H.P. agreement.

When the budgeted interest earned has been calculated (line 9 in Table XXV), forecast expenses can be deducted to give estimated

TABLE XXV. HIRE-PURCHASE PROFIT AND LOSS BUDGET

← Four-Weekly Periods →

		Period 1	Period 2	Period 3	Period 4	Period 5	Budget 1968
1.	Sales per budget	£ 288,000	£ 402,000	£ 439,000	£ 500,000	£	£ 4,851,700
2.	Estimated % H. P. to total sales	24·0%	30·0%	32·0%	37·0%		35·0%
3.	Budgeted H. P. sales	69,100	120,600	140,600	185,000		1,699,000
4.	Average expected interest rate	12·5%	12·5%	12·5%	12·5%		12·5%
5.	*Budgeted interest charged*	8,640	15,080	17,580	23,120		212,400
	Add						
6.	Budgeted provision for unearned interest b/f	75,000	72,500	74,000	77,000		75,000
7.		83,640	87,580	91,580	100,120		287,400
	Less						
8.	Budget provision for unearned interest c/f	72,500	74,000	77,000	82,000		82,000
9.	*Interest earned*	11,140	13,580	14,580	18,120		205,400
	Expenses (not recovered in other depts):						
10.	Collection costs and legal expenses	500	500	500	500		6,500
11.	Provision for bad and doubtful debts	2,070	3,620	4,200	5,550		50,300
12.	Stamp duty	100	100	100	100		1,300
13.	Interest on borrowings against H. P.	5,000	5,500	6,000	6,500		75,000
14.	Total Expenses	7,670	9,720	10,800	12,650		133,100
15.	Profit/Loss on H. P. finance (9 less 14)	P3,470	P3,860	P3,780	P5,470		P72,300
16.	Provision for unrealised H. P. profit	P3,100	L2,100	L4,000	L8,500		L39,900

profit or loss. Expenses of outside collection agencies and legal costs arising from repossessing goods can be allocated evenly in each month or period, in the absence of a more noticeable pattern. The provision for bad and doubtful debts will be a variable charge, related either to the H.P. debt outstanding or to the volume of H.P. business, whichever seems to give the more realistic provision. Stamp duty on agreements is so small that it can be allocated evenly in the budget. The final major expense is the interest charged by the finance house under the block-discounting arrangement or the overall debenture. This will be determined by the amount of the H.P. business discounted, since the company may choose (or be requested by the finance house) to carry some of the debt itself. The four-weekly charge in the budget can be computed by taking one-thirteenth of the annual discount rate, multiplied by the budgeted borrowings outstanding against the debt at the end of each period. This will be satisfactory for budget purposes even though actual interest will be calculated on a daily basis.

It will be noticed in Table XXV that the only expenses charged are those which are not recovered in other departments. There will of course, be the salary and establishment costs of the hire-purchase department, *i.e.* the department administering and collecting the debt. These must be deducted from the profit shown in Table XXV to arrive at the true profit (or loss) on financing the debt. But, in order not to depart from the principle of accountability, in this example they have been included in the salaries and wages and head office establishment budgets. Thus, the H.P. manager is responsible for the staff in the H.P. department, and the H.P. profit and loss budget becomes a *financial* budget only, prepared by, and the responsibility of, the accountant or controller.

The H.P. budget is completed by making a provision for the unrealised profit at the time of sale. Practice differs considerably as to the amount of profit which is deemed to be unrealised. Some companies contend that the whole of the gross profit is unrealised initially and carry forward, say, 33% of outstanding H.P. debt. Others carry forward, say, 10% on the basis that it is the *net* profit which is unrealised, rather than the gross profit, selling expenses being paid at the point of sale. In Table XXV 10% is provided on the total debt outstanding. Thus, in the periods when the H.P. debt is rising, the profit and loss account is charged and the provision for unrealised profit increased, and when the H.P. debt is falling the provision is reduced and the profit and loss account credited. The monthly breakdown of the movement of this provision is therefore essential for correct forecasting.

It will be understood that for credit sale agreements (as distinct from H.P.) there is no need to provide for unrealised profit, since

D

the legal title to the goods passes immediately to the purchaser at the point of sale.

Monthly Reporting

As we have said before, full management control stems from accurate and timely reporting on the significant aspects of the business. The budget, which may be excellent in itself, will be largely vitiated if it is not integrated into a fully developed system of monthly reporting. This does not mean that a thick dossier of paper should be produced every month. It will not be read by the management and by the time that it is circulated the opportunity for effective action may be lost. Reports should take the form of easily digestible tables, with just enough commentary to explain the exceptional variances and the recommended action to be taken. The important factor is to cover all "profit-determining" variables. For a retail company these will essentially be sales, gross profit and expenses. We deal later with the sort of regular reports which should cover source and disposition of funds and the structure of the balance sheet.

The method of monthly reporting will normally be to produce one summary of the overall trading results (contained if possible on one sheet of paper) supported by a number of subsidiary reports which expand in more detail on the major profit-determining areas. Depending on the size of the company, the summary will be directed at the top management, whilst the subsidiary reports will chiefly concern operating and functional managers, e.g. sales, buying, personnel. In a small company all information will be of vital concern to the top management.

Before we consider the monthly summary of results, it would be as well to review briefly the purpose and scope of the subsidiary reports:

(a) *Sales.* This should cover total sales at each outlet: four-weekly and cumulatively, actual and budget, and the variances. The totals should agree to the sales line in the summary of results. A brief explanation should be given where sales deviate significantly from the budget and any action proposed.

(b) *Gross Profit.* The fullness of this report will depend on the amount of stock and sales analysis by individual products made in the financial/cost accounts. Where items with differing gross profit percentages are sold, the overall gross profit percentages at branch level will be determined by the sales "mixture," *i.e.* the proportion of high gross-profit to low gross-profit lines sold. This is vital control information because it is the explanation for differing margins at outlets and for differing margins at the various seasons of the year. The report should at least cover the sales at selling value (and by quantity, if relevant) and the purchases at cost of all the major merchandise groups and the monthly stock movements of each group, if the accounting system does not permit cost of sales to be determined by product. It will be mainly in tabular form for brevity, with verbal commentary reduced to a minimum.

(c) *Expenses*. The monthly report on expenses has been dealt with in the previous chapter and nothing need be added to what was said there.

It may also be necessary to produce reports on special areas or departments in the business in addition to the above. The financing of the H.P. debt may require a separate report, as might the activities of any service department which is profit-earning or subsidised, *e.g.* a department repairing faulty equipment returned by customers, in or out of guarantee. These reports will be specifically directed at the appropriate operating management.

The summary of the monthly trading results is exemplified in Table XXVI. The budget figures are taken from the trading and profit and loss budget (of which Table XXII is an example), and the actual figures are extracted as a matter of routine from the financial accounts. The monthly and cumulative position should be shown, but there is usually no need to provide columns for the variances, since they have already been shown and explained in the subsidiary reports. In the cumulative section the previous year's performance should be shown, so that the management can see not only how the actual results differ from the budget but also what progress has been achieved over the same period in the previous year. The vertical headings in Table XXVI are the same as in Table XXII with the addition of lines to show the results on financing hire-purchase sales.

A summary of trading results is not complete unless it gives an indication of how the year will end. Annually declared profits are the yardstick by which a company is measured, especially public companies, and it is highly important for the management of such companies to have a clear idea of the likely year-end position when planning dividend policy, raising of further funds, acquisition of other companies, and other financial policies. The three right-hand columns of Table XXVI provide this information. They enable the controller to tell the management what the results for the year are likely to be if the business maintains its present pattern, and to show the expected variation from the annual budget and from the previous year. The controller will use for his estimates the techniques of

TABLE XXVI. MONTHLY TRADING AND PROFIT AND LOSS SUMMARY

	Period 6				Cumulative						Year-end Position					
	Actual £	%	Budget £	%	Actual £	%	Budget £	%	Previous year £	%	Latest forecast £	%	Budget £	%	Previous year £	%
Sales	382,669	100·0	395,200	100·0	2,622,816	100·0	2,599,700	100·0	1,893,994	100·0	4,930,000	100·0	4,851,700	100·0	3,554,207	100·0
Gross profit	129,775	33·9	130,400	33·0	884,990	33·7	894,500	34·4	616,212	32·5	1,679,000	34·0	1,666,000	34·3	1,137,104	32·0
Expenses:																
Advertising	5,811	1·5	7,800	2·0	95,328	3·6	91,800	3·5	56,506	2·9	130,000	2·6	127,100	2·6	84,319	2·4
Branch salaries	19,693	5·2	20,000	5·1	163,477	6·3	156,600	6·0	85,763	4·5	300,000	6·1	285,000	5·9	178,835	5·0
Head Office salaries	15,467	4·0	16,000	4·0	91,175	3·5	88,600	3·4	66,807	3·5	210,000	4·3	188,700	3·9	102,223	2·9
Establishment costs	37,335	9·8	35,000	8·8	178,550	6·8	182,500	7·1	105,540	5·6	385,000	7·8	400,600	8·3	250,207	7·0
Overheads:																
Financial	1,307	0·3	1,250	0·3	7,243	0·3	7,460	0·3	5,442	0·3	15,000	0·3	15,330	0·3	9,885	0·3
Legal	985	0·3	1,000	0·3	5,899	0·2	6,950	0·3	3,907	0·2	11,000	0·2	12,570	0·3	8,489	0·2
Distribution	3,825	1·0	3,600	0·9	31,341	1·2	30,630	1·2	16,638	0·9	56,000	1·1	54,500	1·1	35,066	1·0
Others	5,476	1·4	6,000	1·5	38,777	1·5	40,110	1·5	22,105	1·2	75,000	1·6	79,400	1·6	48,771	1·4
Total expenses	89,899	23·5	90,650	22·9	611,790	23·4	604,650	23·3	362,708	19·1	1,182,000	24·0	1,163,200	24·0	717,795	20·2
Trading profit	39,876	10·4	39,750	10·1	273,200	10·3	289,850	11·1	253,504	13·4	497,000	10·0	502,800	10·3	419,309	11·8
H.P. finance result: Profit/loss on H.P. charges	P2,786	0·7	P3,600	0·9	P32,604	1·2	P35,000	1·3	P22,743	1·2	P70,000	1·5	P72,300	1·5	P49,672	1·4
Provision for unrealised profit	L882	0·2	L1,000	0·3	L18,212	0·6	L19,400	0·7	L15,255	0·8	L38,000	0·8	L39,900	0·8	L27,474	0·8
Net Profit before tax	P41,780	10·9	P42,350	10·7	P287,592	10·9	P305,450	11·7	P260,992	13·8	P529,000	10·7	P535,200	11·0	P441,507	12·4

variable forecasting described under Volume and Profit Relationships, above. Bearing in mind the relationships between fixed and variable costs at various sales volumes, he will project forward the current levels of costs and sales revenue, if he thinks that the present trends are likely to continue, and arrive at a new estimate of annual pre-tax profit. By seeing alongside the budget figures, the management can quickly pin-point the reasons for the revised estimate and take any action possible and appropriate.

It must not be thought that variable forecasting replaces budgetary control and renders the budget in any way obsolete. This is by no means true. Interim forecasts of year-end results must necessarily be made quickly and it is not possible to lavish on them the care and thought which will go into the annual budgetary exercise. Furthermore, it is essential that a fixed standard be used for comparison purposes, otherwise the actual results are being compared with a moving standard and effective control is jeopardised. Only when the budget has significantly lost contact with actual events should it be scrapped, and even then it should be replaced by another firm budget, albeit a less detailed and extensive one.

It will not normally be necessary to make a verbal report on the monthly trading and profit and loss summary, since the variances will have been sufficiently explained in the subsidiary reports. Sometimes, however, a few brief notes will be necessary to explain the revised estimates of the year-end position and any other exceptional events that have happened or are likely to happen. If the subsidiary reports are necessarily numerous and full, it may be essential to make a brief précis of them, and submit this with the monthly trading result summary to top management.

Summary

The acceptance of the trading "budget" depends on the adequacy of working capital to fulfil the proposals implicit in the budget. This can be established in general terms by making an approximation of annual revenue and expenditure. The budget, modified if necessary, then becomes a firm statement of intent by the management. Interim estimates will be made during the year of likely profit changes based on variable forecasting techniques. These will give management an up-to-date view of the likely annual out-turn. They will in no sense replace the budget but rather be a clearer explanation of the variations between actual and budgeted results.

CHAPTER 7

CAPITAL EXPENDITURE

Introduction

Most of the now formidable body of literature concerning capital expenditure decisions has developed from, and deals almost exclusively with, industrial investment projects. Virtually no mention is made of capital investment in distribution and the evaluation of likely returns on one or another type of retail or wholesale outlet. This is despite the fact that the basic concepts of measuring yields on capital employed are common to all forms of investment: industrial plant and machinery, shops and hotels. Whether this neglect by writers on business economics is the cause or the effect of the somewhat unsophisticated approach to capital expenditure often found in the distributive trades is difficult to say. It is a fact, however, and one which militates against improved profitability.

It must be admitted, firstly, that the range of alternative investments is often more limited in retail distribution than in manufacturing industry. A manufacturer may have the choice of several machines to produce a given product but the retailer may find only one suitable site in a high street, and he may have to wait years to obtain this site. Investment in distribution is usually a property/location decision for which fewer possibilities naturally exist. Secondly, it is argued that forecasting the likely return on an investment is more difficult in distribution than in manufacturing. The time-scale is longer in distribution (a shop may be leased for, say, twenty-one years) and the more distant estimates of sales are therefore more hazardous owing to the possibilities of competition, re-routeing of traffic, and so forth. Thirdly, so far as multiple retailing is concerned, the company's own image may largely dictate the capital cost of a project: for example, it may require a distinctive shop-front and interior fitting common to all shops. Fourthly, the income which a retail outlet makes on the initial capital outlay is usually significantly larger than that made on an industrial capital project of the same value, and the attitude is possibly that capital costs need be less stringently examined in relation to expected yields in distribution.

All these "reasons" explain but do not excuse the "hit or miss" approach to capital budgeting decisions often found in retail distribution. If the choice of possible investments is more restricted, the period of the investment longer and the likely return higher, the most critical examination of alternative capital costs and estimated yields is demanded.

The starting-point in the evaluation of any capital project is the estimate of the likely income from the investment. In retail distribution this will normally be the gross profit on turnover less the running expenses of the outlet. Clearly the estimate of sales is the most difficult variable to forecast, the gross profit rate and expenses being largely controllable. It is not proposed here to go into detail about the methods which should be used to predict as accurately as possible the sales possibilities of a new outlet, since they extend outside the boundaries of financial control, requiring knowledge of matters such as town-planning, urban redevelopment, highway improvements, and population movements. We may, however, briefly list some of the important points which must be considered when assessing the sales potential of a projected outlet:

1. The floor-area and shape of the unit and its position in the shopping block and shopping centre.

2. The window-space available and promotional aids permissible, e.g. illuminated signs.

3. The facilities for unloading merchandise without hindering customers and breaking parking regulations.

4. Competition from own company and rival outlets, as it is now and as it may develop.

5. Possible traffic re-routeing plans (such as one-way streets), parking restrictions, proximity to adequate car-parks, local transport facilities.

6. Urban redevelopment plans, e.g. a new town being built around an older one, or the construction of a completely new shopping area.

7. The social and economic status of the great mass of the buying public. Surveys of local buying power can be helpful here, e.g. those produced by Comart Research Ltd.

8. Government-sponsored plans for population movements, such as aid for under-developed and depressed areas, and private plans for labour concentration, e.g. "factory-towns" such as Dagenham, Corby, Port Talbot.

9. The availability of good quality local staff for sales and other duties.

10. The distance of the proposed outlet from the company's head office and possible loss of control. Distance from head office may also lower morale in the local unit and prevent effective participation in "national" advertising and promotional schemes.

Over a period of time the significance of each of these points, one against another, can be fairly accurately determined when assessing the sales potentials of new outlets. Also the experience of similar units already opened will be a good guide. The extent and depth of relevant statistical coverage in capital budgeting is most important since we are concerned with a forecast of sales over many years, not merely for one or two years, as in the annual budgeting exercise. The shape of the forecast sales curve, taking into account the factors listed above, is highly significant because the expectation of rewards later may be worth less than rewards now, as we demonstrate in the next section.

Capital Investment Appraisal

The capital expenditure decision is most critical when the company is faced with *alternative* uses of its funds available for expansion. If it is in the position of securing a single investment project which is self-evidently more rewarding than other possible projects, then there is little point in making a detailed investment appraisal of all possibilities. This situation might well obtain in the early years of a retail group's development. Outlets will be opened first in the biggest towns, such as London, Birmingham, Manchester, Glasgow, because these towns offer the best returns, significantly and obviously better than those obtainable in smaller towns. But after the bigger cities have been "exhausted," the approach to capital expansion must become more selective. Not only does the law of diminishing returns begin to become very apparent (*i.e.* capital outlay beyond a certain point produces a rapidly decreasing rate of income) but also the range of possible outlets broadens, and the decision whether to develop here or there becomes more difficult. The following example shows how alternative investment projects can be evaluated to give, on balance, the best choice.

Table XXVII shows the estimated net cash income over twenty years of two retail outlets in different towns. The expression "net cash income" means gross profit on sales turnover less running expenses (*e.g.* rent, rates, salaries, light, heat) and less tax. This definition is significant in capital project appraisal because it includes only *cash* income, and specifically excludes items such as depreciation and contributions to head office expenses, which are not monetary outflows at the point of investment. Thus, the capital outlay in cash terms can be meaningfully related to the cash income, and like compared with like. If, of course, any one new sales outlet does incur head office expenses which are attributable solely to that outlet then they should be included in running expenses, but usually the addition of one or two new branches to a

TABLE XXVII. CAPITAL PROJECT APPRAISAL

YEAR	PROJECTED OUTLET A		PROJECTED OUTLET B	
	Net cash income £	Capital outlay £	Net cash income £	Capital outlay £
0	—	15,000 at 0 yr.	—	17,000 at 0 yr.
1	7,500		7,200	
2	7,200		6,300	
3	8,400		6,400	
4	9,200		6,800	
5	10,000	5,000 at 5 yr.	7,200	
6	10,400		7,600	
7	10,800		8,400	
8	11,000		9,200	
9	11,200		10,000	
10	11,000		10,600	5,000 at 10 yr.
11	10,800		10,800	
12	10,400		11,200	
13	9,800		11,500	
14	9,000		11,600	
15	8,600	3,000 at 15 yr.	11,800	
16	8,400		11,900	
17	8,000		12,000	
18	8,000		12,200	
19	8,000		12,300	
20	8,000		12,400	
Total	185,700	23,000	197,400	22,000

Capital Outlay

	£		£
A: 0 yr. =		B: 0 yr. =	
Cost of modernisation	3,000	Complete shop fitting	7,000
Cost of stock	12,000	Stock	10,000
	15,000		17,000
A: 5 yr. = Shop refit	5,000	B: 10 yr. = Shop refit	5,000
15 yr. = Shop refit	3,000		

retail chain does not materially affect total head office expenses. Similarly, if some of the business at the new outlet will be on H.P. terms, an adjustment should be made to the estimated annual cash income for that part of the H.P. turnover which will be financed by the company itself.

Also shown in Table **XXVII** are the capital outlays for each

D*

branch and the points in time at which they are expected to occur. Outlet A is an already established retail branch which has been left to run down both in management and fitting-out by its previous owners. It will cost £3,000 to modernise it inside and out and £12,000 to stock it with the company's merchandise. At the end of five and fifteen years' trading it will require refits estimated to cost £5,000 and £3,000 respectively. Outlet B is a new branch in a newly developed shopping centre. Slightly smaller than Branch A, it will require a stock investment of £10,000, but the complete shop-fitting necessary will cost £7,000, giving an initial outlay of £17,000. In its tenth year of trading it will need a refit costing an estimated £5,000. Both branches are on twenty-one-year leases at flat rentals, but there is an option to renew on expiry of the leases at negotiated rentals. For capital outlay and return assessment we have considered a period of twenty years only, which takes us to the limit of reasonable forecasting, given the hazards of competition, urban redevelopment and so on.

Before attempting to decide which project is the better investment (assuming that shortage of expansion funds necessitates a choice being made between them) we must look more closely at the net cash incomes of each project and the periods when they are expected to accrue. Fig. 14 shows the net cash incomes graphically. Obviously they reflect the expected sales patterns of each outlet, the inevitable inflationary growth of running expenses being more or less offset by improved gross margins over the years. The exceptionally high net cash income in year 1 for both outlets results from the initial tax allowance on the fixed capital expenditure which will be claimed.

The differing incidence of revenue during the foreseeable life of each investment is very apparent from Fig. 14. In fact, the sales pattern of each outlet can be divided into three phases. For Branch A the improved management and appearance will give annually increasing sales for some nine years. Known plans for shopping centre redevelopment (expected to begin at about year 7) will cause a phase of declining sales from year 9 to about year 17, after which a period of stability will begin. For Branch B development in the new shopping centre will be comparatively slow for the first six years, followed by a period of more quickly growing sales as the surrounding town expands. The third phase, from about year 12, will be increasing annual sales, but at a less fast rate.

It is not claimed that the more distant estimates of branch activity will be anything better than approximately accurate when compiling forecasts which extend over a period of twenty years. The important point, however, is to have sufficiently sophisticated research and intelligence techniques, so that balanced consideration can be given to *all* relevant factors. In this way the forecasts made, although extensive in time, will be more accurate and the consequent investment decisions more rewarding.

We now turn to consider the question of deciding which of the two outlets is the more attractive investment proposition. As we stated earlier, in making our decision, we must give due weight to the *timing* of expected receipts, and not merely consider the initial (or total) capital outlay in relation to total receipts. This means that

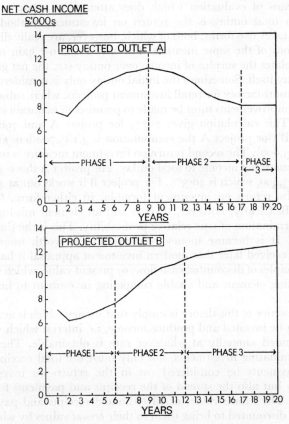

Fig. 14. Forecast cash income on alternative capital projects.

we must use the now commonly accepted method of discounted cash flow to evaluate the projects and bring them to a common denominator. But before we enlarge on this technique we must dispose of the other (traditional) methods of investment appraisal.

A widely used method of comparing two investment projects is the pay-back period. This calculates how long it takes for the investment (usually the initial outlay) to be repaid in income. In Table XXVII it can be quickly calculated that for project A the pay-back period of the initial investment of £15,000 is 2·04 years and for project B it is 2·55 years. This makes project A slightly more attractive than project B, but it is obviously an inadequate appraisal of the two possibilities since it takes no account of the *subsequent* capital payments, nor of the *total* income which the two investments can be expected to produce.

A means of evaluation which does attempt to relate total income to total outlay is the return on investment method. This method takes two forms, both of which, however, are really different expressions of the same measure. The first is the net gain method which relates the surplus of income over outlay (*i.e.* the net gain) to the outlay itself. Sometimes the initial outlay only is considered, but this is unsatisfactory for retail investment projects, where subsequent capital improvements must be made to premises to maintain earning power. This calculation gives 707% for project A and 796% for project B (for project A the computation is £185,700 less £23,000 over £23,000). The second return on investment measure is to relate *average annual* net income to total outlay. For project A this is £9,285 over £23,000, which is 40·3%. For project B it works out at 44·9%. Thus, the return on investment formula, in either form, favours project B. Clearly, however, there is still an element missing from the determination of true relative profitability. This is the timing of receipts. It is because money received now is worth more than money received later that modern investment appraisal is based on the principles of discounted cash flow, or present value, which supply the missing element and enable competing investment to be fairly assessed.

The essence of this theory is simply that money which is available now can be invested and produce income, *i.e.* interest which will be compounded annually at whatever rate is obtainable. Therefore, when evaluating investments, not only must the total receipts and total payments be considered (as in the return on investment method) but also the spread of the receipts and payments forward in time. The future values of all estimated receipts and payments must be discounted to bring them to their *present* values by whatever rate of interest is forgone by investing in the capital project under review. In this way capital expenditure proposals can be fairly compared. The effect of this method of appraisal is that projects whose income takes a long time to mature appear less attractive than projects which give a more immediate return. This is quite right because it acknowledges the interest forgone by waiting, the long term decline in the value of money and the general uncertainty of the future.

The present values of sums to be received or paid in the future can be obtained from tables which are given in most up-to-date books on capital investment. In the absence of such tables, the appropriate discount factor can be quickly computed by taking the reciprocal of the compound interest factor. Thus, from compound interest tables we see that £1 invested at 5% compound interest (with annual rests) amounts to £1·2763 in 5 years. Therefore, the *present* value of £1 receivable in 5 years' time, discounted at 5% compound interest, is

$$\frac{1}{1·2763} = £0·7835.$$

Table **XXVIII** shows the evaluation of the two investment projects considered above by means of the discounted cash flow technique. An interest rate of 9% has been selected to discount the future receipts and payments because this is taken to be the minimum rate at which the company could invest its funds. For example, it could save the 9% block discounting charge by financing its H.P.

TABLE XXVIII. CAPITAL PROJECT APPRAISAL BY DISCOUNTED CASH FLOW

Year	PRESENT VALUE OF £1 AT 9% COMPOUND INTEREST £*	PROJECTED OUTLET A				PROJECTED OUTLET B			
		Net cash income £	Present value £	Capital outlay £	Present value £	Net cash income £	Present value £	Capital outlay £	Present value £
0	1·0000	—	—	15,000	15,000	—	—	17,000	17,000
1	0·9174	7,500	6,880			7,200	6,600		
2	0·8417	7,200	6,060			6,300	5,300		
3	0·7722	8,400	6,480			6,400	4,940		
4	0·7084	9,200	6,520			6,800	4,820		
5	0·6499	10,000	6,500	5,000	3,250	7,200	4,680		
6	0·5936	10,400	6,170			7,600	4,510		
7	0·5470	10,800	5,910			8,400	4,600		
8	0·5019	11,000	5,520			9,200	4,620		
9	0·4604	11,200	5,160			10,000	4,600		
10	0·4224	11,000	4,650			10,600	4,480	5,000	2,110
11	0·3875	10,800	4,190			10,800	4,190		
12	0·3555	10,400	3,700			11,200	3,980		
13	0·3262	9,800	3,200			11,500	3,750		
14	0·2992	9,000	2,700			11,600	3,470		
15	0·2745	8,600	2,360	3,000	820	11,800	3,240		
13	0·2519	8,400	2,120			11,900	3,000		
17	0·2311	8,000	1,850			12,000	2,770		
18	0·2120	8,000	1,700			12,200	2,580		
19	0·1945	8,000	1,560			12,300	2,390		
20	0·1784	8,000	1,430			12,400	2,210		
Total	—	185,700	84,660	23,000	19,070	197,400	80,730	22,000	19,110

$$* V = \frac{C}{(1+r)^n}$$ where V = present value
C = cash paid or received
r = rate of interest
n = number of years

debt itself, but it ought to be able to do better than this by investing in new sales outlets, so that 9% is the *minimum* acceptable rate.

The interest rate to be used in arriving at present values will thus depend on the circumstances of the company. A company which is expanding fast by exploiting a new and profitable product or market will be justified in using a high discount rate because this will emphasise in investment appraisal the desirability of cash income realised soon rather than later, which can be further reinvested in the (at the moment) very profitable activity. Eventually, competition and the progressive saturation of the market will lower investment yields, and therefore a lower discount rate will be used. A company with a large surplus of liquid funds which is consolidating rather than expanding may choose to use a discount rate near or equal to the current return on long-term borrowing or lending. This will reflect its less critical attitude to present rather than future returns. It will be clear that a company's *average* rate of return on capital employed is not a very satisfactory discount factor for investment evaluation, since the expanding company will obtain a much higher *marginal* return (on extra capital investment) and the consolidating company may have to accept a lower marginal return than this average.

When the capital incomes and expenditures of the two investment projects are discounted (in Table XXVIII) by 9%, the present value of the two projects can be meaningfully compared. Incomes and expenditures are multiplied by the appropriate factor to reduce them to present values. On this basis, the net gains of the two projects are as follows:

	Project A	Project B
	£	£
Present value of Income	84,660	80,730
Less Present value of Outlay	19,070	19,110
Net Gain	65,590	61,620

$$\text{Net Gain on Outlay} = \frac{65,590}{19,070} = \frac{61,620}{19,110}$$
$$= 344\% = 322\%$$

Project A is therefore slightly more attractive than project B, which reverses the decision of the conventional method of investment appraisal. This is because the earlier expectation of income for project A (*see* Fig. 14) enhances its value in comparison with project B. In the absence of any other information project A is the more attractive and should be selected.

The Capital Expenditure Budget

The appraisal of major capital expenditure projects will be done by the managing director and financial/budget controller. In larger companies a capital budget committee will be formed, normally consisting of the managing director, financial controller and marketing/sales director. Other functional managers may be co-opted on to the committee, as required. Whatever method is adopted for the formal discussion of capital projects it is important that there should be a method. Not only does it give specific authorisation and control of capital expenditure, but also it enables a detailed capital budget to be made up by the budget officer. The amount and source of the cash to meet the capital expansion programme can then be determined and less essential projects can, if necessary, be scrapped or postponed before the capital budget is finalised.

A typical capital expenditure budget is shown in Table XXIX. In this example expenditure has been divided into four main categories: premises, fixtures and fittings; plant and machinery; office equipment; and motor vehicles. Expenditure in the first category has been further sub-divided between branch and head office, since it is the branch capital expenditure which chiefly contributes towards increased earnings. This is also the area in which the most detailed appraisal of outlay and return must be made, other capital expenditure generally being of smaller value and more obvious in the likely benefits which will accrue.

As in previous budgets, the expenditure in the previous year is shown and the percentage of each category to the total. This enables the management to see which class of asset absorbed most of the available expansion funds and the shift in capital development proposed in the new financial year. The budgeted expenditure in each month or four-weekly period can then be inserted by reference to the date of outlay for each capital project. A standard capital authorisation form will greatly assist in summarising the capital budget into periods.

A useful adjunct to the capital budget is the depreciation information also shown in Table XXIX. The annual rate for each category of asset is shown, to which can be compared the actual rate for the (part) year under review. The actual rate and amount of depreciation will again be summarised from the capital authorisation forms and the closeness of the actual to the standard annual rate will reflect the timing of the capital outlay throughout the budget

TABLE XXIX. CAPITAL EXPENDITURE BUDGET

TYPE OF EXPENDITURE	1966–67 Actual £	1966–67 Actual %	Period 1 £	Period 2 £	Period 12 £	Period 13 £	1967–68 Budget £	1967–68 Budget %	Depreciation Rate p.a. %	Depreciation Actual %	Depreciation Amount £
Branches: New shop fronts	22,531	31·0	5,600	7,200	3,000	3,000	49,900	26·8	10	7·2	3,593
Fixtures and fittings	12,602	17·3	2,000	2,100	1,500	1,800	23,700	12·7	10	5·9	1,398
Renovations	13,593	18·7	3,000	3,700	4,000	—	36,500	19·6	10	5·7	2,080
Electrical work	2,160	2·9	1,600	2,000	—	—	5,300	2·8	10	8·2	435
Head Office: Partitioning	—	—	—	—	—	—	2,200	1·2	10	5·1	112
Fixtures and fittings	6,219	8·6	2,000	2,000	—	—	15,700	8·4	10	7·7	1,209
Electrical work	540	0·7	—	1,500	—	—	1,500	0·9	10	9·2	138
Other	2,112	2·8	500	1,500	300	1,000	7,000	3·8	10	5·7	399
Sub-total Premises, fixtures and fittings	59,757	82·0	14,700	20,000	8,800	5,800	141,800	76·2	10	6·6	9,364
Fork lift truck	—	—	—	300	—	—	300	0·2	15	13·8	42
Equipment for service dept.	2,170	3·0	2,000	2,700	—	—	4,700	2·5	15	14·3	674
Other	315	0·4	100	100	100	100	1,000	0·5	15	8·2	82
Sub-total Plant and machinery	2,485	3·4	2,100	3,100	100	100	6,000	3·2	15	13·3	798
Furniture	4,521	6·2	1,000	2,500	500	—	13,000	7·0	15	7·9	1,027
Machines	1,670	2·3	4,000	3,000	—	—	8,000	4·3	15	14·3	1,142
Sub-total Office equipment	6,191	8·5	5,000	5,500	500	—	21,000	11·3	15	10·3	2,169
Cars	3,490	4·8	4,000	700	—	—	10,000	5·4	20	11·1	1,110
Vans and lorries	891	1·3	1,000	—	—	—	7,200	3·9	20	12·5	900
Sub-total Motor vehicles	4,381	6·1	5,000	700	—	—	17,200	9·3	20	11·7	2,010
GRAND TOTAL	72,814	100·0	26,800	29,300	9,400	5,900	186,000	100·0		7·7	14,341

year. The monthly depreciation charges on the proposed capital expenditure (totalling £14,341 in Table XXIX, just 7·7 per cent of the budgeted total of £186,000) can then be added to the known charge on existing assets, rounded to the nearest hundred pounds, and taken straight to the establishment costs and overheads budgets. In this example, depreciation is based on the straight-line method and calculated from the first day of the four-weekly period in which the capital outlay is to be made. The annual depreciation rates used in the budget will, of course, be the same as those used in the actual financial accounts, *i.e.* governed by the expected useful life of the asset. A multiplicity of rates should be avoided as this unnecessarily complicates computation of the depreciation charge.

When the capital expenditure budget is completed, the four-weekly outlays can be transferred to the cash forecast. It will be clear that an important part of the monthly report on the company's financial position must be devoted to the comparison of the actual with budgeted capital expenditure. This can either be done as part of the monthly financial report, or, if the capital budget is very large in relation to total cash payments, as a separate capital expenditure report. When commenting on the variances between actual and budgeted expenditure the following elements must be clearly distinguished:

(*a*) Excess (or shortfall) of actual over authorised expenditure on specific projects.

(*b*) Actual date of outlay on authorised projects compared with budgeted date.

(*c*) Amount of unauthorised (or ex-budget) expenditure, and the reasons for it.

In this way management can see clearly why actual differs from forecast expenditure and what must be done to correct the situation.

To cut down on administrative work and tighten control, small items should not be capitalised (managers will be called to account for such expenditure via the expense analysis) and strict rules must be made and observed as to which managers can take capital expenditure decisions above a certain money level. Major capital outlays must always be sanctioned by the budget committee.

Summary

Capital development in a retail organisation is the chief factor affecting sales volume and long-term profitability. Capital investment decisions should therefore be taken only after the expected yields have been scientifically evaluated. The financial controller can make a contribution as important as that of the commercial and marketing managers in this process, by using critical techniques to ensure that competing investments are fairly assessed. He must also guide the management on acceptable yields so that the overall return on capital is not depressed. Control of expenditure is achieved by a proper system of budgeting and monthly reporting.

CHAPTER 8

CASH FLOW AND THE
PROJECTED BALANCE SHEET

The Long-term Cash Forecast

The availability of sufficient working capital, or "ready money," is critical to the health of any expanding company. Under-capitalisation is perhaps the biggest single factor which contributes to business failure. The cash budget is therefore the next most important after the sales budget (to which it is, of course, closely linked) and should be given the utmost care in preparation. It is helpful to divide the financing of a company's activities into three phases: long-term, annual and short-term. Many companies of quite substantial size make up only an annual cash forecast, as part of the once-yearly budgetary exercise. This is in most cases seriously inadequate. As much, if not more, thought must be given to long-term development plans and ideas; and at the other end of the time scale, a company in its day-to-day business must never be caught out unable to meet bills of exchange due or pay weekly wages.

To say that a company should regularly review its long-term financial position and prospects is to say only that it should know where it is going over, say, the next five years; it should know, for example, what sort of products it proposes to sell, which markets it feels it can compete in or capture, its planned growth in market share and its size and range of outlets. The managing director and board will no doubt discuss these questions, perhaps daily, but if such discussion is to be useful and purposeful the variables must be quantified. Then, a long-term operating plan, albeit rather sketchy, can be prepared which will do much to ensure that liquid funds are available when the opportune moment for expansion and development arrives. Such a financial forecast will fulfil the equally important task of indicating what rate of expansion is permissible within the framework of the company's short and long-term borrowing facilities, and thus guard against over-trading.

Table XXX shows the projected trading results and cash position of a medium-sized retail chain over a five-year period. The forecast is in four sections: trading and profit and loss account, cash flow, rate of stock turnover and cash flow safety margin. In this example, the management anticipate a 10% increase in turnover on each

TABLE XXX. LONG-TERM CASH FORECAST

	1968	1969	1970	1971	1972
(A) TRADING ACCOUNT	£000s	£000s	£000s	£000s	£000s
Sales	2,880	3,160	3,460	3,800	4,170
Gross profit (say 33⅓%)	960	1,053	1,153	1,270	1,390
Less Cash expenses	625	700	750	800	850
Trading profit	335	353	403	470	540
Less Depreciation	60	65	75	85	97
Profit before tax	275	288	328	385	443
Less Tax (say 35%)	96	101	115	134	155
Net profit after tax	179	187	213	251	288
(Trading profit as % of sales)	11·6%	11·2%	11·6%	12·4%	12·9%
(B) CASH FLOW					
Trading profit	335	353	403	470	540
Add Increase in creditors	10	15	18	20	22
	345	368	421	490	562
Less Increase in stock	100	130	100	80	80
Increase in debtors	20	20	25	30	35
Capital expenditure	50	110	150	120	80
Tax	96	101	115	134	155
Dividends	53	57	65	75	85
	319	418	455	439	435
Cash inflow/outflow	+26	−50	−34	+51	+127
Overdraft brought forward	250	224	274	308	257
Overdraft carried forward	224	274	308	257	130
Overdraft limits	300	300	300	300	300
Deficiency	Nil	Nil	8	Nil	Nil
(C) RATE OF STOCK-TURN					
Opening stock at cost value	720	820	950	1,050	1,130
Closing stock at cost value	820	950	1,050	1,130	1,210
Average stock	770	885	1,000	1,090	1,170
Average rate of stock-turn p. a.	1,920	2,107	2,307	2,530	2,780
(=cost of sales ÷ cost of stock)	770	885	1,000	1,090	1,170
=	2·49	2·38	2·31	2·32	2·38
(D) CASH FLOW SAFETY MARGIN					
Sales estimate error (5%)	144	158	173	190	208
Gross profit reduction (33⅓%)	48	53	58	63	69
Adjusted cash inflow	−22	−103	−92	−12	+58
Overdraft brought forward	250	272	375	467	479
Overdraft carried forward	272	375	467	479	421
Overdraft limits	300	300	300	300	300
Deficiency	Nil	75	167	179	121

preceding year, so that the sales curve, if plotted on a logarithmic scale, would be a straight line. The purpose of the forecast is to answer two questions. One, can the company finance this rate of expansion on its existing overdraft arrangements? Two, what financial risks are run if sales do not reach the expected levels, or put another way, should some more permanent form of finance be looked for other than bank borrowing to cushion the company against more difficult trading conditions?

Section (A) of Table XXX shows the trading and profit and loss forecast for five years. Gross profit is estimated to remain at $33\frac{1}{3}\%$ over the period. Expenses will rise owing to advertising and promotional costs and increased head office and branch wages, reflecting the expansion in the number of outlets. Nevertheless trading profit as a percentage of sales turnover will increase from $11 \cdot 6\%$ in 1968 to $12 \cdot 9\%$ in 1972. The depreciation charge will, of course, increase as a result of fixed capital expansion: branch shop-fronts, fixtures and fittings, motor vehicles, etc. Tax is estimated at 35%, *i.e.* 40% corporation tax less capital allowances. Net profit after tax, therefore, shows a steady increase over the period, and the overall forecast seems satisfactory.

Section (B) of Table XXX shows the cash flow resulting from the planned sales and its utilisation in financing fixed and circulating assets. Creditor and debtor balances are expected to show a net increase each year as the volume of purchases and sales increases. Likewise, there will be a net annual increase in inventories to stock the extra number of outlets. Stock control and turnover is so important in a retail company, however, that special consideration is given to it in section (C). Expenditure on fixed assets is the chief factor generating the higher volume of sales, and the estimates made will be based on a critical appraisal of investment projects, as described earlier. Tax is taken to be the same figure as in the profit and loss account, for simplicity. Dividends are estimated at approximately 30% of net profit after tax, giving a satisfactory growth in earnings per share over the five-year period. A further simplification made is that there is no change in financial provisions and reserves between years.

On these estimates the yearly net cash flow can be calculated and thus the cash position at the end of each year. An overdraft limit of £300,000 is assumed. It will be seen that, although the company will use this overdraft, in only one year will it exceed the maximum allowed, and this by only a very small margin. On the face of it, therefore, the company can finance its planned operations "internally," *i.e.* in the existing overdraft limits.

Clearly, however, the forecast cannot be accepted as it stands. First, the projected stock increase requires further consideration.

The forecast made for each year will be based on the number of new outlets to be opened and the average stock held at existing outlets in relation to turnover. By calculating the average stock-holding during the year and dividing it into the cost of sales, we obtain the rate of stock turnover per year. This is shown in section (C) of Table XXX. The target rate of stock turnover is assumed to be three times per year in this example, but the forecast growth in stock depresses the rate to around $2\frac{1}{2}$ times per year. This suggests either that the outlets used to make up the stock forecast are not typical or that bulk buying on the higher turnover will raise inventories, in which case some benefit in the gross margin should be felt. Fortunately, stock policy is capable of substantial modification in a period as long as that under review, and some slowing-down in the growth of stock should be considered to hold the rate of stock turnover at three times per year or even to increase it.

The important fact revealed by the long-term cash forecast is the sensitiveness of the liquid position to the accuracy of the sales forecast. In section (D) of Table XXX, the effect is shown of the sales forecast being overstated by 5%. The reduction in cash inflow is then the loss of gross profit, assuming that a 5% lower turnover will not materially reduce variable expenses. In 1968 instead of there being a net cash inflow of £26,000 there would be a net outflow of £22,000 (£26,000 − £48,000 = −£22,000). In 1971 the deficiency over the overdraft limits would be as much as £179,000. A forecasting error of 5% is not at all unlikely over a five-year period, and the conclusion must be that the company is running far too close to its bank borrowing limits.

Clearly a generous safety margin of cash must be allowed for, however attractive the prospective development plans may appear, especially for a company which is largely financed on a bank overdraft. In a period of five years' duration, there is no telling how tight money may become. Dependence on bank borrowing could mean jeopardising the whole development programme if the overdraft (which the management had come to regard as a semi-permanent loan) were suddenly and drastically reduced. In this example, therefore, thought would be given to the question of more permanent finance being obtained: a rights issue or debenture, depending on the circumstances of the company, *e.g.* the existing capital structure, the availability of unpledged assets, family control of shares or otherwise, and similar factors.

Apart from the *method* of financing the growth of the business, the long-term cash forecast also invites criticism and review of the projected utilisation of funds as between fixed and circulating assets and the yield shown on the increasing capital investment. If we assume, in Table XXX, that the company's balance sheet at the end of 1967 showed fixed assets of £500,000, stock at cost of £720,000, debtors of £50,000 and depreciation of fixed assets amounting to £55,000, then the return on total capital invested in each year is as follows:

	1968 £000s	1969 £000s	1970 £000s	1971 £000s	1972 £000s
Total Assets before depreciation b/f	1,270	1,440	1,700	1,975	2,205
Additions during year	170	260	275	230	195
Closing Assets c/f	1,440	1,700	1,975	2,205	2,400
Less Depreciation	115	180	255	340	437
	1,325	1,520	1,720	1,865	1,963
Average Assets (less deprec'n.)	1,270	1,422	1,620	1,792	1,914
Profit before Tax	275	288	328	385	443
Return on Capital Employed %	21·6	20·2	20·2	21·4	23·1

The figures show that the overall results of the development programme are satisfactory. Return on capital employed has a downward movement in 1969 and 1970 but this is to be expected in view of the heavy expenditure on fixed assets. In a retail organisation there will be an inevitable delay between spending and return on capital investment since customer goodwill takes time to build up. The important feature of the forecast return on capital employed movement is that after 1970 it begins to climb again, thus justifying the earlier expenditure and the assumptions underlying the development programme.

The weak points in the forecast are still the high level of stocks in relation to turnover and the dangerous narrowness of the cash safety margin. These points would seem, however, to be capable of simultaneous solution. A stock-turn of $2\frac{1}{2}$ to 3 times per year is inadmissible in a retail organisation, and the management should make strenuous efforts to improve it to, say, 5 to 6 times per year. In Table XXX, if the average rate of stock turn per year could be improved to 3 times in 1968 and then gradually up to 6 times in 1972, this would save £257,000 over the five years, and give a satisfactory cushion to a short-fall in sales against the estimates.

The Annual Cash Budget

This is an integral part of the annual budgetary exercise. Its value lies more in analysing the cash movement into months (or four-weekly periods) than in estimating the end-of-year cash position, which can be more easily done by the "profits" method, as in

TABLE XXXI. ANNUAL CASH BUDGET

	Period 1 £	Period 2 £	Period 3 £	Period 11 £	Period 12 £	Period 13 £	Total £
Overdraft b/f	137,000	109,350	96,020	110,000	154,530	113,820	137,000
Purchases	300,000	320,000	350,000	220,000	150,000	274,670	3,373,500
Salaries and wages	29,500	30,290	32,600	37,100	37,800	37,800	473,700
Advertising and display	1,000	2,000	7,000	2,300	25,800	14,300	127,100
Rent payable	—	—	52,150	—	59,900	—	229,430
Rates	—	—	15,730	—	17,460	—	66,430
Cleaning	1,100	1,200	1,200	1,300	1,300	1,310	16,580
Light and heat	1,570	1,610	1,700	1,910	2,000	2,100	24,630
Telephone	1,430	1,470	1,500	1,620	1,700	1,750	20,960
Financial expenses	200	200	4,030	200	4,030	200	15,330
Legal expenses	—	300	150	6,000	1,500	750	12,570
Distribution expenses	3,550	5,400	3,850	5,300	3,650	4,100	54,500
Other expenses	4,000	6,200	3,700	3,800	4,000	6,500	79,400
Capital expenditure	15,000	19,000	21,700	10,000	9,500	6,700	186,000
Tax	—	—	—	75,000	—	—	158,000
Dividends	—	—	—	25,000	—	—	63,000
Total £ Payments:	494,350	497,020	591,330	499,530	473,170	464,000	5,038,130
Cash sales	385,000	401,000	470,000	310,000	350,000	370,000	4,834,700
Rent receivable	—	—	9,350	—	9,350	—	37,430
Sale of leases/investments	—	—	15,000	35,000	—	—	72,000
Total £ Receipts:	385,000	401,000	494,350	345,000	359,350	370,000	4,944,130
Overdraft c/f	109,350	96,020	96,980	154,530	113,820	94,000	94,000
Overdraft limits	150,000	150,000	150,000	150,000	150,000	150,000	150,000
Deficiency/surplus	+40,650	+53,980	+53,020	−4,530	+36,180	+56,000	−56,000

Chapter 6, page 77 above. Table XXXI shows how the annual cash budget can be presented. In any company with a strong seasonal sales pattern a breakdown of receipts and payments into months is essential. Periods of low cash income (and therefore particular financial strain) can then be highlighted and trading and financial policy can be adjusted accordingly. It is sometimes argued that the cash budget should be broken down into weeks or even days if, for example, bills payable and receivable figure largely in the cash flow. For most companies this is far too ambitious and not even necessary. A more realistic and flexible method is to make up a monthly cash budget as in Table XXXI and to supplement it during the year with short-period cash estimates of up to, say, six weeks' duration. We deal with short-term cash forecasting in the next section.

In Table XXXI, the assumption is made that the company is permitted, and uses, an overdraft. This is reasonable for a yearly forecast, given comparative stability of the economic situation, but, as we have said above, it would be unwise to base a long-term cash forecast on such a method of financing. A further simplifying assumption in Table XXXI is that no H.P. business is undertaken, and that trade is mainly on a cash basis with a small number of monthly settlement accounts. Payments are listed downwards, starting with trading account items (purchases are shown net, *i.e.* after cash discounts have been taken), then expenses, and finally capital items and tax and dividends. Receipts are shown in a similar order. Care must be taken to allocate expenses according to the time of *payment* and to allow for any prepayments and accruals at year-ends. The estimated overdraft at the end of each four-weekly period can then be shown together with the overdraft limits, thus giving the deficiency or surplus carried forward.

In this example, although purchases are heavy in the first three periods, the rising volume of cash sales covers the outlay and keeps the overdraft well within the limits. In period 11, however, the incidence of £100,000 of tax and dividend payments coupled with low turnover pushes the overdraft £4,530 over the limit. This is a dangerous situation and the management must consider ways of easing the strain, for example, by deferring some of the tax payment (if possible), or postponing capital expenditure, or reducing purchases. Thus, within the limitations of inevitable forecasting errors and day-to-day changes of policy, the management can *plan* the financing of its trading activities, making full use of available resources but at the same time leaving a realistic safety margin.

Before finalising the annual cash budget, its accuracy should be checked in total by the "profits" method, as in Chapter 6, p. 77, above. When adjustments are made to profit (before depreciation and tax) for year-end changes in stocks, debtors, creditors, provisions, the resulting cash flow must be the same as in the detailed method, items such as tax, dividends, capital expenditure and special receipts and payments being common to both methods.

The completion of the cash budget also enables the charge for bank interest in the overheads budget to be computed. For it will be clear that the bank overdraft both determines and is determined by the amount of bank interest payable. The solution to this is to leave bank interest open in the expense budget and to compute it (after the overdraft, without interest added, has been calculated) by the following formula:

$$Bank\ Overdraft\ without\ interest = \frac{100 - 6}{6}.$$

where, for example, 6% per annum is the interest rate payable. The resulting sum can then be added to the overdraft and inserted in the expense budget, and the cash flow will show the correct interest payable on the overdraft, which itself contains the same interest charge.

The Short-period Cash Forecast

The annual cash forecast will not be sufficient for day-to-day control of the cash position. Every financial movement—stock, expenses, capital expenditure—is reflected in the cash flow, and therefore the cash budget is the most likely of all to differ significantly from actuality. This does not mean that the long-term and annual cash forecasts should not be attempted. They are obviously vital to financial planning. Short-term cash control, however, needs a flexible tool to ensure that immediate trading commitments can be met and a sufficient safety margin left over.

Table XXXII shows how the short-term cash position can be controlled. The forecast should cover a period of four to six weeks ahead, in any event long enough to span the cyclical peak cash outflow, which is usually the end and beginning of each month. It should be prepared weekly, the correct bank balance being the opening figure each week. Previous "mistakes" in forecasting should be ignored (unless there is an error of principle) but, of course, the aim should be to make the estimates of receipts and payments as accurate as possible. This will necessitate the accountant or controller keeping in close touch with all executives who initiate or authorise payments of large amounts: the manager of the bought ledger department, the advertising manager, etc. Estimates of receipts from cash sales (and hire purchase instalments) should be fairly accurate if close attention is paid to the seasonal pattern of sales and the likely influence of any exceptional circumstances, *e.g.* bargain sales, political events such as the Budget, and so on. Other items—salaries,

TABLE XXXII. SHORT-PERIOD CASH FORECAST

	Week ending 19th June	Week ending 26th June	Week ending 3rd July	Week ending 10th July	Week ending 17th July	Total
	£	£	£	£	£	£
Overdraft b/f	131,600	73,990	61,950	240,340	150,880	131,600
Payments:						
(a) inflexible						
Purchase bills	7,750	5,250	—	11,000	12,500	36,500
Salaries	5,370	12,700	5,370	5,370	5,370	34,180
P.A.Y.E.	5,600	—	—	—	—	5,600
National insurance	570	950	570	570	570	3,230
Rent payable	—	52,160	—	—	—	52,160
Rates	—	16,500	—	—	—	16,500
Financial expenses	1,050	750	6,000	—	500	8,300
Distribution expenses	800	1,000	850	850	850	4,350
Capital costs (contract)	5,000	—	7,000	2,500	—	14,500
Tax	—	—	—	—	—	—
Dividends	—	—	—	12,000	—	12,000
(b) Slightly flexible						
Capital expenditure*	—	—	20,000	—	—	20,000
				— ⟶ 20,000		
Purchases (monthly A/c)*	—	—	238,700	—	—	238,700
			158,700 ⟶ 80,000			
Advertising and display*	500	300	4,600	300	300	6,000
			600 ⟶ 4,000			
Cleaning	300	300	300	300	300	1,500
Light and heat*	150	600	4,800	150	150	5,850
			— ⟶ 4,800			
Telephone*	—	—	3,900	—	—	3,900
			— ⟶ 3,900			
Legal expenses	300	300	300	1,500	500	2,900
Other expenses	1,000	1,500	1,000	1,000	1,000	5,500
Total payments	28,390	92,310	293,390	35,540	22,040	471,670
Receipts						
Cash sales	86,000	95,000	115,000	125,000	130,000	551,000
Rent receivable	—	9,350	—	—	—	9,350
Other receipts*	—	—	20,000 ⟵		20,000	20,000
Total receipts	86,000	104,350	115,000	125,000	150,000	580,350
Overdraft c/f	73,990	61,950	240,340	150,880	22,920	22,920
90% overdraft limits	135,000	135,000	135,000	135,000	135,000	135,000
Deficiency			105,340	15,880		
O/d after adjustment	73,990	61,950	107,640	130,880	22,920	22,920

* Deferred or brought forward. Italic figures denote adjustments.

rents payable and receivable, capital expenditure—will be in the immediate control of the accountant.

When listing the payment items it is helpful to distinguish those that are almost totally inflexible from those which are capable of some short-period deferment. If the cash position does look very tight, then attention can be given to the latter payments and their possible rearrangement. Where a company is trading on an overdraft, as in the example in Table XXXII, a smaller figure than the maximum allowable overdraft should be used as the limit, to give a margin of safety for unforeseen contingencies and forecasting errors. A 10% allowance is made in this example, but some companies might well prefer a larger one.

The usefulness of short-period cash forecasting can be seen from Table XXXII. Although the overdraft in the five-week period shows a reduction of more than £100,000, the incidence of the monthly purchases settlement pushes the overdraft well over the safety limit in weeks ended 3rd and 10th July, unless some correcting action is taken. The proposed correcting action is shown by the arrowed lines in the table. Capital expenditure amounting to £20,000, and £80,000 of the purchases account will be deferred from the week ended 3rd to the following week (with probably a loss of some cash discount for prompt settlement). Likewise, £4,000 of the advertising agency's monthly account, and the quarterly accounts for light and heat and telephone will be deferred for a week. In addition, the sale of trade investments (unquoted securities) which was planned for the week ended 17th July (£20,000) will be brought forward to the week ended 3rd July. The effect of making these adjustments is shown in the bottom line of Table XXXII. The overdraft in the two critical weeks, 3rd and 10th July, is reduced to £107,640 and £130,880 respectively, i.e. within the safety limits.

By scheduling forward commitments in this way and rearranging them if necessary, a temporary shortage of funds can be overcome and the progress of the business remain unimpeded by a cash position which is not intrinsically adverse.

It is not suggested that deferring settlement of accounts, even by a week, is an ideal method of trading. To have sufficient funds always to be able to settle accounts promptly is obviously preferable and should be the aim of progressive financial stewardship. However, the growing company may not be able to attain this happy position for some time. In the meantime, a close watch on the day-to-day cash position, as in Table XXXII, will avoid major embarrassment and bring nearer the time of permanent liquidity.

It may be argued that a business which is compelled to watch the immediate cash position so closely is overtrading and risking its shareholders' capital. On the other hand, a company's directors have a duty to obtain the *maximum return* on the capital invested and this can often be achieved in an expanding company by making the available funds "work" as hard as possible. Overtrading can be said to have begun when the overdraft shows no signs of reducing. In the example in Table XXXII the overdraft between the beginning and end of the five-week period falls substantially. Indeed, an oscillating bank balance is almost inevitable in a retail company where the income is spread throughout the month but the settlement for purchases falls at one time during the month. As long as good relations with creditors are not prejudiced by temporary accommodation of a few days, little harm can be done. Experience will tell the controller which suppliers will allow such accommodation.

The short-period cash forecast is useful not only to the company which is trading up to its borrowing limits. It is just as useful to the company with surplus funds, because if the management is to obtain the maximum yield on short-period trade investments it must know the amount of cash in excess of normal trading requirements and the period for which it is likely to be available. This may necessitate a cash forecast of up to, say, six months, but provided that a suitable safety factor is built into the estimates, short-term lending at the present high interest rates can be a very lucrative source of revenue.

Balance Sheet Projection

The trading budget is not complete unless its effects on the balance sheet are projected forward to the end of the budget period. Any imbalance in the growth of fixed and circulating assets can be detected before the budget is finalised and modifications made to plans if necessary. The importance of having a sound balance sheet cannot be overstated. It is the only detailed statement of trading results which a company is obliged by statute to publish, and it therefore receives close scrutiny by investors, both private and institutional. Public companies do or do not find it easy to raise further capital by what their balance sheets reveal. Private companies are helped or hindered by their balance sheets when seeking credit from banks and other institutions. It therefore behoves the financial controller to tell the management what the balance sheet will look like at the end of the year, given reasonable approximation of actual to forecast events.

Table XXXIII shows in a simplified way how the balance sheet at the beginning of the budget year can be projected forward to the end of the year. As the budget is usually prepared before the start of the new year an estimate may have to be made of the opening balance sheet, but this should be fairly accurate if full monthly accounting is operated. It is quite possible from the budget working papers to produce a quarterly or monthly forecast balance sheet, and this is in most cases desirable. In the example in Table XXXIII, however, we have only considered a projection to the year-end, although the principles involved are the same for any period. The left-hand column shows the actual or estimated balance sheet at the beginning of the year, the middle columns the changes in assets and liabilities which the budget implies, and the extreme right-hand column shows the projected balance sheet at the end of the year. It is helpful to divide the forecast movements in assets and liabilities

TABLE XXXIII. BALANCE SHEET PROJECTION

Balance Sheet at 31st Dec., 1967	£000s	£000s	Forecast Movements 1968	Other Accounts Dr £000s	Other Accounts Cr £000s	Cash Book Dr £000s	Cash Book Cr £000s	Profit and Loss Account Dr £000s	Profit and Loss Account Cr £000s	Balance Sheet at 31st Dec., 1968	£000s	£000s
			Profit before depreciation and adjustment to provisions			462			462			
Fixed assets		1,000	Depreciation		130			130		Fixed assets		827
			Capital expenditure	75			75					
			Sale of properties		118	160						
Investments		42	Sale of investments		36	30				Investments		6
Subsidiary companies		250	No change							Subsidiary companies		250
Current assets										Current assets		
Stocks	1,253		Increase in inventory	146			146			Stocks	1,399	
Debtors	125		Increase in trade debtors	10			10			Debtors	135	
Cash	21		Balance on cash a/c cols.							Cash	209	
	1,399										1,743	
Current liabilities										Current liabilities		
Creditors	291		Decrease in creditors	25			25			Creditors	266	
Current tax	108		Increase in provision		75			75		Current tax	75	
			Amount payable	108			108					
Final dividend	30		No change in rate				100	100		Final dividend	30	
	429										371	
Net current assets		970								Net current assets		1,372
		2,262										2,455
Less Future tax		150	Increase in provision		30			30		Less Future tax		180
		2,112										2,275
Share capital		800								Share capital		800
Capital reserve		150	Sale of properties and investments		36					Capital reserve		186
Unapprop. profits		1,162	Balance on Profit/Loss a/c cols.							Unapprop. profits		1,289
		2,112	Total	364	425	652	464	335	462			2,275
								—	—			

into three columns: other accounts, cash, and profit and loss appropriation account. This conveniently separates the main accounts and enables full double-entry to be used, so checking the accuracy of the extensions.

Profit before depreciation and adjustment to provisions is brought down from the forecast trading account and debited to cash and credited to profit and loss account. Then the forecast change in each asset and liability is made, with the appropriate effect on the cash book and profit and loss account. Thus, fixed assets will be affected, *inter alia*, by the depreciation charge, capital expenditure and any disposal of fixed assets. Receipts, payments and appropriations are taken from the budgeted cash forecast and trading account, and the double-entry made. This gives horizontally the projected change in all assets and liabilities except the balance of cash and unappropriated profits, for which the two vertical columns (cash book and profit and loss account) provide the answer. The check on the accuracy of the extensions is to ensure that, on inserting these two final balances, the projected balance sheet balances, and also that the cash balance equals that shown by the detailed cash forecast.

In cases where a forecast transaction affects two or more "other accounts," the double-entry cannot be made on the one horizontal line. For example, in Table XXXIII the proceeds of sale of properties will exceed the book value, but a loss is expected on the sale of investments. The net "surplus" will be credited to capital reserve, which balances the entries in the fixed asset and investment accounts.

If the projected balance sheet movements can be summarised on to a form no more detailed than that shown in Table XXXIII, it may be worth while incorporating the form as it stands into the master budget, since it usefully summarises much of the financial and trading policy of the company. If, however, the forecast balance sheet movements are highly complex or the management has no feel for accountancy, then it is better to show merely the opening and closing balance sheets and omit the detailed movements in between.

Balance Sheet Ratios

In the day-to-day running of the business close attention will be given by the managing director and controller to particularly significant ratios: *e.g.* expenses as a percentage of sales revenue, net profit to sales revenue, cost of sales to stock. These operating ratios will be highlighted each month in the trading report, since they measure the operational efficiency of the company. Equally important are certain balance sheet ratios, and their movements during the year should be the subject of a separate financial report. No difficulty should be experienced in obtaining the figures if full monthly accounting is the practice.

Similarly, when projecting forward the balance sheet for budget purposes, comment should be made on the forecast changes in the important ratios, as they may reveal an unsatisfactory disposition of funds between fixed and circulating assets, or an inadequate surplus of current assets over current liabilities, and so on. The trading policy implicit in the budget may then be modified, if practicable, to improve the financial position.

The most important of these ratios is the return on capital employed. Capital employed is defined either as the total of all fixed and current assets or as fixed and current assets less current liabilities. There are arguments for and against both definitions, but the choice of one or another will not greatly matter so long as it is consistently used over a period of time. The trend of the yield on capital employed is more important than the absolute percentage, although where current liabilities are large in relation to net worth, it would seem to be overstating the return on capital employed to deduct them in total. A fair definition, depending on the activity in which the company is engaged, can usually be arrived at by excluding some current liabilities and including others in the calculation of capital employed. Return also has a dual definition. Sometimes it is net profit before tax, sometimes net profit after tax. Again, consistency in use is more important than the particular definition. Generally speaking, net profit before tax is more meaningful, as the tax charge can fluctuate considerably from year to year. In either definition care must be taken to exclude (or explain) any special or non-recurring profits or losses.

To improve, or at least to maintain, the return on capital employed is obviously the aim of management in any company. In a retail organisation this will be achieved by expanding the sales volume, widening gross margins (buying cheaper and tightly controlling selling discounts) and holding down expenses, inventories and debtors. Of course, this is easy to say, but more difficult to achieve. But if, when the monthly review of these essential ratios is produced, the management knows where to look to explain significant movements in them, an important step has been taken towards improved financial control. A properly installed system of budgetary control and monthly reporting will direct the management's attention to the areas that need investigation and save time which might otherwise be wasted on probing into parts of the business which are functioning satisfactorily. Thus, in addition to the budgetary control and monthly reporting on sales, margins and expenses, which we have described earlier, the separate financial report will highlight both the level of stock and the rate of stock turnover, and the reasons for changes from the budget and from previous periods. The debtors' position will also be dealt with: the ratio of sales to debtors, both for monthly settlement accounts and hire-purchase transactions. If the hire-purchase business is significant in size, the tightest control will be necessary to maintain the cash flow and prevent accounts slipping into arrears. This should take the form of complete analyses of sections of the H.P. ledger, usually by day number, with full statistical reporting on the percentage by value of accounts in arrears.

Table XXIV shows the type of analysis sheet which should accompany the monthly financial report. The important balance

TABLE XXXIV. MONTHLY BALANCE SHEET ANALYSIS

	BALANCE AT MONTH-END		RATIO		RATIO FORMULA
	Actual	Budget	Actual	Budget	
	£000s	£000s	% or no. of times p.a.	% or no. of times p.a.	
Stocks	1,450	1,439	3·9 times	4·5 times	M.A.T. cost of sales Average stock at cost
Monthly debtors	147	138	14·8 times	14·0 times	M.A.T. monthly invoice sales Average monthly debtors
H.P. debtors	1,090	950	1·3 times	1·5 times	M.A.T. H. P. sales Average H. P. debt
Trade creditors	243	266	15·2 times	15·0 times	M.A.T. purchases Average creditors
Working capital	1,261	1,372	4·4 times	4·7 times	Current assets Current liabilities
Fixed assets	1,070	1,027	4·9 times	5·3 times	M.A.T. sales Fixed assets (average)
Provisions: Stock Monthly debtors H. P. debtors	37 4 35	40 3 32	2·6% 2·7% 3·2%	2·8% 2·2% 3·4%	Provision to asset Provision to asset Provision to asset
H. P. Interest unearned	110	105	10·1%	11·0%	Provision to H. P. debt
H. P. profit unearned	301	295	27·6%	31·0%	Provision to H. P. debt
Depreciation	175	200	16·3%	19·5%	Provision to gross fixed assets

sheet figures should be given, both actual and budget, with the appropriate ratio which signifies the degree of efficiency in employment of assets. It is better to show assets *gross,* and give a separate

E

analysis of provisions made against them, as the adequacy of reserves can then be more easily judged. For retail and distributive companies with a marked seasonal sales pattern, it is also better to relate assets and liabilities to *moving annual* sales, purchases, etc., rather than to cumulative (financial year-to-date) figures. Moving annual totals used in conjunction with average monthly assets calculated over a complete year will eliminate wide fluctuations in ratios and show more clearly the true trend.

The ratios relating to stocks, debtors and creditors in Table XXXIV will tell the management how efficiently they are using the funds at their disposal and why the return on capital employed is exceeding or lagging behind the budget expectations. From the point of view of liquidity the working capital ratio is important, *i.e.* the number of times current assets cover current liabilities. If a retail company is to maximise its return on capital employed it must be flexible in its trading policy, able to buy new lines and capitalise on short-term changes in the strength and pattern of demand. Further, a satisfactory surplus of current assets over current liabilities will guard against a downturn in activity and enable a company to weather a period which might otherwise be a very difficult one if fixed asset expansion is allowed to absorb too much of the available finance. What the working capital ratio in precise terms should be will depend on the nature of the company's business, but the controller should ensure, when projecting forward the balance sheet, that a satisfactory growth in net current assets is provided for, as in Table XXXIII.

The efficiency of fixed capital utilisation can be measured by relating fixed assets to sales, thus giving the speed of fixed capital turnover. Capital development at new and existing outlets unmatched by a corresponding growth in sales volume will be detected by a slowing-down in this rate. The causes of such slowing-down, which are not usually difficult to find, should also be explained in the financial report. As before, to avoid the problems caused by seasonal turnover, moving annual sales should be related to average fixed assets and so give a meaningful ratio.

Summary

The availability of funds for expansion is determined by the long-term cash forecast, which also sets the pace for development and quantifies more specifically the amount of external finance required. The annual cash budget highlights periods of strain during the year. Day-to-day financial management is greatly facilitated by short-period cash forecasts. Balance sheet projection and the regular review of significant ratios enable unhealthy trends to be detected and corrective action taken.

CHAPTER 9

BRANCH PROFITABILITY, EXPENSE ALLOCATION AND PRICE POLICY

Branch Profitability

In Chapter 6 the profitability relationships between fixed and variable expenses and sales volume were examined from the point of view of the company as a whole. We must now reconsider these relationships in the context of the day-to-day management of the company's affairs, *i.e.* the profitability of branches and departments, the practical problems of allocating central expenses to branches and products, and the construction of selling price policy for the guidance of management.

We have said before that there are circumstances when it is very important for the manager of a retail branch to know as precisely as possible his break-even sales—that level of turnover which yields neither a profit nor a loss. (This applies equally to the buyer in a department store. Indeed throughout this book where we have been speaking of the head office and branches of a retail company we describe by analogy the administrative areas and selling departments of a department store. The two retailing methods, though different in character, are conceptually identical for budgetary control and costing purposes.)

The value of knowing the break-even turnover is twofold. First, it exerts a downward pressure on expenses and an upward pressure on sales from both branch and top management when sales are below the break-even level. Second, it gives both levels of management an approximate idea of profitability, on the assumptions that a large part of branch or department expenses are fixed and that gross profit on turnover averages out to a more or less constant figure at most seasons of the year. Thus, a buyer in a department store knows that if his "fixed" expenses (cost of floor-space, proportion of light and heat, allocation of administrative department expenses, staff salaries, etc.) amount to, say, £250 per week and that gross profit is normally 25% of sales at retail value, then £1,000 sales per week will recover fixed expenses, and gross profit on turnover above £1,000 per week will be "net" profit, ignoring the incidence of variable expenses for the moment. The assumptions made are admittedly large, but a rough idea of profitability is immediately available to the department manager, which may be more useful than an exact profit and loss account some weeks later.

The *detailed* branch or department profit and loss statement must, of course, be produced as a matter of routine, otherwise the break-even turnover calculations cannot be corrected to take account of changes in expense levels and gross profit ratios. Further, when more serious decisions have to be taken (*e.g.* whether an outlet should be closed down or not) such decisions must be supported by exact figures in fairness both to the local and top management.

Full-scale branch profitability analysis is probably most useful when the budgetary control system extends to branch level. This is a highly desirable degree of sophistication. Break-even figures, whilst obviously very valuable, should not be a pre-occupation at all times of the year, unless the business is operating at very low profit levels. In a highly seasonal business they will be very informative at the low points of the season, but at the peaks of the season the break-even turnover becomes less meaningful. What is important all the year round in any type of business is the variation of actual from budgeted results. This applies as much to the individual branches and departments as it does to the company as a whole. If a branch is doing substantially less well than forecast then the local and the top management should be concerned to know whether their expectations were too great or whether a serious loss of efficiency has taken place.

The extension of the budgetary analysis to cover branches will not present many administrative problems, if the techniques described in earlier chapters are used. Sales will be forecast (using statistical methods) by branch or department. The gross profit percentage by branch will be known for basic costing purposes, and will either be applied overall to forecast sales or will be analysed by the forecast sales mixture, if variable rates of gross profit apply. Branch direct expenses must be available since total company expenses are built up from these figures. It only remains to assemble the figures to produce a forecast trading result by branch, with which the actual branch profit and loss accounts can be compared. The variances disclosed will enable the management to take corrective action in those outlets whose results are seriously adrift from the forecast and will influence, among other things, the capital development programme, personnel and salary policy and buying and stock policy.

Expense Allocation

A problem which often militates against the use of branch break-even and profitability analysis is the allocation of central or head office expenses to departments or branches. As we have said in an earlier chapter *all* expenses must be recovered from the revenue-earning outlets, and if a branch is said to have made a profit its expenses in that profit calculation must include a due proportion of head office costs. If in a break-even cost computation only branch expenses are included, turnover will fall short of the required total company figure by the amount necessary to recover head office expenses and the management will get a quite unrealistic picture of the sales volume necessary to yield a profit. The snag is finding a useful and equitable means of apportioning central expenses to branches.

This problem appears to be an intractable one for retailers because the maintained price system has for so many years been an integral part of resale business. Retailers selling at the "recommended" price by legal contract or threat of withdrawal of supplies have been largely absolved from the necessity of "costing" their merchandise by adding expenses to buying price and arriving at retail price by the addition of a suitable profit margin. They have traditionally worked from the other way, *i.e.* being given selling price and gross profit (as a fixed discount), they have kept expenses low enough to yield a working profit. This has undoubtedly put a restraining pressure on retailers' fixed and variable expenses, but it has had the unfortunate effect of limiting the development of cost and profitability analysis in retail companies which the breakdown of resale maintenance now demands.

Under conditions of "free" resale prices the retailer is in the same position as the manufacturer so far as the fixing of selling prices is concerned. He must build up to his selling price by recovering direct costs, overheads, and a suitable profit margin. In industry this is usually done by the process known as "absorption" costing, by which overhead expenses are allocated to direct product costs on some basis so that at the point of sale all expenses are "absorbed" in the selling price. The techniques which industrialists have developed to allocate overhead expenses to products must now be generally used by retail companies if they are to set profitable yet competitive selling prices and judge scientifically those lines which are worth stocking and those which are not.

The process of absorbing overhead costs in selling prices also provides a convenient means of allocating the same overhead expenses to branches (in a multiple retail chain) and to departments (in a department store). In a department store the merchandise groupings and sales departments are usually homogenous, so that the allocation of overheads to, say, the hardware department is the same as the allocation to hardware merchandise. For example, £5,000 is the estimated share of overheads which must be recovered in total by the hardware department. The same £5,000 can be allocated to the individual lines sold in the hardware department as a flat percentage addition to the purchase price of each item sold. The department manager can then arrive at his true break-even turnover and the top management will know that the selling prices which they have set will fully recover all overhead cost, if actual turnover approximates to the budget.

In multiple retail companies the problem is slightly more complex because each branch sells a variety of merchandise and there is not the same identity between branch and product group sales as there is in a department store. However, the same method of "absorption" costing can be used. Overhead expenses can be apportioned to merchandise groups in the same way as in department stores and can then be further distributed to branches on the basis of the forecast turnover of each product group in branch sales. This gives each branch manager his estimated allocation of overhead (or head office) expenses for break-even purposes and at the same time enables the price-structure of individual lines to be correctly built up. It is desirable to avoid having two methods of allocating central expenses, one to branches and one to products.

How should overhead expenses be apportioned to product groups? Obviously as simply, cheaply and yet as effectively as possible. It must be remembered that the purpose of such apportionment is to *improve operating efficiency*, by determining profitable selling prices and thence merchandise policy, not to do an academic accounting exercise which satisfies some theoretical ideal. Table XXXV shows how central expenses can be conveniently allocated to merchandise groups and to branches in a multiple retail organisation. The top half of the table gives horizontally the head office expenses which must be recovered in total company turnover and vertically the various merchandise groups. The basis of recovery of each category of expense is also shown. Thus central advertising and display department costs (press and television advertising, magazine inserts, display media) can be closely identified to particular merchandise groups—those lines which the management are specially promoting. If one item is the subject of a special television commercial the cost of the promotion should be earmarked to that item if the true cost and therefore the correct selling price are to be known. Where advertising is not so specific an estimate must be made of the amount which should be borne by each product group and for this purpose the advertising and display budget will provide a realistic and convenient method of apportionment. Head office establishment costs (rent, rates, depreciation), salaries and overheads can similarly be allocated to merchandise groups on the most satisfactory basis available, so that all central expenses are eventually recovered in turnover.

Again it must be stressed that an expedient compromise has to be reached between the degree of analysis possible and the value derived from such analysis. For most companies no greater detail than that shown in Table XXXV will suffice to reflect accurately the proportion of head office expenses that must be recovered by each merchandise group, from which correct pricing policy can be built up. Thus, of total head office expenses budgeted at £372,600 for the full year, merchandise group A will recover 10·7% (£40,000)

TABLE XXXV. ALLOCATION OF CENTRAL EXPENSES TO MERCHANDISE GROUPS AND TO BRANCHES

		ADVER-TISING AND DISPLAY	ESTAB-LISH-MENT COSTS	SALARIES			
				Financial Admin-istration	Buying Dept.	Stock Records	Total
Basis of Allocation		Product Advertising Budget	Product Sales Budget	Product Sales Budget	Estimated number of Purchase Orders	Estimated number of Sale Dockets	
Merchand-ise Group							
A	£	24,000	6,300	1,540	1,000	750	40,000
	%	18·9	11·7	11·7	12·5	10·5	10·7
B	£	10,500	4,400	1,080	500	700	32,000
	%	8·3	8·2	8·2	6·2	9·8	8·6
C	£	2,000	810	200	190	260	5,000
	%	1·6	1·5	1·5	2·4	3·7	1·3
etc.							
Total	£	127,100	53,900	13,200	8,000	7,100	372,600
	%	100·0	100·0	100·0	100·0	100·0	100·0

	Total			Branch 1		Branch 2		Branch 8	
	Budget Sales	Expense Re-covery	%	Budget Sales	Expense Re-covery	Budget Sales	Expense Re-covery	Budget Sales	Expense Re-covery
Mer-chand-ise Group	£	£		£	£	£	£	£	£
A	570,600	40,000	7·0	12,000	840	10,000	700		
B	400,000	32,000	8·0	20,000	1,600	13,000	1,040		
C	77,500	5,000	6·5	7,000	450	5,000	320		
D etc.									
Total	4,851,700	372,600	7·7	60,000	5,560	40,000	3,920		

which is the horizontal total of the individual head office expenses allocated to that merchandise group. Each of the other merchandise groups recovers its estimated share of head office expenses until the total amount of £372,600 is fully absorbed.

The lower half of Table XXXV shows how the same head office expenses can be apportioned to branches in a multiple retail group. For a department store this second stage is usually unnecessary since the merchandise groups and departments in the top half of the table are for practical purposes identical. The simplest method of allocating head office expenses to branches is on the basis of branch forecast sales. From the top half of the table it can be seen that merchandise group A must recover in total £40,000 of head office expenses. Forecast sales of this group are £570,600 taken from the annual budget. Thus, each branch's turnover of group A must recover 7% for head office "contribution." A similar recovery factor is calculated for each merchandise group so that finally the total head office expense allocation can be determined for each branch. (In the table, Branch 1 must recover £5,560 of head office expenses, Branch 2 £3,920, and so on, until the whole £372,600 is recovered.) This enables the branch managers to compute their break-even turnover by adding this allocation to their own branch direct expenses, so giving total expenses which must be recovered before a profit is made. Generally, allocating central expenses on the basis of forecast turnover is quite satisfactory and would only require amendment if actual sales turned out to be very materially different from the budget.

In this example of head office expense allocation it has been assumed that the company in question operates a chain of retail shops only. The inherent uniformity of each outlet enables the method of apportionment described to be easily and effectively used. Some modification might be necessary, however, if one or more outlets were significantly different in character from the other. For example, if a retail group operated a substantial mail order business as well as shops a different treatment of the mail order expenses recovery would be arguable. In this case it would be desirable to isolate as far as possible the expenses which the mail order business directly incurred, e.g. the relevant part of the press advertising budget, the clerical staff engaged in dealing with orders, and the packing and stores staff dealing with mail order only. Expenses which related to shop turnover (lorry and van expenses for re-stocking branches, area supervisor's salaries) would be excluded. A more correct estimate of the true break-even turnover of the mail order business would thus be obtained, which would obviously be more informative to management.

It is clear, however, that this requires two (or more) analyses similar to that shown in Table XXXV: a distinct split must be made of central expenses by type of outlet and their respective allocations to product groups. This may give widely differing expense recoveries for the same merchandise group in each of the two outlets, and if both outlets sell the same merchandise, a problem will arise as to which recovery factor to use when setting retail prices. Clearly, the same article must be sold at the same price both in the shops and in the mail order department. The only solution is to have one cost "matrix" which allocates central expenses to outlets for break-even sales computations and another which allocates precisely the same expenses to merchandise groups for selling price determination. However, this can easily lead to difficulties if it is not very carefully applied and the reasoning behind it is sometimes difficult to explain to management. Therefore, unless the arguments to the contrary are very compelling, one method of central expense recovery should be used which provides both break-even turnovers and selling price information.

Selling Price Policy

The determination of minimum selling prices is obviously critical to profitability. Not only does it allow management to take a searching look at lines which are shown to be yielding little or no profit, but, as resale price maintenance breaks down, it gives a flexibility to price policy which under highly competitive conditions may mean the difference between substantial profits and substantial losses. Table XXXVI shows how the expense recovery matrix of Table XXXV can be used to build up minimum desirable selling prices. The first step is to represent the selling price as 100%. Then, we know that merchandise group A, for example, must recover 7% of sales value for central expenses. This figure can be put in the table against "central expense allocation." The direct costs of the selling department must now be inserted, which we have assumed to be 14% of sales revenue. (In a multiple retail company an average, or standard, percentage recovery for branch direct costs must be arrived at, since items must be sold at the same price in all branches. In a department store the actual direct expenses of each department can be used, or an average, whichever gives the better result.) If the desired net profit in this class of merchandise is, say, 10%, the cost price can be computed, which is 69% of sales value. Thus, cost is arrived at by deducting from retail price net profit, central expense allocation (or overheads) and branch direct expenses.

To say that cost price is 69% of sales value when selling prices have to be determined from purchase prices is not very helpful. So we translate the cost build-up to equate *purchase price* to 100% rather

E*

than selling-price. This merely involves multiplying each item in the first column of Table XXXVI by a factor of 100/69. The results are shown in the adjacent column. We can now easily determine the minimum desirable selling prices of merchandise in group A by adding on the appropriate percentages to cost value to cover expenses and the desired profit margin. An example is given in the lower half

TABLE XXXVI. DETERMINATION OF MINIMUM DESIRABLE SELLING PRICES

Merchandise Group A	Selling Price =100%	Cost Price =100%
Cost price at purchase value	69·0	100·0
Standard { Department } Direct expenses { Branch }	14·0	20·3
Central expenses allocation	7·0	10·1
Total cost	90·0	130·4
Desired net profit	10·0	14·5
Minimum desirable selling price	100·0	144·9

EXAMPLE: Determine the minimum desirable selling price of an item in merchandise group A costing £1 0s. 0d.

	£	s.	d.
Purchase price	1	0	0
Standard branch direct expenses (20·3% of £1)		4	1
Central expense allocation (10·1% of £1)		2	0
Total cost	£1	6	1
Desired net profit (14·5% of £1)		2	11
Minimum desirable selling price	£1	9	0

of Table XXXVI for an item with a purchase price of £1 0s. 0d. This shows that the minimum desirable selling price is £1 9s. 0d. but that cost plus expenses amount to £1 6s. 1d. The management can trim their price policy according to the dictates of the market, knowing the lowest price which will yield a 10% net profit.

It will be clear that the real value of this cost-price analysis is the flexibility it gives to retailers. No suggestion is made that selling prices will be rigorously fixed according to a formula. Where market conditions permit a 100% or 200% net profit it will obviously be made. Market conditions and the retailer's attitude to the other competition must determine the overall strategy of price policy. The important point is to *know* when costs are not being recovered in the retail price, and to take appropriate action. But, here also, we must be careful how we interpret the cost build-up information.

Table XXXVII shows a company which is assumed to trade in three classes of merchandise, two of which yield a net profit and the third (group B) a net loss. Variable expenses are known for each group and directly charged, but "fixed" expenses are an allocation of central service expenses based on the best estimate of the benefit which each merchandise group obtains from them. For product group B competition prevents an increase in selling price, so gross profit is abnormally low, resulting in a net loss of £450. In total the company makes a net profit of £2,820.

TABLE XXXVII. PRICE POLICY, SALES VOLUME AND PROFITABILITY
Trading with a "loss-making" Merchandise Group

| | \multicolumn{6}{c} Merchandise Group | | | | | | Total | |
| | A | | B | | C | | | |
	£	%	£	%	£	%	£	%
Sales	9,000	100·0	15,000	100·0	25,000	100·0	49,000	100·0
Gross profit	3,000	33·3	3,000	20·0	7,500	30·0	13,500	27·5
Fixed expenses	900	10·0	1,950	13·0	2,000	8·0	4,850	9·9
Variable expenses	1,080	12·0	1,500	10·0	3,250	13·0	5,830	11·9
Total expenses	1,980	22·0	3,450	23·0	5,250	21·0	10,680	21·8
Net profit/loss	P1,020	11·3	L450	3·0	P2,250	9·0	P2,820	5·7

Closing down the "loss-making" Merchandise Group

| | A | | B | | C | | Total | |
	£	%	£	%	£	%	£	%
Sales	9,000	100·0	—	—	25,000	100·0	34,000	100·0
Gross profit	3,000	33·3	—	—	7,500	30·0	10,500	30·9
Fixed expenses	900	10·0	1,950	∞	2,000	8·0	4,850	14·3
Variable expenses	1,080	12·0	—	—	3,250	13·0	4,330	12·7
Total expenses	1,980	22·0	1,950	∞	5,250	21·0	9,180	27·0
Net Profit/loss	P1,020	11·3	L1,950	∞	P2,250	9·0	P1,320	3·9

The lower half of Table XXXVII shows the effect of closing down the "loss-making" group. Direct variable expenses are eliminated, but the "fixed expenses which were allocated to the group remain. In fact, of course, they would not be allocated to a merchandise group which has ceased to trade, but because they are fixed they are a charge on the company as a whole, which reduces total company profit to £1,320. Although group B was making a loss on its combined direct and allocated expenses its gross profit (although below average) was helping to recover the company's total fixed expenses, which do not reduce as a result of closing down this group. Central expenses, such as head office establishment costs, head office salaries, financial and general overheads, are scarcely affected by the closing down of one product group or branch, which is why they are described as "fixed."

In the jargon of accountants, gross profit less variable expenses "contributes" towards covering fixed expenses, and although the cost build-up calculations (which must rightly contain a proportion of fixed expenses) may show that the market price is below total cost, it may be more profitable to sell at that price simply to help to pay for the central administration. In Table XXXVII it will be seen that total company net profit falls as a result of closing down group B by the gross profit less direct expenses of that group. This is the fixed expense contribution no longer made.

If the impression is given that we have set up a price guidance formula which now turns out to be unreliable this can quickly be dispelled. For it will be readily appreciated that if central expenses *are for immediate purposes* fixed, then selling price can be set as low as that price which just covers purchase price plus direct expenses, and still be an economic proposition. Returning to the example in Table XXXVI, selling price could be as low as £1 4s. 1d. and still be contributing to total profitability. Obviously, any price which fails to cover cost plus direct variable expenses will result in a loss not only to the merchandise group but to the company as a whole. Similarly, a branch in a multiple retail group which does not completely recover its "head office" expense allocation may still be contributing to *total* head office expenses. But at a sales level which is so low that it fails to recover its "direct" expenses (shop salaries, rent, rates, light and heat, etc.) it will make a real loss for the company.

This approach to selling price problems and decisions whether or not to close down a selling department or branch is known as "marginal" costing. It contends that profit should be expressed as sales revenue less *variable* cost only, the resulting surplus being a contribution to fixed expenses. If the surplus exceeds fixed expenses a net profit is made. If not a net loss results. Marginal costing will tolerate a selling price which just covers purchase price plus variable expenses on the basis that at this price a contribution is made to fixed expenses. This approach is contrasted by accountants to the "absorption" method of setting prices which recovers *all* expenses in selling price. This is where we began our discussion of selling price build-up.

In fact, there is no mutual antagonism between these two methods, or at least, there need not be. Both approaches can be valuable in the same business, provided that we fully understand the interpretation we are putting on the figures. Essentially, a different approach to price and other decisions is justified by the time-scale which we are considering. A very large part of total costs in retailing is described as "fixed": *e.g.* head office establishment cost, salaries, overheads, branch rents, rates. But, of course, they are not permanently and inescapably fixed. In the medium term they are semi-fixed, in the long run they are completely variable. Furthermore, they are fixed or variable for different *decisions*. For management, deciding whether to close a branch, the "fixed" expenses of that shop (rent, rates, depreciation, minimum operating salaries) are variable costs. In price decisions it is quite justifiable for management to accept cost plus variable expenses as a minimum selling price for a short period of time (and for a limited range of items) because in the short period "fixed" costs *are* for practical purposes fixed. But falling prices and contracting sales revenue must be followed quickly either by a switch out of the loss-making lines into merchandise which does recover total cost, or by a reduction in fixed expenses—head office overheads, salaries—and possibly by a closure of outlets. Precisely what proportion of total sales can be sold below total cost and for how long will depend on a number of circumstances, but which course of action is likely to be most profitable can be determined, even though the analysis may be somewhat complex.

Briefly, therefore, the total cost method of building up selling prices is the correct basis for price-fixing. Only by this method will management construct a profitable price policy in the long term. Short-term decisions to sell below total cost to contribute to the immediate permanency of fixed costs are perfectly justifiable (and profitable) *provided* that management are aware that they are not recovering total cost and know the extent and duration of such trading.

Summary

Break-even analysis and budgetary control of branches and departments are essential to full managerial control. To operate them a way must be found of allocating central expenses to outlets. This is best achieved by recovering central expenses via merchandise groups and then allocating them to outlets on the basis of forecast sales. The foundations are at the same time laid for the construction of a profitable price-policy, which becomes more than ever necessary with the break-down of resale price maintenance.

Decision-orientated accounting (marginal costing) is a valuable adjunct to the absorption cost method of setting up minimum desirable prices. The importance of the contribution which gross profit less variable expenses makes towards fixed expenses must be clearly understood. But the time-scale in which we are deciding selling price and other policy must be equally clearly measured. How long any costs are "fixed" is the crucial issue, which resolves the apparently opposing approaches of marginal and total cost methods to managerial decisions.

In the next chapters we consider in more detail ways of reducing costs and improving operating efficiency.

CHAPTER 10

COST REDUCTION: DISTRIBUTION AND STAFFING EXPENSES

Introduction

We have now covered in some detail the fundamentals of tight financial control: realistic and analytical sales forecasts; task-setting budgets for gross profit and expenses; critical methods of capital investment appraisal; cash planning and balance-sheet projection; branch profitability, expense recovery and price guidance. The installation of a budgetary control system which provides for the foregoing will immeasurably help top management in making the right decisions at the right time. But budgetary control in itself is not enough unless the budgets themselves are continuously being scrutinised to see where and how economies can be effected and efficiency improved. This does not mean negatively that a cheese-paring approach should be adopted when reviewing expenditure levels, but positively that if a service or function can be performed more economically the attempt should be made to achieve this objective.

Every trading company is subjected to constant cost-inflation pressures, distributive and retail companies no less than manufacturing ones. The selective employment tax is at the time of writing the most recent burden to be carried. Unless expense increases are offset pound for pound by expense reductions or wider margins, the net margin is eroded, to the detriment of long-term growth. Wider margins from suppliers are not easy to obtain for the same cost-inflation reasons and therefore in this chapter we consider some tried and proved techniques of cost reduction. By these and other methods budgetary control is made doubly effective: not only is a standard set up (which is in itself control) but that standard is continuously reviewed to bring it to its most efficient level.

Cutting Distribution Costs

Since we are mainly concerned in this book with distributive companies, distribution expenses are a logical starting-point in our discussion of cost reduction; the more so as there is an inherent tendency for distribution expenses to absorb a greater and greater share of sales revenue as the multi-branch company expands. This is because the newer branches tend to be opened further and further away from the central warehouse and may in addition contribute a reducing average turnover, on the assumption that the areas with the greatest potential are exploited first. As new branches are opened, therefore, it becomes necessary to ask, among others, the following questions:

(a) Is the central warehouse now in the best possible place, given the new distribution of outlets throughout the country?

(b) Should one or more feeder warehouses be opened up to supply regional groups of outlets?

(c) Are the present delivery routes from warehouse to branches the very best possible in that they satisfy branch demand with minimum total transport costs?

These are clearly searching questions to which an obvious answer cannot easily be given. Sometimes, a precise answer is impossible because of the absence of sufficiently detailed costings, but more often it is due to a disinclination by management to become involved in the quasi-mathematical techniques required. Thus, decisions are taken at less than optimal level by hunch or "common sense." There are, however, techniques available to the forward-looking business-man which, applied under specialised supervision, can make significant reductions in distribution expenses with no loss of efficiency. These techniques form part of the growing body of knowledge known as operational research. They are admittedly based on mathematical principles, but management need not fear mathematics if it is applied intelligently and if it gets results. Five hundred guineas' worth of professional consultation is a good bargain if it reduces transport costs by £5,000 per year.

It is not proposed in this chapter to go into the mathematics of transportation and network techniques. There are many excellent books on these subjects available to those who wish to pursue the mathematical theories involved and acquire a deeper understanding of business mathematics. We are more concerned here to show which techniques can be profitably applied to certain situations and we discuss applications in non-mathematical language.

Network methods are used to reduce distribution costs because they systematically explore alternative delivery routes to find the most economic route. A map (or network) is made up of the various possible routes with the mileages labelled against each one. It can then be very easily found which is the shortest route by considering in a logical manner the alternative ways from the starting to the finishing point. This example is trivial because it takes no account of the loads to be delivered at each stopping point and the fact that the routes are largely predetermined by their location. A more practical problem is where selling outlets must be restocked from a central warehouse by a fleet of vans at minimum total transport costs. Assuming for simplicity that transport costs are directly variable with distance covered, the problem becomes one of trying to minimise the total mileage covered by all vans. A further variable to be introduced is the capacity of each van. Networks are drawn of all possible routes with the loads which must be delivered to each outlet. Then loads are added together to form a total van-load (bearing in mind the capacity of the vans) for a particular route, and this is compared with another route to see if a saving in expenses results. This process is continuously repeated until the maximum possible savings are achieved.

Clearly for a company with a large number of outlets and a large transport fleet the problem does not lend itself easily to manual calculation. However, as a very large number of repetitive calculations are involved, a computer can be employed to cope with the mathematical aspects at great speed. Computer programmes have been written to give optimal solutions to distribution problems of this type, which may well yield substantial cost-savings to companies which are at the moment "solving" such problems by intuition or approximation. Reputable operational research consultants can be invited to advise companies on this and other computer orientated problems.

Another technique which has been successfully used to reduce distribution expenses is linear programming. This rather formidable-sounding phrase is another quasi-mathematical method of obtaining an optimal solution to problems which permit alternative courses of action, but which involve some restrictions on the possible choices. If the choices and restrictions can be expressed numerically and in linear form then the best solution possible can be determined, albeit after some complex mathematics has been carried out, often requiring a computer. The word linear means, as we saw in Chapter 2, that a *proportional* relationship exists between the variables, *e.g.* if transport costs are 6*d.* per mile, 10 miles will cost 5*s.* and 30 miles 15*s.* This linearity is not often found in the real business world, but linear programming can sometimes cope with this difficulty by breaking up a curved function into linear "pieces," rather as the straight sides of a threepenny bit can be said to approximate to a circle.

The sort of distribution problem which can be tackled by linear programming is where a company has a number of depots or warehouses to service its retail outlets and wishes to reduce total transport costs to a minimum. It will, we assume, locate its depots as conveniently as possible among large groups of outlets, but there will be a number of outlets on the fringe of depot areas where uncertainty will exist as to the best choice of servicing depot. Now, linear programming will not only solve this problem, but it will also produce an optimal solution for the *total* distribution of goods from depots to outlets. The results may well fly in the face of "common sense" by showing that total costs are at a minimum when the depot in one area services some of the outlets in another area as well as some of those in its own area. The "common-sense" solution may not be the best one.

In this type of problem the transport costs from each depot to each outlet must be numerically specified, as well as the quantities of merchandise required by each outlet. Freight costs per van-load will vary from route to route because of the differing distances of outlets from depots. Demand by outlets may have to be specified as average weekly sales, allowing for a realistic buffer stock. Given this information the linear programming technique then proceeds as follows. It begins with any pattern of shipments from depots to outlets which meets the basic restriction that demand at each outlet must be satisfied without any build-up of inventory in excess of the allowed buffer-stocks. It then systematically evaluates every route not at present being used to see what potential savings it offers. When no unused route offers a reduction in total costs the optimal distribution pattern is obtained. Thus it examines without bias and exhaustively every possible solution. It makes no assumption that because this outlet is close to this depot then it must obviously be serviced by this depot, an unwarranted assumption when it is considered that it is *total* costs which must be reduced.

Clearly this problem is similar to the one which we considered by network methods. In fact, the two techniques can be used together in the more realistic situation where several depots service a greater number of outlets, but one van-load is sufficient to "top-up" the stock at more than one outlet. The analysis can be further extended to consider the benefits of relocating one or more of the servicing depots to reduce total costs even further.

Enough has been said to make the reader aware of the powerful analytical tools which are on call nowadays to bring substantial savings in distribution and other costs. The development of these tools has been stimulated by the availability of high-speed arithmetic and algebraic calculation from computers. This facility not only enables computation to be done in seconds which would previously have taken days to perform manually, but it also permits more and more variables and restrictions to be introduced, so making the mathematical theories more and more useful in the practical business world. Notwithstanding this, operational research techniques as a whole should be applied realistically, sensibly and with a full understanding of the limitations involved. To expect a little from them and to gain a lot is better than to expect too much and be disappointed.

Increased Profitability through Incentive and Bonus Schemes

Incentive schemes can be a very effective method of reducing costs and improving profitability in retail and distributive companies. Sales outlets, which are static so far as size and location are concerned over a number of years, lend themselves easily to bonus systems for reduced costs or higher turnover or both. A very positive stimulus is then given to increased efficiency, namely, one which directly affects the pay-packets of the manager and staff of the outlets.

A drawback to many of the schemes actually applied in practice is that, for administrative convenience, they are over-simple in operation and can therefore be abused by staff and managers. For example, the incentive scheme which provides a bonus on weekly or monthly turnover may well result in higher sales, but the higher sales may be at the expense of gross profit (staff pushing high value but low gross profit items, or giving cash or other discounts or part-exchanging at unfavourable prices), or at the expense of overheads (granting credit to bad-risk customers resulting in high H.P. collection costs and bad debt write-offs). Lower rather than higher profits may in these circumstances be the result.

Similarly, incentive schemes which concentrate exclusively on reducing running expenses may also defeat their own ends. Staff and overheads (such as light and heat) are cut down and customers are put off going to cold, badly-lit and inadequately staffed premises.

If an incentive scheme is installed to improve *profitability* (and this can be the only logical reason), then it must take account of all the factors which affect profits. For retail and distributive companies these are:

(*a*) Sales volume.
(*b*) Gross profit (where this is variable with products).
(*c*) Expenses.

A scheme which is comprehensive enough to cater for these variables will be more expensive to set up and run, but it should, properly introduced and applied, result in a more than compensating increase in profits.

When introducing an incentive scheme it should be clearly established to whom the incentive is being offered and the extent to which that person can improve his income by greater effort or efficiency. Some staff by the nature of their job cannot make a calculable contribution to increased profitability and should therefore be excluded from any but the most general bonus schemes, *e.g.* the profits of the company as a whole. Other staff can only make a contribution in one direction, by increasing sales, for example. The increased efficiency must therefore be measurable and directly attributable to individual effort, if the scheme is to be a real incentive and fair in its operation.

The precise nature of the scheme must be carefully suited to the particular business, its methods of trading, type of staff, size of outlets. It is not proposed here to cover all the possible schemes which can be used by retail and distributive companies but rather to explain in some detail a particular scheme which the writer constructed and installed, and which is working successfully. It is hoped that this will more usefully acquaint the reader with the practical points to be considered and the benefits which are likely to accrue, when bonus schemes are under discussion.

The writer was concerned with a medium-sized multiple retail organisation trading in consumer durable goods. An incentive scheme of traditional type was already in operation for the managers and salesmen of the retail outlets, namely, a basic salary (varying from some £10 to £35 per week) plus a commission of $x\%$ of the weekly branch turnover. Cashiers and non-sales staff were excluded from the scheme. The company marketed a wide range of merchandise, much of which was bought exclusively from manufacturers at better prices than those obtained from wholesalers. Thus, gross margins varied widely from product to product and it was obviously the aim of the company to promote sales of its own exclusive lines when customers requested goods roughly in the same price bracket. The method of payment gave managers and salesmen a fair income (although the pronounced seasonal pattern of sales caused too great a variation in income throughout the year), but it gave no incentive towards reducing branch running costs and tightening gross margins by promoting exclusive lines and being selective in part-exchange deals. Thus profits suffered because only turnover was the aim.

On investigation it became clear that a reasonable basic salary plus a commission on sales was the best method of paying the salesmen. Commissions were not individually assessed but were related to the total turnover of the branch, thus avoiding the evils of "customer-grabbing." The salesmen's job was essentially to obtain turnover and they were best rewarded as a joint effort on this basis. The manager, however, was in a very different position. His job was certainly to lead his sales team, but just as important, to reduce running costs where possible and maintain the overall gross margin as high as possible. He should therefore be rewarded on overall branch profitability, rather than merely on turnover.

This aim was achieved by developing the existing branch profitability analysis so that it could be used as a profit-sharing medium

TABLE XXXVIII. BRANCH PROFIT-SHARING STATEMENT

BRANCH PROFIT-SHARING STATEMENT

Branch ....

Branch Category ....

Period from .... to .... (.......weeks)

STATISTICAL ANALYSIS

MAJOR STOCK GROUPS	SALES-UNITS	SALES-£	GROSS PROFIT %	% OWN LINES	CLOSING STOCK
ALL STOCK GROUPS					

EXPENSES

	THIS PERIOD THIS YEAR	THIS PERIOD LAST YEAR	INCREASE—RED DECREASE—BLK
RENT/RATES			
STAFF SALARIES			
PETTY CASH			
TELEPHONE			
LIGHT/HEAT			
H. O. EXPENSES			
SPECIAL DEBITS*			
TOTAL			

GROSS PROFIT

THIS YEAR	LAST YEAR	INCREASE—BLK DECREASE—RED

NET PROFIT

THIS PERIOD	LAST YEAR	INCR./DECR.

DIVISIBLE PROFIT

THIS YEAR	LAST YEAR	INCREASE—BLK DECREASE—RED

SALES

THIS PERIOD	LAST YEAR	INCR./DECR.

	DIVISIBLE PROFIT THIS YEAR
PROFIT SHARE	
BASIC SALARY	
EFFICY BONUS	
SPECIAL BONUS	
TOTAL INCOME	

W.107

for salary payment. Table XXXVIII shows the profit-sharing statement which accompanied each manager's four-weekly pay-packet. The somewhat curious lay-out of the form was adopted merely to enable the calculations to be carried out on a National Cash Register book-keeping machine.

The left-hand side of the form showed the branch four-weekly running expenses for the current year and for the previous year, the essence of the scheme being that managers were paid a share of the increased profits which they earned during the year. The increases or decreases in expenditure were automatically thrown out by the machine and the totals added. Gross profit for the two periods was also shown from which were deducted expenses to give divisible profit. Managers were paid a share of the increased divisible profit earned according to their branch category. These categories were determined by the size of the various outlets. Thus the manager of a small branch could earn 30% of the increased divisible profit, whilst the manager of a large unit might be restricted to 15%. The reason for this was that it was easier for the bigger outlets to make large absolute savings in expenses than for the smaller ones; the potential for significant increases in profitability obviously expands with the size of the outlet.

Most of the expense items shown in Table XXXVIII are self-explanatory. Head office expenses were included to show the manager the value of the services which he was receiving from the central establishment: advertising, H.P. collection, credit control, personnel and welfare services. They were allocated to each branch by the method described in Chapter 9 but as the manager had no control over them the same figure was entered in the comparison period, thus giving a nil variance. Special debits covered charges made to a manager for such items as loss of stock, bad credit sanction, excessively low stock turnover, and the reason for the charge was detailed on the profit-sharing statement.

Normally a manager's profit-share was added to his basic salary to give total income for the period under review. The basic salary was fixed for each category of manager to leave room for a very powerful incentive to higher income by way of profit-sharing. If a manager showed a decrease in divisible profit (*i.e.* a loss over the two periods) he was only paid his basic salary. On the other hand, "excess" divisible profits above a certain level were carried forward to offset possible losses, thus removing wide fluctuations in earnings from period to period. A further incentive was provided by giving an "efficiency" bonus to managers who achieved exceptional increases in profitability and a "special" bonus to managers who sold more than their quota of certain promotional lines.

When the manager's total income was deducted from divisible

profit branch net profit resulted, the manager's salary being the only item to be deducted at the divisible profit stage. Branch net profit was thus available as a by-product for statistical purposes. The final item to be inserted was sales for the two periods under review.

The scheme therefore gave the manager a very good idea of his branch performance: the movement in sales, gross profit and expenses was clearly shown. This by itself, however, was not enough. Since the company marketed its own range of goods and gross profits varied widely between merchandise groups it was important to tell the manager the composition of sales. The statistical analysis in the profit-sharing statement catered for this requirement (*see* Table XXXVIII). With the aid of a computer (time hired through a computer bureau) stock was unit controlled and costed. Gross profit per item and per main stock group was thus available, as well as the percentage of exclusive to total lines sold. By studying the statistical analysis the manager could see, for example, how he had been depressing gross profit by bad part-exchanging or selling too great a volume of non-exclusive lines. He could also calculate the average realised price of each major product group by dividing sales revenue by units sold and he could watch his stock levels period by period. Thus, the profit-sharing statement provided him with a unique insight into his own trading activities which enabled him to take corrective action to the mutual benefit of himself and the company.

Measuring Staff Efficiency

Measuring the efficiency of labour utilisation and attempting to reduce wage costs per pound of turnover are obviously of cardinal importance in the retail trade. Wage and salary costs usually absorb the greatest share of the gross margin and this share has been increased by the imposition of selective employment tax. Somehow the retail trade must offset the effects of S.E.T. by greater efficiency of staff utilisation. In an earlier chapter (5) we considered ways of measuring head office staff efficiency. In this section we consider the efficiency of direct staff in the sales outlets.

The problems involved in reducing direct wages must not be under-estimated. In this respect the distributive trades are in a far worse position than manufacturing industry. Production planning in a manufacturing business can ensure that only a small fraction of the working day is lost in idle time, under normal operating conditions. In the retail trade much of the week (and much of the day, in some trades) is idle time. Saturday can contribute anything from 20% to 50% of the week's turnover, which means that on the quietest day perhaps only 5% of the week's business will be done.

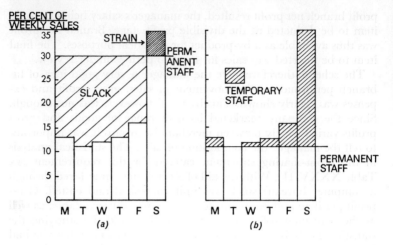

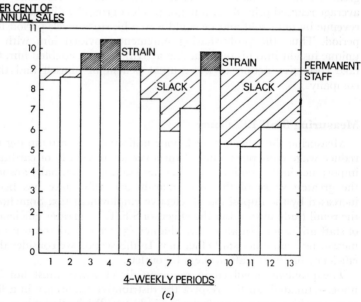

Fig. 15. Inefficiency of labour utilisation in retail business.
(a) *Top left:* "normal" situation with no temporary staff.
(b) *Top right:* "ideal" situation with unlimited temporary staff.
(c) *Above:* problems of high seasonal sales.

Fig. 15 shows more graphically the inherent inefficiency of labour utilisation in the retail trade. Diagram (a) shows the percentage of total weekly business done each day in a typical specialist multiple group. In the absence of an adequate supply of good-quality temporary staff the level of permanent staff must be kept high enough to cope with Saturday's business. The immense amount of slack which is available during the week can be clearly seen. In fact, to save money the level of staff is very often kept below that needed to deal with the weekly peak, so that there is slack from Monday to Friday, but strain on Saturday, often resulting in rushed and discourteous service. Diagram (b) shows an unattainable ideal in which there is an unlimited supply of part-time staff. It is shown merely to emphasise the dramatic reduction in permanent staff which could be effected under ideal conditions.

For many companies there is not only the irregularity of demand during the day and week: a marked annual seasonal pattern must also be contended with, as exemplified in diagram (c) of Fig. 15. Here also there are periods of slack and strain if the level of permanent staff is kept somewhere between that required for the highest and lowest point of the season. The weekly cycle is, of course, superimposed on the seasonal pattern, which further complicates staffing requirements, it being necessary to obtain temporary staff for the season and often additional temporary staff on Saturdays. Dependence on a high proportion of temporary staff in a specialist trade can bring as many problems as it solves, and there is no doubt that a point can be reached where the poorness of customer-service exceeds the inefficiency of a permanent staff coping with extremes of demand.

Very considerable headway has been made towards solving some of the practical problems of reducing wage costs in retailing: *e.g.* self-service stores, supermarkets, automatic vending machines. We discuss the implications of these techniques on cost reduction in the next section. It is the writer's opinion, however, that much can be learned and profitably applied simply by studying the relative staff efficiency in the individual branches or departments of one's own company. It will be invariably found that labour efficiency differs considerably from outlet to outlet within the same concern. If some of the reasons for this variation can be isolated an important step will have been taken towards cost reductions and improved operational efficiency.

Table **XXXIX** shows a summary of the individual percentages of wages to sales in all the 83 outlets of a retail group (*see* Table XL). Wages as a percentage of sales has been taken as a starting-point in the measurements of staff efficiency because this is the primary ratio. Other ratios such as average turnover per sales assistant or number of transactions per sales assistant may be considered to be secondary ratios, in the sense that they help to explain the primary ratio.

TABLE XXXIX. WAGES/SALES RELATIONSHIP IN A
MULTIPLE RETAIL CHAIN (data from Table XL)

Percentage of annual salaries to annual sales	Number of outlets
3·1– 4·0	1
4·1– 5·0	2
5·1– 6·0	8
6·1– 7·0	19
7·1– 8·0	21
8·1– 9·0	18
9·1–10·0	10
10·1–11·0	4
Total	83

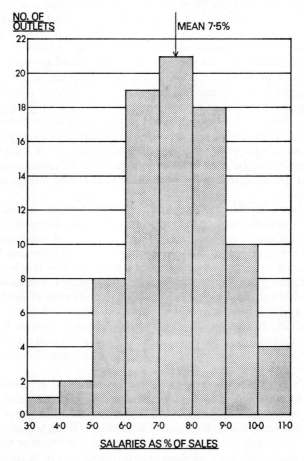

Fig. 16. Frequency distribution of data from Table XXXIX.

Suitable class intervals have been determined to summarise the 83 percentages into eight classes, or groups. The frequency distribution of Table XXXIX is graphically expressed as a bar-chart (or histogram) in Fig. 16. The roughly symmetrical nature of the histogram is immediately noticeable—it has the appearance of being a "normal" curve, like the distribution of sales variations from budget which we discussed in Chapter 3 (Fig. 8). The fact that the histogram approximates reasonably closely to a "normal curve of error" enables us to compute a measure of variation known as the *standard deviation*. This tells us the number of outlets where the ratio of wages to sales falls outside tolerable limits from the average, from which we can go on to find out the reasons for such extremes. These reasons may be obvious at a glance or they may be very hard to find, and we must, in any case, expect a *certain amount* of random variation, because wages cannot be rigidly controlled in relation to turnover. The crucial point is how much random variation we can reasonably accept without query (clearly not from 4% to above 10% as in Table XXXIX). The standard deviation gives us a good starting-point in assessing acceptable levels of variation.

The computation of the standard deviation is very simple and is shown in Table XL. The first step is to find the average percentage of wages to sales for all outlets. This is the total of all the percentages (631) divided by 83. It will be noted that this is an unweighted average, *i.e.* it takes no account of the relative size of each outlet in terms of wages and sales. In order to compute the standard deviation we must use the unweighted average, rather than the weighted, although the latter is obviously relevant as an *overall* measure of efficiency. The next step is to calculate the deviations of each percentage above and below the average of 7·6%. The small residual total of +0·2% in this column arises from taking this part of the calculation to one place of decimals only. This is perfectly adequate for the purposes we have in mind. The final step is to square the deviations from the mean and sum them. On squaring the deviations the signs disappear, and the total squared deviation divided by 83 is 2·0883. This figure is also known as the variance. The standard deviation is the square root of the variance, and by using logarithms, it is found in this case to be 1·44, to two decimal places.

The standard deviation is a fundamental measure in statistics. Other measures of dispersion can be calculated (textbooks on statistics will explain them to the interested reader) but only the standard deviation has such a wide application: in sampling, quality control, correlation, indeed in every field of applied statistics. We do not need to go into the mathematical reasons why the standard deviation is so useful, as against other measures of variation. Its practical value in our study is that it gives a measure of the variations

TABLE XL. WORK-SHEET FOR COMPUTATION OF STANDARD DEVIATION
(mean percentage of wages to sales 7·6%)

Branch No.	Wages as % of sales	Diff. from mean x	Diff. from mean squared x²	Branch No.	Wages as % of sales	Diff. from mean x	Diff. from mean squared x²
1	8·9	+1·3	1·69	43	9·6	+2·0	4·00
2	6·2	−1·4	1·96	44	6·2	−1·4	1·96
3	6·8	−0·8	0·64	45	6·5	−1·1	1·21
4	7·6	—	—	46	5·9	−1·7	2·89
5	6·6	−1·0	1·00	47	9·1	+1·5	2·25
6	6·6	−1·0	1·00	48	6·6	−1·0	1·00
7	9·2	+1·6	2·56	49	8·7	+1·1	1·21
8	6·2	−1·4	1·96	50	8·7	+1·1	1·21
9	7·3	−0·3	0·90	51	10·0	+2·4	5·76
10	6·5	−1·1	1·21	52	7·8	+0·2	0·04
11	7·1	−0·5	0·25	53	8·8	+1·2	1·44
12	7·5	−0·1	0·01	54	8·3	+0·7	0·49
13	7·4	−0·2	0·04	55	8·4	+0·8	0·64
14	8·3	+0·7	0·49	56	7·0	−0·6	0·36
15	7·7	+0·1	0·01	57	7·9	+0·3	0·09
16	8·2	+0·6	0·36	58	3·6	−4·0	16·00
17	6·1	−1·5	2·25	59	7·9	+0·3	0·09
18	8·5	+0·9	0·81	60	9·7	+2·1	4·41
19	7·6	—	—	61	5·6	−2·0	4·00
20	8·1	+0·5	0·25	62	8·2	+0·6	0·36
21	7·1	−0·5	0·25	63	8·5	+0·9	0·81
22	6·9	−0·7	0·49	64	7·1	−0·5	0·25
23	7·5	−0·1	0·01	65	6·2	−1·4	1·96
24	6·6	−1·0	1·00	66	6·0	−1·6	2·56
25	7·2	−0·4	0·16	67	8·6	+1·0	1·00
26	4·8	−2·8	7·84	68	6·8	−0·8	0·64
27	4·9	−2·7	7·29	69	10·5	+2·9	8·41
28	7·5	−0·1	0·01	70	10·5	+2·9	8·41
29	9·5	+1·9	3·61	71	5·6	−2·0	4·00
30	8·0	+0·4	0·16	72	8·4	+0·8	0·64
31	6·8	−0·8	0·64	73	9·2	+1·6	2·56
32	9·2	+1·6	2·56	74	7·7	+0·1	0·01
33	7·3	−0·3	0·09	75	7·8	+0·2	0·04
34	7·0	−0·6	0·36	76	9·2	+1·6	2·56
35	6·3	−1·3	1·69	77	8·6	+1·0	1·00
36	9·6	+2·0	4·00	78	10·5	+2·9	8·41
37	8·6	+1·0	1·00	79	8·9	+1·3	1·69
38	7·5	−0·1	0·01	80	5·1	−2·5	6·25
39	5·9	−1·7	2·89	81	10·7	+3·1	9·61
40	5·6	−2·0	4·00	82	8·6	+1·0	1·00
41	6·5	−1·1	1·21	83	5·3	−2·3	5·29
42	8·0	+0·4	0·16				
				Total	631·0	+0·2	173·33

of labour efficiency in the 83 retail outlets which we can use at intervals to monitor progress towards higher productivity. For retail groups with several hundred outlets it can also be used for sampling purposes, to obtain an estimate of the overall variation in efficiency from a sample number of outlets, where time and effort preclude an analysis of them all.

Where the frequency distribution is normal (or approximately so) the standard deviation tells us the spread of the data. One standard deviation plus and minus from the mean covers 68·3% of the items, two standard deviations plus and minus cover 95·45% of the items. In our example the mean of 7·6 plus and minus 1·4 gives 6·2 to 9. Thus, we should find that 68·3% of the outlets (=57) have a wage/sales ratio of between 6·2% and 9% both extreme values included. This is exactly the number that we do find, which shows the "normality" of our distribution.

When studying wage/sales ratios in retail outlets we are interested in two measures: the average and the standard deviation. We must ask ourselves, firstly, is the *average* ratio acceptable or is to too high? And secondly, is the *variation* round the average acceptable, or is that too high? Clearly, we have to expect a certain amount of variation round the mean. Although management policy may be to try to keep wages, say, at approximately 7·5% of turnover (this *was* the policy in the example we are considering) it is not possible to maintain this ratio across the whole company. We can accept the mean of 7·6% as being close enough to our standard. But we cannot accept extremes around the mean from 3·6% to 10·7% (that one outlet should effectively have three times the wage bill of another for the same sales turnover) without enquiring into the causes of such a variation. To simplify our task we say that we will tolerate variations of one standard deviation either side of the mean as being inevitable differences in labour efficiency, given the different size, location, type of trade, and other factors, of the outlets. This is perhaps too high a variation, but it enables us to eliminate from our study the fifty-seven outlets which have wage/sales ratios from 6·2% to 9%. We then go on to find the reasons why the remaining twenty-six outlets should have either extremely high or extremely low ratios. It should be noted in passing how this study reveals the inadequacy of the average by itself as a measure of efficiency. Although it is only 0·1% different from the predetermined standard it nevertheless conceals very wide fluctuations, which only the standard deviation (or other estimate of variation) truly measures.

Causes of Varying Labour Efficiency

Determining the reasons for variations in labour-efficiency in retail outlets involves associating the extreme outlets with a series of factors which may *cause* these extreme ratios. Thus, we list the factors which may tend to reduce staff-efficiency (and so give higher than normal wage/sales ratios) and then correlate them in turn with the extreme outlets to see if we really can say that one or more factors causes high or low staff-efficiency. The sort of factors which may affect staff efficiency are as follows:

1. Higher than average weekly or seasonal sales peaks, causing staff "wastage" at points of low sales turnover.

2. The type of trade carried on in the branch: a large volume of low-value transactions or a small number of high-value transactions may affect sales turnover per sales assistant.

3. The range of stock carried. An unusually wide range may necessitate specialist staff who cannot easily be switched from counter to counter to ease pressure in busy times.

4. The type of branch: whether it is partly self-service, a concession department in a department store or a conventional retail shop (completely self-service stores must be treated separately for wage/ sales analysis). Also, the physical characteristics of the shop: whether long and narrow or wide and shallow, which may affect customer-flow; or whether inconveniently placed for unloading, resulting in one or more assistants being away from counters to help unload quickly.

5. The size of the outlet. Larger shops are perhaps more efficient than smaller ones because staffing can be more flexible. There is an irreducible minimum of staff which must be carried to cater for lunch-breaks, daily banking of cash, and so forth, in small shops.

6. The efficiency of the local branch manager or area supervisor. This may be a very important factor, though somewhat difficult to quantify.

7. The locality in which the outlet is situated. Possibly higher-quality, better-paid staff must be employed in "upper-class" towns (York, Cheltenham) than in "working-class" towns.

8. Local labour conditions. A reasonably plentiful supply of good quality permanent and temporary staff will obviously increase efficiency, other things being equal.

9. Local advertising (product-promotion). This may cause higher than average sales per sales assistant, resulting in a "concealed" efficiency factor.

10. Local competition. Intense rivalry in the same town may push wage-levels higher than average as firms bid up for trained sales staff.

These are some of the factors which may affect labour-utilisation, but it is not claimed that this is an exhaustive list. In the study of the twenty-six extreme branches an attempt was made to associate each of these factors with high or low staff efficiency. On the whole, the results were rather disappointing. Out of the ten factors listed only two seemed to show a significant association with staff efficiency, but it must be remembered that several of the factors were themselves difficult to evaluate numerically (especially numbers 6 to 10). The conclusion seemed to be that random elements affected labour-utilisation to a much greater extent than had been supposed, or indeed was desirable. This reinforced the necessity of a regular survey of wage/sales ratios with particular reference to the standard deviation, insofar as much of the variation around the mean appeared to be due simply to lack of managerial control both at branch and head office level. Wage/sales ratios could be improved upon, if only the information and the will to do so were there. (The introduction of the incentive scheme described in an earlier section was a powerful stimulus to greater staff efficiency at branches.) It should be noted that although only two of the ten factors listed above were statistically significant in relation to wage/sales ratios it was nevertheless a useful exercise to identify them. For companies in different trades other conditions may stand out more clearly as being associated with staff efficiency and in any analysis of staff efficiency all possible causal factors should be itemised.

The two factors which did seem to affect staff efficiency significantly were numbers 2 and 5 above: the average transaction value and the size of the outlet. We deal with the latter first. Table XLI shows the outlets which were outside one standard deviation from the mean, *i.e.* with wage/sales ratios below 6·2% and above 9% (twenty-five outlets rather than twenty-six are listed because one was known to have an unusual wage/sales ratio for special reasons). Also shown is the annual sales volume of each outlet. We then calculated the average wage/sales ratio and average annual sales of the two extreme classes. These are given at the foot of the table. It will be seen that the average wage/sales ratio varies almost exactly in inverse proportion to average annual sales, *i.e.* 5·4% (the average for the most "efficient" twelve outlets) is to 9·7% (the average for the least "efficient" thirteen outlets) as £35,100 is to £64,700. Too much cannot be read into these averages because an important factor (as we have already seen) is the variation of the wage/sales ratios around the two means. But without going into details there is clearly some correlation between staff-efficiency and sales volume.

This is not an altogether surprising result since we have already suggested that in smaller shops the size of staff may be higher than is justified by sales alone: (*a*) owing to the necessity of staffing the

TABLE XLI. ASSOCIATION BETWEEN STAFF "EFFICIENCY" AND TOTAL SALES VOLUME AT BRANCHES WITH EXTREME STAFF EFFICIENCY RATIOS

Branch	Wages/sales percentages one standard deviation or more *above* mean		Wages/sales percentages one standard deviation or more *below* mean	
	Wages/sales percentage	*Annual sales*	*Wages/sales percentage*	*Annual sales*
	%	£000s	%	£000s
7	9·2	52·4		
17			6·1	85·1
26			4·8	74·1
27			4·9	80·8
29	9·5	47·8		
32	9·2	25·7		
36	9·6	59·6		
39			5·9	70·7
40			5·6	61·3
43	9·6	58·0		
46			5·9	48·3
47	9·1	39·0		
58			3·6	116·3
60	9·7	48·3		
61			5·6	60·0
66			6·0	86·9
69	10·5	20·0		
70	10·5	14·1		
71			5·6	31·5
73	9·2	28·6		
76	9·2	31·0		
78	10·5	14·5		
80			5·1	37·3
81	10·7	17·5		
83			5·3	24·0
Total	126·5	456·5	64·4	776·3
Average	9·7	35·1	5·4	64·7

shop in lunch-hours; (*b*) because people are discrete units, *i.e.* it is not easy to employ half-persons; (*c*) because the ratio of junior to senior sales assistants can be increased in larger branches. Other reasons can no doubt be found, but the implications on policy are apparent: small branches opened up in "C grade" positions in cities, or in small provincial towns, or as concession outlets in department stores, are less economic from the point of view of labour-utilisation than larger shops. This may be an inevitable penalty of expansion. On the other hand, a regrouping of two or three outlets into one bigger one may prove to be significantly profitable, not only from the staff-efficiency aspect, but also because rent and rates per pound of sales may fall, distribution of stock from warehouse to branches may be simplified, managerial problems may be reduced, and so on.

The other factor which seemed to be related to staff-efficiency was the average value of transactions at branches. In order to obtain a more comprehensive picture of this factor over the company as a whole it was decided to take a *random* sample of twenty out of the eight-three outlets, rather than study only the extreme outlets. Twenty numbers from 1 to 83 were drawn from a table of random numbers and these were the branches selected for a study of average transaction values. Because of the considerable amount of work involved in listing transactions, it will be appreciated why a sample number of branches, rather than all, were surveyed. Also, it was decided to relate transaction values to *average weekly sales per salesman*, rather than to wage/sales ratios. This is permissible since, if any association exists, it is more likely to be between transaction size and sales per person than between transaction size and wage/sales ratios. Average sales per sales assistant is a secondary ratio which helps to explain the primary wages to sales ratio. It is less comprehensive because it takes no account of differing wage rates paid to the various classes of sales assistants, but if a relationship can be inferred between transaction size and sales per sales assistant, it can reasonably be extended to exist between transaction size and "staff efficiency," as measured by the percentage of wages to sales.

Table XLII (columns 2 and 3) shows the average transaction value and average weekly sales per salesman of the sample twenty branches. Before attempting to measure precisely the degree of association (if any) between these two variables, we plotted them on a scatter diagram, which is shown in Fig. 17. Each dot (crosses are sometimes used) marks the point of intersection between transaction value and average weekly sales per salesman of one branch. The independent variable (the one we think *causes* movement in the other) is normally plotted on the x-axis, and the dependent variable on the y-axis. It will be seen that the twenty dots do seem to follow some sort of pattern: smaller average transaction values seem to be associated with lower average weekly sales per assistant and higher transaction values with higher sales per assistant.

To measure precisely how much association existed between these two variables we then computed the coefficient of correlation. This is a very simple calculation, and the workings are shown in Table

F

TABLE XLII. ASSOCIATION BETWEEN SIZE OF TRANSACTION AND AVERAGE WEEKLY SALES PER SALESMAN

1	2	3	4	5	6
Branch	Average transaction value £x	Average weekly sales per salesman £y	xy	x^2	y^2
1	4·27	181	772·87	18·23	32,761
2	2·72	112	304·64	7·40	12,544
3	2·18	129	281·22	4·75	16,641
4	2·27	122	276·94	5·15	14,884
5	3·36	132	443·52	11·29	17,424
6	1·66	57	94·62	2·76	3,249
7	3·55	124	440·20	12·60	15,376
8	5·13	161	825·93	26·32	25,921
9	3·87	145	561·15	14·98	21,025
10	3·39	155	525·45	11·49	24,025
11	3·45	106	365·70	11·90	11,236
12	3·86	148	571·28	14·90	21,904
13	5·17	298	1,540·66	26·73	88,804
14	4·75	238	1,130·50	22·56	56,644
15	5·07	244	1,237·08	25·70	59,536
16	4·86	307	1,492·02	23·62	94,249
17	6·87	254	1,744·98	47·20	64,516
18	5·24	188	985·12	27·46	35,344
19	3·28	146	478·88	10·76	21,316
20	3·31	156	516·36	10·96	24,336
Total	78·26	3,403	14,589·12	336·76	661,735

(A) CALCULATION OF REGRESSION LINE

$$\Sigma y = Na + b\Sigma x$$
$$\Sigma xy = a\Sigma x + b\Sigma x^2$$

I. $3,403 = 20a + 78·26b$

II. $14,589·12 = 78·26a + 336·76b$

Multiplying I by 3·913,

$13,315·94 = 78·26a + 306·23b$

II. $14,589·12 = 78·26a + 336·76b$

Subtracting;

$1,273·18 = 30·53b$

$b = 41·70$

Substituting, $a = 6·98$

Regression line $y = 6·98 + 41·70x$

When $x = 1, y = 48·68$

$x = 7, y = 298·88$

(B) CALCULATION OF CORRELATION COEFFICIENT

$$r^2 = \frac{(a\Sigma y + b\Sigma xy) - \bar{y}\Sigma y}{\Sigma y^2 - \bar{y}\Sigma y}$$

$$= \frac{(6·98 \times 3,403 + 41·70 \times 14,589·12) - 579,020}{661,735 - 579,020}$$

$$= \frac{23,752 + 608,366 - 579,020}{82,715}$$

$$= \frac{53,098}{82,715} = 0·6419$$

$r = 0·80 = 80\%$

Test of significance $\dfrac{r}{\dfrac{1}{\sqrt{n-1}}} > 3$

$$= 0·80 \times \frac{\sqrt{19}}{1} = 0·80 \times 4·36 = 3·49$$

XLII. First of all we calculated the regression line (Table XLII
(A)). This is the line of "best fit" between the two variables—the
computations are exactly the same as for fitting a straight-line trend
equation, which we discussed in Chapter 2. The regression line is
shown in Fig. 17. It will be seen that it passes through the scatter of
dots so that it approximately describes the relationship between
transaction value and sales per assistant. Thus we would say that an
average transaction value of £3 10s. 0d. would produce average
weekly sales per assistant of roughly £150, and £7 would produce
roughly £300, and so on.

AVERAGE WEEKLY SALES
PER SALESMAN £

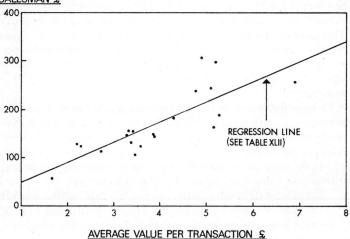

Fig. 17. Scatter diagram and regression line showing relationship
between transaction size and sales per salesman.

But we also wished to know how closely this relationship held, so
that the second step was to calculate the correlation coefficient. The
mathematical formula required is given in Table XLII (B). Having
computed the regression equation the only other workings required
to give the correlation coefficient are squaring the y-values and
summing them. In the formula the bar over the y means that this is
the average of the sum of the y-values. The correlation coefficient is
known statistically as "r" (relationship) and can vary between 0
and 1 (positive or negative). On substituting into the formula it was
found in our study to be 0·80, or 80% in percentage terms. This is
a fairly high coefficient and indicated that some relationship
between transaction size and sales per assistant could reasonably be
inferred. However, since our coefficient was based on a sample

number of outlets rather than the whole, we tested the significance of our result of 0·80 by dividing it by the reciprocal of the square root of the number of outlets in our sample less one. As the result exceeded 3 we concluded that our coefficient was significant for all practical purposes. The foregoing is an accepted statistical test of significance.

This association between transaction size and sales per assistant might again appear to be self-evident, as for staff-efficiency and size of outlet. But the implications must not be dismissed without consideration. It might otherwise have been thought that a natural compensating mechanism operated at retail shops, *i.e.* low value transactions are more quickly dealt with and a greater number can be effected per hour compared with higher value transactions so that average sales value per assistant per hour (or week) is maintained. This appears not to be the case universally. It may well operate at certain very busy times of the day or week, but in the quiet periods when there is a great deal of waiting time a transaction of higher value is a real improvement to sales per assistant and to staff "efficiency."

Perhaps for many companies not very much can be done to raise average transaction values, given the type of trade in which they are engaged. But, where an association between transaction size and sales per assistant is established we should enquire why some outlets within the same concern consistently have so much higher an average transaction value than others. Possible reasons are:

(*a*) The staff in some outlets do not sell "up" as much as others.

(*b*) The locality in which the branch is situated may affect average transaction size, the richer districts yielding a higher value than poorer class districts.

(*c*) The distribution of stock around branches may be bad, some branches always obtaining a greater range of better quality merchandise than others, so giving a higher average sale value.

(*d*) It may be deliberate management policy to sell the same stock at lower or higher prices in different outlets.

Close attention to points (*a*) and (*c*) may well give greater productivity per employee, even if little can be done about points (*b*) and (*d*).

We have dwelt at some length on staff efficiency because it is so obviously fundamental to increased profitability, especially with S.E.T. It will be found in any retail trade that one or more "causes" of greater or lesser efficiency can be fairly easily elicited. Typical of such causes are size of outlet and average transaction value and these go some way to explain variations in productivity per employee. But it will also be found that much of the variation in staff efficiency between one outlet and another cannot be traced to any cause other than lack of managerial control. It is here that very significant cuts in operating costs can be effected by reducing permanent staff and engaging more part-time labour so that the staff complement is more closely matched to the work-load.

We have attempted to show how statistical methods can be used to control wage/sales ratios, the mean and standard deviation being particularly useful to monitor overall staff efficiency. This approach can be contrasted to setting a rigid standard for each outlet, a method of control which may be unworkable. If the mean and standard deviation of wage/sale ratios are plotted regularly (on a moving-annual basis if there is a pronounced seasonal pattern) the outlets which are causing movements in these two measures can quickly be seen and corrective action taken.

Self-service

We cannot leave the subject of cost reduction in relation to staff-efficiency without briefly mentioning self-service shops, supermarkets and other labour-saving techniques of retailing. The need for such developments, specially with S.E.T., requires no emphasis. In the food trades wage costs can absorb up to 50% of the narrow gross margin, and it is not surprising that it is the grocery trade which has made greatest progress in self-service. But in any retail trade wage-costs take a more than desirable share of gross profit, owing to the fundamental inefficiency of labour-utilisation. It therefore behoves all retailers whose business can practically be run on self-service lines to consider this form of trading.

It is not proposed here to argue which retail trades can successfully be converted to self-service, nor to comment on the design and layout considerations which must be borne in mind when converting from traditional to self-service trading. These are subjects involving social, economic and practical issues, which are outside the scope of a book on management accounting. But, assuming that a switch from traditional or self-service trading is feasible, we can outline some of the financial points which must be considered when arriving at a decision whether to convert.

It will be obvious that self-service should achieve two objectives. First, it should reduce the wage bill, certainly as a percentage of sales, and preferably in absolute terms. Second, it should expand sales volume by enlarging the selling area and making available more shelving space, quite apart from new custom being attracted by the modern, stylish shop-front and interior layout. This second objective, however, requires capital, and the likely return on capital invested must be the ultimate determining factor. Sales and trading profits will almost certainly be raised by converting to self-service,

F*

TABLE XLIII. VOLUME AND PROFIT RELATIONSHIPS IN SELF-SERVICE SHOPS

| | Traditional service | | Self-service | | | | | | | | |
| | Volume = 100 | | Volume = 105 | | Volume = 110 | | Volume = 115 | | Volume = 120 | | Volume = 125 | |
	£000s	%	£000s	%	£000s	%	£000s	%	£000s	%	£000s	%
Sales	100·0	100·0	105·0	100·0	110·0	100·0	115·0	100·0	120·0	100·0	125·0	100·0
Gross Profit	18·0	18·0	18·9	18·0	19·8	18·0	20·7	18·0	21·6	18·0	22·5	18·0
Rent, rates, insurance	5·0	5·0	5·0	4·7	5·0	4·5	5·0	4·3	5·0	4·1	5·0	4·0
Depreciation of f/f	0·7	0·6	1·5	1·4	1·5	1·4	1·5	1·3	1·5	1·2	1·8	1·4
Light, heat, refrigeration	0·5	0·5	0·8	0·8	0·8	0·7	0·8	0·7	0·8	0·7	0·8	0·6
Telephone	0·2	0·2	0·2	0·2	0·2	0·2	0·2	0·2	0·2	0·2	0·2	0·2
Cleaning, etc.	0·1	0·1	0·1	0·1	0·1	0·1	0·1	0·1	0·1	0·1	0·1	0·1
Salaries	7·5	7·5	6·8	6·5	6·8	6·2	6·8	5·9	6·8	5·7	7·0	5·6
Total expenses	14·0	13·9	14·4	13·7	14·4	13·1	14·4	12·5	14·4	12·0	14·9	11·9
Branch net profit	4·0	4·1	4·5	4·3	5·4	4·9	6·3	5·5	7·2	6·0	7·6	6·1
Fixtures and fittings	7·0		15·0		15·0		15·0		15·0		18·0	
Quarter's rent in advance	1·0		1·0		1·0		1·0		1·0		1·0	
Stock (T/o per year)	5·5	(15)	4·3	(20)	4·5	(20)	4·7	(20)	4·9	(20)	5·1	(20)
Total capital invested	13·5		20·3		20·5		20·7		20·9		24·1	
Return on capital %	29·6		22·2		26·3		30·4		34·5		31·5	

but the expansion must be sufficient to increase the return on capital outlay from current levels. Capital cost relationships to possible sales volumes must therefore be very carefully evaluated before the decision to convert is taken.

Table XLIII shows the type of working sheet which can be used to explore these relationships so that a decision can be rationally taken. The first column gives the summarised trading account and asset statement of a branch in a multiple grocery chain which is at the moment run on traditional-service lines. For convenience, sales are assumed to be £100,000 per year, giving a volume index of 100. After deducting expenses from gross profit, branch net profit before tax works out at £4,000 per annum which, on the present capital invested in the branch, yields a return of 29·6%. Capital invested includes, in addition to fixtures and fittings, one quarter's rent in advance, representing money "sunk" in the business whilst the shop is a going concern.

The second and remaining columns of Table XLIII show how return on capital is affected by conversion to self-service at various hypothetical sales levels. In order to modernise and re-equip the branch for self-service trading a capital outlay of £15,000 is calculated. The assumption is made that virtually none of the existing fixtures and fittings will be suitable for self-service trading, so that a complete internal refit will be required, in addition to a new shop-front. Other items of major importance in the capital budget are partial resiting and refitting of the stock-room, enlarged refrigeration facilities and better lighting. Any losses on the scrapping of existing fixtures are charged against head office account rather than against the branch results for the profitability comparisons in Table XLIII.

Turning to the trading account, self-service will affect this in a number of ways. Rent, rates and insurance are assumed not to change, but depreciation of fixtures and fittings will increase to £1,500 per year on the new capital outlay. A 10% per annum write-off is provided. Light, heat and refrigeration are expected to increase by £300 per year. Telephone, cleaning and miscellaneous expenses will be contained at the original level. The only saving in running expenses is to be found in wages, where it is estimated that two girls less will be required under self-service, giving a saving of £700 per year.

If sales expand by 5% as a result of conversion to self-service, branch net profit on the new expense levels can be seen to increase to £4,500 per year, an increase of £500 p.a. over traditional service results. However, on the capital outlay this profit is only 22·2%, as against 29·6%, after allowing for the faster turnover of stock (from fifteen to twenty times per year) which should be possible under self-service. A 10% expansion in sales would bring the net return on capital up to 26·3%, but a 15% expansion is required before the return equals that obtained under traditional service. A 20% increase in sales would give a significantly improved return on capital. Therefore we can say that self-service must confidently be expected to increase sales volume by at least 20% before the conversion from traditional trading can be economically justified. It is interesting to

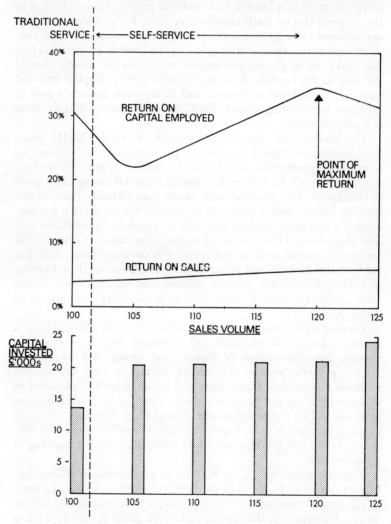

Fig. 18. Return on capital in traditional and self-service stores
(data from Table XLIII).

note that a sales volume above £120,000 in our example might require a further capital outlay of £3,000 for increased selling area to cope with peak periods. Depreciation of fixtures and fittings is then increased and salaries may have to be increased to provide part-time help. Return on capital is then depressed again, as shown in the extreme right-hand column of Table XLIII, although net profit in absolute terms continues to increase.

This oscillating movement in return on capital outlay is shown more clearly in Fig. 18. The capital invested to produce the various sales volumes in Table XLIII is shown in the bar-chart in the lower half of the figure. The graph in the upper half shows how return on capital falls on conversion to self-service if sales volume expands by less than 5%, after which point it rises as volume increases, reaching a maximum at a sales volume 20% higher than the current level. If, within the same premises, sales can be expected to increase by 30% or 40%, then return on capital may move up again. But it is safer to set reasonable limits to theoretical expansion, *i.e.* to assume that after a point the marginal return on capital falls and goes on falling, owing to physical limits of customer-capacity within the same selling area.

It is not suggested that these figures are in any way typical of self-service operations. Ambiguities in the meaning of the expression "self-service" and the range in size and type of retail outlet to which self-service principles are applied preclude any notion of a "typical" self-service store being reached. Rather we have attempted to delineate the criteria which should judge the merits or demerits of going into self-service, supermarkets, automatic vending machines and any other form of labour-saving retailing. The primary consideration must be to improve return on capital employed. This can only be achieved by a detailed and realistic assessment of sales levels, savings on staff, and capital outlay in the new form of trading.

Summary

Budgetary control is incomplete without a continuous review of costs. This applies in good as well as bad times. Retail companies have been especially hard hit by recent fiscal and economic measures. Most operating costs have been unavoidably increased, buying prices have been raised by increases in purchase tax, and at the same time the trade has had to contend with pressures on margins due to contracting demand and the break-down of R.P.M. Nothing could be more important than a searching examination of all costs.

Transport costs have been raised by higher Road Fund contributions and increased fuel costs. These can be offset, however, by more efficient methods of distribution. Mathematical techniques such as network methods and linear programming can often yield significant savings (applied under skilled supervision) by reducing journeys, loading more efficiently, rescheduling van rounds and resiting feeder warehouses.

Labour costs have spiralled under the combined effects of S.E.T. and general wage increases. Inherently inefficient by the sporadic nature of demand, retail labour utilisation can nevertheless be greatly improved by statistical controls, employment of part-time staff and the introduction of self-service methods.

Efficiency gains can often be secured by equitable and intelligently applied incentive schemes. The essential point to be borne in mind is that such schemes must improve *net profit*, not merely sales. Extra turnover at lower margins or with higher expenses may be no real improvement.

This chapter has tended to emphasise the use of "quasi-mathematical" techniques in cost reduction. It should not be thought that common sense or intuition are denied their rightful place in business judgments. The reader is merely reminded that almost every business problem can, if desired, be expressed in numerical terms and is in that sense "mathematical." The available techniques of mathematical analysis may as well be employed if they can contribute to profitability.

CHAPTER II

REDUCING ADMINISTRATION COSTS

Simplified Administration

Reducing administration costs is an area where surprisingly big economies can be made in many medium-sized and large retail organisations. As companies expand, systems, controls and paper-work proliferate to a point where extra revenue is being largely, or entirely, absorbed by administration costs. This situation has led to the development of Organisation and Methods (O. & M.) as a specialist function in larger companies. O. & M. is a justifiable specialisation in big organisations, but it should be remembered that the O. & M. department must not only make savings in operating departments but it must also recover its own expenses in those savings before an overall economy is effected. Fear of increasing rather than reducing costs has led some companies to shy away from setting up a specialist "efficiency" department, and it must be agreed that O. & M. is very largely applied common sense. Very significant savings can be made without any formal training in O. & M. principles if enquiring minds with a knowledge of the business are put to work. The achievements of Marks and Spencer in simplifying paper-work and systems as an internal company exercise must be unique in the retail trade.

It is almost axiomatic that no matter how good we believe our administrative systems to be, they can almost certainly be improved upon somewhere and show real savings, if only marginally. How successful we are in making savings will depend on the approach taken to the problem. Firstly we need the ability to stand away from the business and view the interdependent activities as a complete entity, so that the relationship of one department or function to another can be seen in perspective. For managers absorbed in the day-to-day problems of their own department this can often be extremely difficult, and is a partial justification for calling in an outside observer. Secondly, we need a questioning, almost sceptical, disposition. The question must constantly be in mind: does this department or system or piece of paper provide a service of *real value* to the concern, such that without it profitability would suffer? Again, this is a question which is not always easy to ask, let alone answer. The real costs of clerical procedures are not extracted easily from conventional book-keeping, and proving a case against an established system may require a fresh approach to cost accounting, some unpopularity, as well as much hard work. Thirdly, we need the ability to put the case for change briefly, coherently and convincingly to management. The following few pages attempt to demonstrate how these precepts can be applied in practical situations.

Flow-charting

An essential technique in simplifying administration is flow-charting. In complex clerical procedures it is almost impossible to trace mentally the movement of paper-work through each department. If a map or network of the flow of documentation is drawn, the controls used and the functions they perform can immediately be more easily grasped. Fig. 19 shows a flow chart which traces the flow of documents through four departments of a retail group to fulfil various functions and controls. The departments are shown across the top of the figure and the functions and controls down the left-hand side. At the bottom is given the key to the various symbols used, which are standard O. & M. practice. It must be stressed that this is only a skeleton chart of a fragment of the company's activity; the real value of flow-charting is the detailed analysis of all processes, so that the relationships between each of them can quickly be seen. Only in this way can possible improvements be pin-pointed.

However, even with its inadequacies, Fig. 19 raises some relevant points of administrative procedure. The questions we should be concerned to ask are for example:

1. Are the functions and controls at present maintained necessary at all?

2. Assuming that they are, is the present routing of paper-work the best possible to achieve these objectives?

3. Are any functions and controls duplicated unnecessarily?

4. Is there a positive requirement for each copy of each document?

5. Are the functions and controls performed in the best possible way, e.g. could a clerical operation better be carried out mechanically, by a book-keeping machine, for example?

6. Is the layout of forms and dockets the best possible to achieve the objectives specified?

Questions 5 and 6 will entail a study of all relevant documentation, and a copy of each form used should accompany the flow-chart.

Looking at Fig. 19 in relation to these questions we can say in answer to the first that the functions in themselves are necessary to control the business effectively and give management essential information. Secondly, the routeing of the paper-work is also not capable of modification to any great advantage. When we ask the third question about duplication we see that two functions are duplicated, stock recording and sales analysis. We must now deal more fully with stock recording because it is in this area that many retail companies have made significant savings.

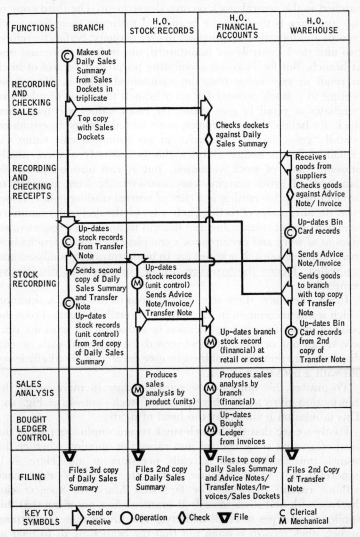

FUNCTIONS	BRANCH	H.O. STOCK RECORDS	H.O. FINANCIAL ACCOUNTS	H.O. WAREHOUSE
RECORDING AND CHECKING SALES	Ⓒ Makes out Daily Sales Summary from Sales Dockets in triplicate Top copy with Sales Dockets		Checks dockets against Daily Sales Summary	
RECORDING AND CHECKING RECEIPTS				Receives goods from suppliers Checks goods against Advice Note/Invoice
STOCK RECORDING	Up-dates stock records from Transfer Note Sends second copy of Daily Sales Summary and Transfer Ⓒ Note Up-dates stock records (unit control) from 3rd copy of Daily Sales Summary	Up-dates stock records Ⓜ (unit control) Sends Advice Note/Invoice/ Transfer Note	Up-dates branch Ⓜ stock record (financial) at retail or cost	Ⓒ Up-dates Bin Card records Sends Advice Note/Invoice Sends goods to branch with top copy of Transfer Note Up-dates Bin Ⓒ Card records from 2nd copy of Transfer Note
SALES ANALYSIS		Produces sales Ⓜ analysis by product (units)	Produces sales analysis by Ⓜ branch (financial)	
BOUGHT LEDGER CONTROL			Up-dates Bought Ⓜ Ledger from invoices	
FILING	▼ Files 3rd copy of Daily Sales Summary	▼ Files 2nd copy of Daily Sales Summary	▼ Files top copy of Daily Sales Summary and Advice Notes/ Transfer Notes/In-voices/Sales Dockets	▼ Files 2nd Copy of Transfer Note
KEY TO SYMBOLS	Send or receive	◯ Operation ◇ Check ▼ File		C Clerical M Mechanical

Fig. 19. Flow chart showing receipt and sales of stock in a retail company.

It will be noted that each branch makes up a daily sales summary from the individual sales dockets. This not only ensures that each docket is recorded but also that head office, who receive the top copy of the summary, have an easy control on the daily cash banked by each branch. It is also important for planning and replenishment of stock that head office should have daily knowledge of unit stock levels, so that the second copy of the daily sales summary is despatched to the central stock records department. The third copy of the summary is used by the branch to maintain their own stock records and for reference purposes in case of query. So far, therefore, two unit stock controls are maintained, one at head office and one at branch. But for financial accounting purposes a control of stock at retail or cost value must be maintained. This is effected by posting to a stock account for each branch the value of sales and purchases at retail or cost value. (If retail values are used then stock, for balance sheet purposes, must be reduced by an estimated overall "gross margin" to arrive at an estimated cost value. As explained in an earlier chapter this is not only a theoretically unsound basis of stock valuation, but it can also be positively dangerous if gross margins vary considerably from product to product or if price cutting is a part of normal trading policy. However, the alternative of costing each entry on the daily sales summary to give a correct stock value and margin means a very considerable amount of work and presupposes a complete analysis of articles into merchandise groups, if margins are to be meaningfully analysed and controlled. Hence the growing use of computers in distributive companies.)

In all, therefore, three sets of stock records are kept, a situation which is not uncommon in many types of retail company. From the point of view of work simplification or reduction we must ask ourselves: can one or more of these records be dispensed with, or can the three functions be combined to give greater or equal efficiency but with a net saving in cost?

To answer this question we must tabulate in more detail the information given at the three points of stock control (*see* Fig. 19). This tabulation is shown at the head of p. 163.

Firstly we see that the branch stock record duplicates part of the head office unit stock control and raises the question whether the branch unit stock record is really necessary at all. (Here, it is important not to extrapolate from other retailers' experience without careful thought. The fact that Marks & Spencer can dispense with unit stock records at branches does not mean that this applies to all types of retail activity.) The justification for keeping branch stock records is often not that the branch needs to refer to these records to obtain its stock balances (which can often be seen

	Branch	H.O. stock records	H.O. financial accounts
Stock in units			
Per article	x	x	—
Per product group	—	x	—
Per product group/per branch	—	x	—
Stock at value			
Per article	—	—	—
Per product group	—	—	—
Per product group/per branch	—	—	—
Per branch only	—	—	x
Per company total	—	—	x

physically), but that maintaining them puts a pressure on the branch manager to keep his paper-work in good order and makes it easier for head office to reconcile their own stocks with those of the branch.

Where this is essentially the main reason for keeping branch stock records it is legitimate to query the assumptions made. For a retail chain, with, say, fifty branches, thirty of which are big enough to require a clerk to maintain their stock records, branch stock recording can cost roughly £20,000 per year. If the loss of stock (at cost value) through defalcation, or shrinkage, is likely to be less than this figure if branch unit stock control is abandoned, then a saving can and should be made. Further, in the twenty branches which do not justify a stock-records clerk, the manager or sales assistant who performs this job can then devote his time to more directly useful jobs. Many retail companies have stopped branch stock recording on the grounds that it simply does not pay for itself. But these companies mostly sell low-value, high-turnover merchandise. For high-value stock selling comparatively slowly, like jewellery, a tight unit control at branches is probably essential: the financial loss through lack of control is likely to be higher and the amount of work required to maintain stock records lower than for fast-moving, low-value merchandise.

Secondly we notice from tabulating the information given at each of the three points of stock control that certain financial figures are not supplied at all: the value of stock (at retail or cost) per article, per product group, and per product group within branch. These are obviously of interest to management. But the information which is missing in value terms is provided in unit form from the H.O. stock records department. Therefore we should ask ourselves whether the stock records and financial accounts department could not be usefully combined for stock control purposes. From the flow-chart we see that both departments use book-keeping machines to record movements on and off stock, which means that two sets of skilled machine operators are employed to do a job in two stages, which can perhaps be done as a unified function. A possible solution would seem to be to insert the unit retail or cost price on each of the unit stock cards in the stock records department and, weekly or monthly, multiply the unit stock balances by price to give stock valuation. This job could be done by comptometer operators and would have the advantage of giving no less information than at present, but in addition supplying the financial accounts department with stock balances per article and per merchandise group.

The flow-chart also shows that sales analysis is partially dupli-cated, the unit analysis by product being carried out in the central stock records department and the financial analysis by branch in the accounts department. Here again, sales by product and merchandise group in financial terms are missing. As for the stock recording function, unit sales could be multiplied by purchase-cost price to give cost of sales per article, main merchandise group and branch. Thus, gross profit per branch would be obtainable, which, when variable margins apply, is invaluable management control infor-mation. Gross profit per merchandise group would require a dis-section of the daily sales summaries into product groups, which might be too heavy an administrative burden.

It will be clear the way the analysis of this problem is proceeding. The flow-chart shows that stock recording and sales analysis are fragmented, and as a result the system fails to provide essential management and financial controls. By integrating these functions so that unit stock movements (purchases, sales and stock balances) are multiplied by purchase-cost prices taken from invoices, dupli-cation of work is removed and the area of control greatly extended. Thus, we envisage a single stock records and sales analysis depart-ment providing both financial and commercial management with the information required to take timely and correct decisions. We discuss in the next chapter the problems which arise when the volume of work precludes a manual extension of unit stock movements by cost-price.

When we are attempting to simplify administrative process, there-fore, we are not solely concerned with reducing the work-load. We must also search for ways of improving efficiency and profitability by providing management with faster and more comprehensive operating data. The initiative in this direction will not always come from management. The value of a detailed flow-chart accompanied by copies of all documents used is that it reveals where the system is wasteful and also where it is lacking and so prompts management into action. Frequently the savings made on cutting out duplication of functions and documents more than offset the extra cost of improving output.

Flow-charting highlights areas of duplicated effort and so shows where time and money is wasted in unnecessary filing. This stems largely from extra copies of documents being produced to satisfy an alleged departmental need. As a principle it can be stated where three or more copies of a document are produced, the necessity of the third and subsequent copies should be seriously challenged. For documents that are "customer-orientated," such as invoices and purchase orders, two copies are, of course, necessary: one for the recipient and one for the company's own record.

But are the other copies (which may be two or three more) really necessary in the sense that without them profitability would materially suffer? Not only do extra copies have to be filed at each point of receipt (which can be extremely expensive in terms of wasted space bought at high rentals, quite apart from mounting wage costs), but almost certainly the receiving departments duplicate fully or partly the work of each other. If two or more departments receive precisely the same piece of paper either they both perform the same task on the piece of paper as a whole, or one department uses one part of the information for its own purpose and another the other part. In both cases a saving can be made (albeit only on filing time and space), if the job is done as a combined function. In Fig. 19, if the head office stock recording and sales analysis functions are unified, one copy of the daily sales summary will suffice for head office purposes, so that the third copy is dispensed with. For a company with fifty branches this eliminates the filing of 300 documents per week (50 ×6 days per week). It will be appreciated how big the savings on filing can be if this approach is taken to, say, a dozen standard company forms.

Costing Administrative Procedures

Examination of administrative and accounting systems will often show that a disproportionate amount of money is being spent on "servicing" a small volume of turnover. Table XLIV gives an analysis of a representative sample of 3,000 invoices made out by a distributive company selling small value items. The invoices are grouped into value ranges and the number of lines on each invoice are collated as well as the sales revenue in each range. The percentage of invoices, lines and sales revenue to the total is also given. (By "lines" we mean the number of entries on each invoice.) Thus, 1,613 invoices comprising 51·8% of the sample produce £1,010, or 3·8% of the total sales revenue. At the other extreme 54 invoices (1·7%) produce £7,020 revenue (26·6%). This relationship between

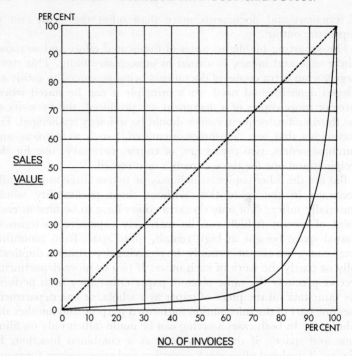

Fig. 20. Lorenz curve showing relationship between invoices and sales
revenue.

invoices and revenue can be forcibly expressed by converting the
figures into a "Lorenz" curve, which is shown in Fig. 20. The
percentages of invoices and sales revenue in each value range are
accumulated and plotted one against another, the invoices on the
horizontal axis and the sales value on the vertical. The "ideal"
relationship, where say 50% of the invoices produces 50% of the
revenue, is shown as the dotted line. How much the actual line bends
away from the ideal line is strikingly obvious: 80% of the invoices
produce only 15% of the sales revenue, and 90% only 35%.

This relationship (known colloquially as the "80/20 rule") almost
deserves to be recognised as a business "law" because it is found to
operate in so many areas of industry and commerce. Very commonly
80% of a company's stock produces only about 20% of sales turnover, or 80% of total customers account for only 20% of total sales,
or 80% of individual creditor balances comprise only 20% of the
bought ledger control, and so on. The significance of this "law" on
administration expenses is that too often an accounting system is set
up which, on a detailed costing, is found to be unprofitable for the
greater bulk of its activity.

In the example in Table XLIV four copies of each invoice were made out, one for the customer, one as an advice note of despatch, one for the sales and stock records department and one for the sales ledger department. A full sales ledger was maintained, each customer having an account card posted on a book-keeping machine. When the total cost in terms of wages and office space was calculated for invoicing, sales and stock recording, debtor control and filing, it was found that the gross profit on the bulk of the invoices was entirely absorbed by administration costs, leaving selling expenses and overheads totally unrecovered. The small number of high value

TABLE XLIV. ANALYSIS OF INVOICES TO SHOW RELATIONSHIP BETWEEN NUMBER PRODUCED AND RELATIVE SALES VALUE

Value Range	Invoices		Number of lines on invoices		Sales Value	
	No.	% of Total	No.	% of Total	£	% of Total
£0–£1	1,613	51·8	4,520	66·6	1,010	3·8
£1–£2	337	10·8	541	8·0	520	2·0
£2–£4	293	9·4	479	7·1	1,060	4·0
£4–£6	144	4·6	279	4·1	720	2·7
£6–£8	112	3·6	179	2·7	800	3·0
£8–£10	72	2·3	124	1·8	690	2·6
£10–£20	221	7·1	294	4·3	3,850	14·6
£20–£30	110	3·5	125	1·8	2,690	10·2
£30–£40	67	2·2	70	1·0	2,570	9·7
£40–£50	27	0·9	41	0·6	1,190	4·5
£50–£60	30	1·0	35	0·5	1,680	6·3
£60–£70	7	0·2	10	0·1	450	1·7
£70–£80	13	0·4	19	0·3	1,000	3·8
£80–£90	5	0·2	8	0·1	440	1·7
£90–£100	8	0·3	9	0·1	750	2·8
Over £100	54	1·7	60	0·9	7,020	26·6
Total	3,113	100·0	6,793	100·0	26,440	100·0

invoices were subsiding a much greater number of unprofitable ones.

The solution to this sort of problem is not to turn away the small value business (which may be important for goodwill purposes), but to simplify the system of control for small orders so that it costs much less. It may be worth while having two systems, an extremely simple one for small orders and a more sophisticated one for high value orders. For the small value orders we might suggest keeping only one copy of the sales invoice which would be filed pending receipt of the remittance. On receipt of cash the invoice would be removed from the file, which would thus become the sales "ledger." Customers would be asked to remit against invoice so that as a rule statements would not be sent, only follow-up reminders to late payers. A section of the warehouse could be divided off as a small-order store, in which no bin cards records would be kept. Stock records would merely be made up from periodic stock counts, the sales analysis being items delivered into the small-order store plus opening stock less closing stock. As an alternative to having a debtors' ledger, small-order customers might be requested to pay cash on delivery. If these suggestions seem radical the cost of servicing a mass of small transactions on a total-control system must be very carefully evaluated before they are dismissed. A simplified system may not ensure 100% control but it will probably be extremely beneficial from the point of view of the profit and loss account.

For any administrative or accounting system, therefore, we should be able to define precisely two variables: one, the basic unit of work being performed, and two, the cost of that unit. Once the problem has been reduced to quantitative terms, it is then possible to suggest alternative systems which will give acceptable levels of control but at a significantly reduced total cost. Almost invariably some savings can be made, which makes such analysis well worth while.

Defining the basic unit of work means finding the factor which, more than any other, influences the total amount of work performed, and therefore total cost. Reflection on the small value order problem, for example, shows that it is not the number of *orders* which is the prime causal factor but the number of *lines* on each order. Most of the functions necessary to process an order from its receipt to collection of cash have to be carried out for each item on the order: order checking (for correct product descriptions), pricing, stock recording, sales recording, invoicing and invoice checking. Work which relates to an order as a complete entity (*i.e.* irrespective of the number of separate items ordered) is confined to sales ledger posting, filing and general supervision.

Table XLV shows the analysis of total cost of order processing for the distributive company under review. The departments involved are shown horizontally and the various processing functions vertically, divided into work per line, per order and general work. The table serves the dual function of showing the proportion of total cost incurred by each department (the order office accounts for 32·6% for example) and, just as important, the proportion of costs which are directly attributable to lines and orders. Work per line absorbs nearly two-thirds of total order processing expenses and is therefore the chief determining factor of total costs.

The significance of identifying the basic unit of work can be seen by returning to Table XLIV. Here, the number of lines for a given sales revenue is shown, as well as the number of invoices. The 1,613 invoices, which account for 51·8% of the total, cover 4,520 lines, or 66·6%. Thus when we consider numbers of lines processed rather than individual orders the disproportion between the administration costs incurred and the sales revenue achieved becomes even more marked. Invoices under £8 in value cover nearly 90% of lines processed (and therefore the major part of total administration costs), but produce only 16% of total sales revenue. When these facts are brought home to directors in this way they quickly see the advantages of a simplified system.

Indeed, having determined total processing costs and the basic work unit, it is possible to show in money terms the savings likely to be realised under a simplified system. Suppose that total order processing costs under the existing system (as outlined in Table

TABLE XLV. ANALYSIS OF ORDER PROCESSING EXPENSES TO SHOW PERCENTAGE OF COSTS ABSORBED BY WORK PER LINE, PER ORDER AND GENERAL WORK

	Total	Order Office	Invoice Dept.	Stock and Sales Records Dept.	Sales Ledger Dept.
	%	%	%	%	%
Work per line:					
Order recording ⎱	10·0	10·0	—	—	—
Order checking ⎰					
Order pricing	8·5	8·5	—	—	—
Stock recording	16·0	—	—	16·0	—
Sales recording	8·5	—	—	8·5	—
Invoicing	18·6	—	18·6	—	—
Invoicing checking	4·5	—	4·5	—	—
	66·1	18·5	23·1	24·5	—
Work per order:					
Ledger posting	5·0	—	—	—	5·0
Cash/invoice queries	2·2	—	—	—	2·2
Filing	8·9	2·8	2·0	3·0	1·1
	16·1	2·8	2·0	3·0	8·3
General work:					
Supervision	9·3	2·8	1·8	2·5	2·2
Correspondence	8·5	8·5	—	—	—
	17·8	11·3	1·8	2·5	2·2
Total %	100·0	32·6	26·9	30·0	10·5

XLV) amount to, say, £30,000 p.a. If the number of lines processed are 120,000 p.a., costs per line are 5*s*. each. A simplified system may save £12,000 p.a., which can be positively identified in fewer staff and smaller space occupied, so that processing costs per line are now 3*s*. each. Table XLIV shows that orders under £1 contain roughly three lines each. Under the existing system, therefore, a typical order for three items at a total value of, say, 13*s*. 6*d*. does not even recover its processing costs, which are 15*s*. Under the simplified system a three-line order of 9*s*. just recovers its servicing costs. If high volume small-value business must be done to maintain goodwill this magnitude of cost reduction can be very important for profitability.

Measuring the true cost of the basic unit of work should not be a problem if care is taken to describe clearly the duties of staff. This is greatly facilitated by the use of flow-charts. Instead of relying on the often misleading description of his duties volunteered by a clerk, the systems analyst can usually define a person's function more accurately by studying the work-flow. To obtain the cost breakdown shown in Table XLV it is then only necessary to arrive at an overall cost per employee. This is best achieved by grading staff so that their employment expenses are conveniently summarised. Thus, for each grade of staff we calculate:

1. Average salary.
2. Average bonus, if any.
3. Pension expenses.
4. Welfare expenses (canteen, nurse, subsidised sports and social club, etc.).
5. Housing expenses (average space occupied per person, multiplied by rent and rates, light and heat costs per square foot).
6. Other expenses (National Insurance, telephone expenses, etc.).
7. Total employment expenses (1 to 6 above).

Having graded staff and analysed their duties as far as possible into functions, it is then a simple matter to cost each function, as shown in Table XLV. It goes without saying that detailed and accurate statistics must be kept of orders, invoices and lines processed to arrive at the cost of the work unit.

Selective Controls

An area of administrative activity which can be very expensive in retail companies is stock checking. But here, too, a careful application of the "80/20 rule" can show significant savings. It is obviously important that stock records should be as accurate as possible, for commercial as well as accounting reasons. Pilferage also must be kept under control. For a number of reasons, however, it is never possible to expect 100% accuracy of stock records (particularly in the retail trade), no matter how tight the system of control. It is obvious too, that it is not good business to spend £25,000 p.a. in stock-takers' salaries and expenses if the maximum stock loss is, say, £20,000 p.a. This is the sort of situation which can occur if a total control system is operated, rather than what we might call a selective, or statistical, control. Granted that a reasonable amount of time and money must be spent on stock-checking, how should this time be spent to achieve optimum auditing results?

We know that in any company's stock there is a spectrum of turnover rates, ranging from items that come into and go straight out of stock to items that take months to move. An analysis of turnover rates and stock values for each item will almost certainly show that 80% (or thereabouts) of the company's sales is provided by only 20% (or thereabouts) of the stock. It will also be found that most of the errors in stock-recording are errors of paper-work. So, if an item of stock has not moved during a period, no paper-work has been raised and there is little point in checking stock. Leaving aside pilferage for the moment, if stock checking can be more closely matched to speed of stock turnover considerable savings should result. Instead of checking the entire stock, much of which has not moved in the period under review, effort can be directed to more frequent checks of the items which are most likely to be in error, *i.e.* the relatively small stock of fast-moving items.

The procedure is to take the stock and sales records of each merchandise group and calculate the rate of stock turnover based on, say, the last six months' sales, taking care to adjust for the seasonal pattern, if any. The stock items can then be arranged in ascending order of turnover rate with the average stock balance for each item shown beside it. If all items within a merchandise group have much the same cost value, unit balances can be used. Otherwise it is better to use stock values at cost or retail value, as this will correctly "weight" the auditing effort towards the higher value items. To obtain the value (or quantity) of stock which turns over in a given period or less it is then only necessary to accumulate the stock balances. The cumulative balances can also be expressed as a percentage of total stock in the merchandise group to arrive at the *proportion* of stock which turns over in a given period of time. The following few entries show how the calculations proceed:

Stock item number	Average turnover rate (weeks)	Average stock value £	Cumulative stock value	% of total stock
054	1·0	320	320	0·6
142	1·2	540	860	1·7
077	1·5	260	1,120	2·2

This distribution of stock value against rate of turnover can be shown graphically, as in Fig. 21. Percentage of total stock value is described on the vertical axis and rate of turnover on the horizontal. A logarithmic horizontal scale must be used because of the wide variation in turnover rates. Each percentage (cumulative stock value to total) can then be plotted against each turnover rate, so that the proportion of stock which turns over in a given period or less can easily be seen. The figure shows, for example, that only 20% of total stock turns over in less than seven-and-a-half weeks, therefore 80%

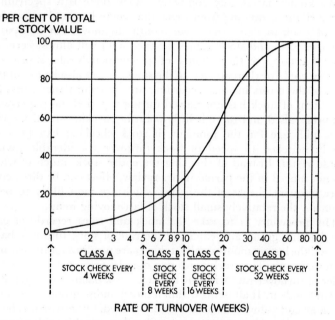

Fig. 21. Diagram to show percentage of stock turning over in a given period or less used as a basis for stock auditing frequency.

has a rate of turn greater than seven-and-a-half weeks. If stocks are checked in total, a great deal of auditing effort may be spent on checking stocks which have not moved since the date of the last check—time wasted, apart from spotting defalcations.

A chart, such as Fig. 21, can thus be used to classify stock items into frequency-of-checking groups. Bearing in mind the limited amount of money which can be spent on stock-auditing we may say that items which turn over in less than five weeks are in class A, items which have a stock-turn of between five and ten weeks are class B, and so on. We then set stock checking frequencies which are practical and realistic for each turnover group. Using the suggested frequencies shown in Fig. 21 it will be seen that only about 12% of total stock value is checked every four weeks and about 30% every eight weeks. The savings in cost by using this selective method as against a total checking system can be readily appreciated. Stock-takers can be sent to branches and warehouses to check a limited number of items, rather than attempt full-scale audits, the very size of which delays the correcting of book stocks and encourages mis-management.

If pilferage is a very severe problem a series of additional random checks may mitigate it to some extent. But a certain random element is inherent in the selective system described above: stock items are constantly changing their rates of turnover, so the frequency of stock checking will be changing too. A certain amount of pilferage is almost inevitable in the retail trade and we must take care that the cost of suppressing it does not outweigh the actual stock loss. Where pilferage exceeds an acceptable level factors other than purely administrative ones must be considered, e.g. security, staff morale.

Summary

Administration costs tend to absorb a larger and larger share of the trading margin. All systems and procedures must be scrutinised to ensure that control is adequate but is obtained at minimum cost. Whether this is done by professional O. & M. experts or by intelligent company staff is immaterial, provided that results are achieved.

Flow charting is an essential technique in analysing systems and can lead to reduced paper-work, a simpler, more effective, and cheaper system, and the elimination of unnecessary filing.

The "80/20 rule" focuses attention on the profit-earning areas of activity and suggests simplified methods to service low-value high-volume business. More efficient stock-auditing and other selective controls also stem from this fundamental business principle.

As in the previous chapter, analysis has been stressed at the expense of practical aids to efficiency. The omission of information on office machinery, form design, office layout and so on is excused on the grounds that these subjects are already covered in many excellent books, and that analysis must precede consideration of practical aids.

CHAPTER 12

THE USE OF COMPUTERS

Introduction

In previous chapters we have stressed the importance of fast and accurate reporting to management. This especially concerns information on sales and stock levels since it is the throughput of stock at a given realised price which is the essence of a retail company's activity. The break-down of resale price maintenance, intensified competition and general economic uncertainty only make the need for fast reporting that much more urgent. Many forward-looking retailers have seen that the problems which medium to large-scale retailing poses nowadays can only be solved by the use of computers (either by outright purchase or on a bureau basis) and this is why a trade traditionally backward in administration is now moving right to the forefront of advanced computer applications.

It is obvious that retailing lends itself naturally to computerisation: an immense number of small transactions must be recorded and controlled, and stocks replenished for a great variety of merchandise. All this must be done quickly and accurately if the management are to take profitable decisions on buying and pricing of stock. Little wonder that one of the pioneers of high-speed data-processing was a big catering and retailing chain—J. Lyons & Co. Ltd. Nowadays, however, companies need not be the size of Lyons to justify the use of a computer. Rapid development in electronic techniques and the growth of computer bureaus have brought high-speed data-processing within the reach of a great number of medium-sized retail companies, both departmental and multiple.

In this chapter we try to remove some of the "mystique" which surrounds computers, and show how a medium-size retail organisation can decide: (a) whether its volume and type of business justify a computer; (b) whether it can afford one and (c) how, assuming (a) and (b) are affirmative, it should select the most suitable medium for its data processing.

Evaluating the Data-processing Problem

When does the management of a company become aware that it has a data-processing problem? Not merely when the existing systems start to break down under the pressure of a mounting volume of business, although this may be an indication to management that they should begin to think about new accounting and control methods. A company can still have a data-processing problem even though its present systems and staff are coping adequately with the administrative load. The problem may be that whilst the *quantity* of work may be manageable, the feedback of vital control information, *i.e.* the *quality* of reporting, may be unmanageable, in the sense that it is too late, inadequate or misleading. Most manual systems of stock control, sales analysis, cash control, can be extended to cope with extra routine work almost without limit, simply by employing more staff. Further, purely routine administration can probably be done cheaper manually than by using a computer. Where human beings fail and the computer succeeds is in giving a limited number of key facts *rapidly* from the mass of routine data-processing, which enables the management to modify their trading policy as circumstances demand.

It is important that companies who are considering a computer should understand this point. The attitude should not be "how can I get my stock control, sales analysis or purchase ledger done more quickly" (although these are obviously laudable aims), but rather "how can I be told quickly where my trading policy is going wrong so that I can rectify it quickly." This latter approach will set the computer study off on the right foot, *i.e.* as a *commercial* exercise in profit maximisation, rather than as an *accounting* exercise in improved administration. The computer must pay for itself. The return on the investment will not usually be found in savings on staff and salaries, but in improved reporting and control, which lead to greater profitability.

So the existence of a data-processing problem is made clear in most cases by a managerial need for faster and more comprehensive operating information (commercial as well as financial), rather than by an overburdened administration. For this reason it is not possible to lay down meaningful rules about the number of sales dockets handled daily which justify a computer, or the number of lines stocked, or the number of sales outlets trading. Size itself is a factor, but not the only one, to be considered. For example, it may be more worth while for a medium-sized company trading in fast-moving, highly competitive merchandise to consider a computer, than for a much bigger company trading in a more leisurely business. In a fast-moving, competitive business mistakes of policy are more likely to be reflected in excessive stocks or reduced margins.

This is where the computer should be able to help. Suppose that a company has a stock investment of £1·5m. which equals three months' sales. The management knows that it could do the same volume of turnover on two months' stock, if only it could be told quickly enough how to adapt its trading policy to changing consumer demands. Suppose a computer costing £100,000 is ordered to achieve this objective, and is successful. Stock investment is now £1m., a saving of £500,000. At 8½% p.a. interest, this represents a reduction in running expenses of £42,500 p.a. The computer pays for itself in under two-and-a-half years on faster stock turnover alone, quite apart from any other applications programmed, such as hire-purchase ledger or bought ledger. (This also ignores the substantial capital allowances now available to companies purchasing computers.)

In some trades, where resale price maintenance is breaking down, control of margins may be critical to profitability. Selective price cutting demands a knowledge of the earned margin on all lines if it is to be really profitable. We have mentioned in previous chapters the necessity of keeping book stocks at cost value, rather than retail, where conditions of variable gross profits apply. The drawback to this for many companies carrying a wide range of merchandise is the immense amount of calculation involved. But this is no problem to a computer. The computer will constantly up-date the purchase-price file in its memory from new purchase invoices, and give stock and cost of sales per line at weighted average value, LIFO (last in, first out), FIFO (first in, first out) or any other basis of valuation. This is where the computer is not merely doing the existing job at greater speed, but providing new management control information to keep pace with the rapid developments in modern retailing.

Evaluating the data-processing problem, therefore, requires a critical reappraisal by the management of the information which they are now receiving (and whether it comes in time to be useful) and the information which they think they should have but are not getting. It helps in this reappraisal actually to specify the management's objectives. Fig. 22 is a diagrammatic representation of how a computer can help in achieving management's aims of maximising profitability and return on capital employed. The four primary objectives are, of course, a major preoccupation in any business— indeed they *are* business. But where the achievement of some or all of these objectives is being hindered by slow and cumbersome administration or the absence of appropriate controls, it is time to consider the use of a computer. As the figure shows, a computer can help in all areas of profit-maximisation, and it should be looked at from this point of view: as a piece of capital equipment which will positively increase productivity, just as a fork-lift truck or delivery van will.

Is it possible, then, to lay down *any* rules about the annual turnover or stock investment a company should have before it is worth while considering a computer? In the writer's opinion the answer must be no. Obviously a company with a turnover of less than, say, £2 million p.a. would have a job to justify buying its own installation. I.B.M. have suggested that it is not generally worth while computerising a retail company with an annual turnover of less than about £8 million. But this seems to take too little account of the diversity of retailing problems, as well as of the range of equipment now available to potential users. Every company has its own special requirements and a turnover of much less than £8 million may handsomely repay a computer if a large part of that sales volume is on H.P. Possibly for a stock control and replenishment application alone £8 million may be near the smallest economic turnover level, but one of the aims in computerising must be to obtain, as far as possible, an *integrated* control system, not only stock recording and sales analysis on the computer, but bought ledger, sales ledger, payroll, branch profitability analysis, and so on.

We conclude, therefore, that the size of the company, either in terms of turnover, profits or capital employed, must not be the guiding factor in the data-processing decision. The sole determining criterion must be whether the computer would, by giving faster, more comprehensive and more accurate information, really pay for itself. This is not an easy case to prove because it will involve guesses and estimates and a quite radical approach to administration. But the evidence of both sides must be fully heard before a verdict is reached.

Costing the Computer

In assessing whether a computer would materially improve profitability, obviously some fairly broad generalisations must be made. It may not be possible at this stage to identify the particular computer (its configuration, hardware, software, and so on) which is likely to be most suitable because the problem has not been evaluated in sufficient detail. There is a danger in trying to be too specific at this early stage. To become involved in detailed discussions with manufacturers' representatives before the terms of the data-processing function have been worked out by the company itself may prove to be a costly mistake. Although the manufacturers insist that they are selling a system as much as a computer, it may not be the best system for the company's particular problems. Nor is there a great deal of merit in calling in "computer-consultants" to examine the system and give impartial advice on the type of computer which it demands. Such consultants would spend a lot of extremely expensive time learning the company's business, which the management knows intimately. Moreover, a much better system will eventually be designed if the management itself does the pre-liminary research. Then, when the selected manufacturer puts forward (in many cases unworkable) proposals, the management will be able to argue from a position of strength. There is no reason to suppose that either consultants or computer-representatives can evaluate the data-processing needs of a company better than the informed, intelligent management of that company, at least to the point of being able to give a categorical answer to the question whether or not to have a computer.

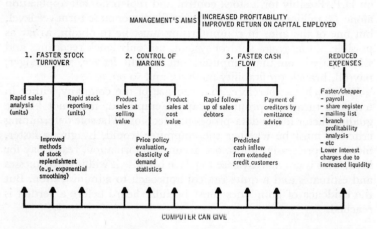

Fig. 22. Diagram to show how a computer would help to achieve the aims of management.

Fig. 22 gives a guide to the way the computer-costing can be started. It should be possible, against each of the four primary objectives, to put a notional financial saving, against which can be set the approximate cost of a suitable computer. Consider this very simplified profit and loss account and balance sheet of a retail company.

	£000	%		£000
Sales	2,400	100·0	Fixed assets	500
Gross profit	720	30·0	Stock	600
Less Salaries	240		Debtors	220
Bank interest	16		Bank overdraft	*Cr.* 200
Other expenses	284	540 22·5	Creditors	*Cr.* 400
Net profit	180	7·5	Net assets	720

Return on net assets 25%   *Net current assets* £220

This company is considering buying a computer with the chief purpose of improving net profit on sales, reducing stocks (which at the moment turn over only four times p.a.) and thus becoming self-financing, rather than dependent on short-term borrowing. Fig. 22 shows how it can put some financial estimate on the four primary benefits which the computer might give. These are outlined below.

1. *Faster Stock Turnover*

It is a proven fact that the better unit control of stock which the computer should give and the faster feedback of information should significantly increase sales. A very substantial amount of turnover is lost to retail companies because the customers' requirements are not in the right branch at the right time. By following branch sales trends closely and providing a rapid liaison between buying and selling departments the computer should be able to capture more of the available market. Let us estimate an increase in sales volume of 3% from £2,400,000 p.a. to £2,472,000. Further, because the buying and selling functions are more closely linked, the actual day-to-day inventory carried should be considerably reduced. Let us say that the computer should enable average stock carried to be turned over six times p.a. instead of four. This will reduce the stock investment from £600,000 to £412,000 (on the estimated sales of £2,472,000).

2. *Better Control of Margins*

By giving unit sales at retail and cost value the computer shows the true gross profit on each item sold. The management can thus see which merchandise is "watering down" the target gross margin and the reasons why this is so: *e.g.* disadvantageous part-exchange transactions, authorised or unauthorised price cutting, buying mistakes. Probably for the first time, the management sees quickly and concisely a full analysis of the trading account by product or product group. With such information available on a regular basis the buying and selling departments can avoid buying mistakes, set better selling prices and make a real improvement in the gross margin. Let us estimate the effect of this tighter control as an increase in the gross profit percentage from 30% to 31%.

3. *Faster Cash Flow*

As well as enabling stock to be turned over more rapidly the computer should be able to improve the cash flow by giving a better control of debtors and creditors. Assuming that the debtors' ledger is put on the computer (which will certainly be worth while if the number of accounts runs into several thousands) overdue accounts can be automatically "chased," by the computer taking over the whole job of issuing reminders and statements. This should materially reduce the average debtor period. Similarly, if the creditors' ledger is computerised, payment will be made to suppliers not on their statements but on remittance advices covering only invoices which the company is prepared to pay. This shifts the onus of establishing the creditor position from the creditor to the company and should result in a longer period of credit being taken. Generally, also, the comprehensive management information provided by the computer should enable cash budgeting to be more accurate. Let us estimate that the computer will reduce average debtors from £220,000 to £200,000 and increase average trade creditors from £400,000 to £420,000.

4. Reduced Expenses

It is unlikely that the computer will reduce overall net expenses p.a. because the savings made will not in most cases more than offset the rental or hire of the machine and the increased salary bill resulting from the recruitment of higher-paid computer personnel. In a hire-purchase application, for example, savings on staff will occur, but the wastage is usually of low paid staff, which will not cover the cost of programmers and systems analysts. But the computer should lead to reduced expenses in *individual* areas of the business. Perhaps the most important of these for many companies is the increased liquidity which results from points (1), (2) and (3) above, so giving significantly reduced interest charges on borrowed money. In the trading account above (p. 178), bank interest is shown at £16,000 p.a., being 8% on the overdraft of £200,000. The effect of the anticipated improvement in sales, margins and stock turnover which the computer should give is to wipe out the overdraft and give a cash surplus, thus eliminating bank interest. Also, in the example we are considering, salaries (apart from those which relate to the computer itself) are estimated to decrease by £8,000 due to putting the payroll, share register, mailing list and branch profitability analysis on the computer.

5. Overall Result

The total effect of points (1) to (4) on the trading account and balance sheet described above can now be shown. (In the cash flow, which gives the bank balance shown below, capital expenditure is estimated at £50,000 and is offset by a like amount of depreciation, thus leaving fixed assets unchanged at £500,000. Tax is estimated at £88,000.) The annual cost of the computer, including computer personnel, is estimated at £30,000, which is a reasonable approximation for the configuration required:

	£000	%		£000
Sales	2,472	100·0	Fixed assets	500
Gross profit	766	31·0	Stock	412
Less Salaries	232		Debtors	200
Other expenses	284		Bank	160
Computer	30	546	22·1	Creditors	*Cr.* 420
Net profit		220	8·9	Net assets	852

Return on net assets   25·8%   *Net current assets £352*

Thus, net profit before tax increases from £180,000 to £220,000, net current assets from £220,000 to £352,000, and return on net assets is maintained. It is not suggested that such a transformation would happen in a single year. American experience suggests that the initial reaction to the computer may be for stocks to rise with the better customer service provided. But as the experience gained is applied, the increased sales volume will overtake the stock increase and so give a faster stock turnover. It will be noted in this example how comparatively modest are the expectations made individually of the computer. It is the *total* effect of the tighter controls and faster feedback of information which is so impressive.

The approximate costings, therefore, show that the computer seems to be a very worth-while proposition, if it does in fact produce the planned increase in productivity. On this point much will depend on the attitude of the company's directors and senior managers towards the computer. It will have been noted in the discussions above that practically every aspect of the business is affected by the new method of data-processing: sales, buying, stock policy, finance, payroll, branch profitability, etc. In some cases jobs will change as the computer takes over routine output of statistics and control data. In nearly all cases staff will have to adapt themselves to new paper-work, reports, systems and time-tables, which may not be easy in established companies. Provided, however, that both management and staff clearly understand that the computer only removes much of the drudgery from the daily round, and still leaves the job of *managing* in the hands of people, much heartache will be avoided.

Obviously a critical factor in the costings is the estimate of £30,000 for the computer and the necessary personnel. How wrong is this initial estimate likely to be? The answer is that if a properly constituted working party is set up in the company to study the computer project, it should be able to obtain from manufacturers a good guide to the size of the installation likely to be required, and the necessary programmers and systems analysts. As wide a variety

G*

of opinion as possible should be canvassed, either discreetly or by open tender, provided that no commitment is entered into whilst the project is under discussion.

If, when the costings have been fully evaluated, it seems that the computer is only marginally profitable, the chances are that the management are considering electronic data-processing (E.D.P.) too early in the company's life. More often than not the anticipated savings of the computer are greater than those actually realised, and in a marginal decision it is only prudent to decide against a heavy capital purchase, which if unsuccessful, might set the company back some years. It is hardly necessary to say that the very worst reason for buying a computer is for prestige purposes, although this has been known.

In cases where the purchase of an entire installation seems unjustified it may still be worth while considering E.D.P. in a more limited way, i.e. on a bureau basis. This is particularly likely to appeal to a great number of medium-sized retail companies, so we now consider this method of using E.D.P. in more detail.

Using a Computer Bureau

A computer bureau is a computer centre to which companies and other organisations send input (punched cards or paper tape prepared by the companies themselves) which is then processed at the bureau and sent back to the companies in the form of output: reports, statements, analysis. It may be as well to show diagrammatically the basic units of a computer and these are given in Fig. 23.

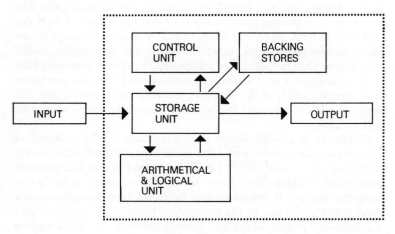

Fig. 23. Basic units of a computer.

The input medium will usually be a punched document of some sort, either card, tape, or tag, or possibly magnetic ink characters, as on cheques. Preparation of this input is effected on appropriate card or tape punches from the basic documents (invoices, sales dockets) and the cards or tapes are then "read" into the storage unit on input devices. The computer performs the necessary calculations by making use of the control unit and arithmetical and logical unit. Output is produced in the form of tabulations, reports, analyses, by the line printer. The main memory of the computer (storage unit) will usually be "backed up" by backing stores in the form of magnetic tape or discs, holding the information which it is not necessary to retain in the main memory.

In the figure above the area inside the dotted line shows the computer equipment which the bureau requires to carry out its data-processing function. In other words, the only physical equipment which the company must have to obtain the services of a bureau is input devices, normally either card or tape punching machines. This means that a company can begin electronic data-processing with a relatively small capital investment, the bureau having the responsibility of housing, maintaining and financing most of the expensive electronic and electro-mechanical equipment. We may summarise the advantages of using a computer bureau as follows:

1. The capital outlay is comparatively modest.

2. The running costs are not excessive in relation to the savings to the company which should accrue.

3. The space required to house the input machines and associated equipment is small.

4. The company can gain valuable experience in E.D.P. without a large capital commitment.

5. When the company's data-processing needs justify the acquisition of a complete installation, the staff will be familiar with E.D.P., and the systems will have been adapted to computer operation.

6. Using a bureau enables a company to have the advantages of E.D.P. whilst it waits for the particular computer most suitable to its needs to be developed and tested.

Practically every commercial and industrial application of computers is catered for by one bureau or another, although proximity is obviously an important factor when selecting the bureau. Care must be taken also to ensure that the computer which the bureau uses is suitable for the particular application which the company has in mind. This will necessitate at least one senior member of the company (the one who will be the data-processing manager, for preference) becoming a real computer expert, such that he will not be misled by the technical jargon of computer people.

Many of the bureaus are run by the computer manufacturers and it is clearly advantageous to use the bureau whose company will eventually supply the machine, assuming that the transition to ownership will eventually be made. Having E.D.P., whether by purchasing a computer or using a bureau, is not simply obtaining the appropriate equipment. It is also a question of forming a relationship with the staff of the computer manufacturer which will be mutually profitable to both parties. Personal contact and mutual evaluation of problems play a bigger part in E.D.P. than in any other commercial transaction. The manufacturer stands to gain as much from helping a customer solve a complex E.D.P. problem as the customer himself, because in this way the manufacturer adds to his "software" programmes, which may have an application to numerous other companies. The larger manufacturers are obliged to carry a number of specialist staff, experts in operational research, statistics, O. & M., or production control, for example, and it behoves a company thinking about E.D.P. to take advantage of this free quasi-consultancy service. Therefore if a company is considering initially a limited application of E.D.P. (say payroll) but with a much more comprehensive system in mind (say additionally stock control, hire-purchase, and bought ledger), it should select the bureau whose parent organisation will later supply the computer, thereby creating extremely valuable goodwill and orientation towards the particular approach to E.D.P. which the manufacturer takes.

In May 1968 there were over a hundred computer bureaus in use commercially, of which about sixty were in London and the South. Since then the number has undoubtedly grown to meet the demand for this service, and a potential user should have little difficulty in finding a suitable bureau. A growing trade is being established in sharing of computers, where a company with its own installation will take up its excess capacity of computer time by hiring it out on a bureau basis to companies in the vicinity. This further widens the field for potential users of E.D.P.

There is at the moment no set scale of charges common to all bureaus. Some bureaus charge on the basis of lines of input and output processed, or a combination of both. Most contracts are the subject of individual negotiation, but whatever basis is used the company should be able to work out reasonably accurately the approximate annual cost, against which can be set the estimated savings which E.D.P. should bring. Most bureaus charge for reprogramming a customer's job if modifications are necessary (this is not surprising in view of the high salaries demanded by programmers), so these should be kept to a minimum by ensuring, as far as possible, that all contingencies have been foreseen. The cost of the initial programming is also usually charged to the customer, but at a less expensive rate than for reprogramming. It is not easy to give examples of actual costs charged since the bureaus are naturally chary of revealing the terms of individual contracts. A stock replenishment and sales analysis application known to the writer, which gives comprehensive output data for some 500 lines, costs about £10,000 p.a. This should not be taken in any sense as a guide, however, since every company has its own particular problems, which will affect the basis of charge. As stated before, the yardstick to measure the bureau's cost by is not another bureau's charge for a similar application (because no two applications are similar) but how much the expected savings exceed this cost.

Adapting the Systems to Electronic Data Processing

So far we have discussed the evaluation of the data-processing problem, the approach to costing the computer, and the advantages of using a bureau for a limited application. We must now assume that the decision to have E.D.P. has been taken, either by purchase of a complete installation or by use of a computer bureau. In both cases the existing administrative systems will almost certainly have to be altered if the transition to E.D.P. is to be successful, and we consider below the points which should be borne in mind when making the conversion.

If the question is asked: "Why alter the systems at all? Why not get the computer to do exactly what is done manually at the moment?" the answer is twofold. Firstly, the present systems are probably not even best as a manual operation and can be improved on in a number of ways. Secondly, it is a paradox of E.D.P. that the jobs which take a human being so long to do can be done in seconds by a computer, and the jobs which can be done quickly and easily by human beings cannot be done at all by computers, except at prohibitive expense.

On the first point, the introduction of E.D.P. will require a thoroughgoing analysis of all systems in use simply to determine how best to convert them to E.D.P. This analysis will take the form of flow-charts, showing the movement of paper-work through each department, assessment of document volumes, both present and planned, form design, and so on. In this review anomalies, duplications of effort, inessential processes, and other deficiencies will come to light, and can be reviewed before the conversion to E.D.P. gets under way. Sometimes the systems review is not done until the computer manufacturer's staff are actually on site preparing the feasibility study, but, as explained earlier, this is undesirable because it puts the company on the defensive, unable to examine critically enough the implications of the feasibility study. The systems review should be done as part of the process of deciding whether to have E.D.P. and before inviting comment from the manufacturer or bureau.

On the second point, the paradox of E.D.P. is that whilst it is incredibly fast in operation it is also incredibly inflexible. Human beings are by comparison extremely slow yet extremely versatile. A digital computer (one for commercial use) operates simply on the principle of an electric current either flowing or not flowing. Therefore, in a complex process every step has to be painstakingly reduced to a "yes/no" decision. All calculation must be done in binary arithmetic, *i.e.* in a number system using only zero and one. This massively cumbersome approach to clerical operations is only justified by the immense speed of computation, measured in thousands of millionths of a second. So a compromise is struck (an extremely valuable one for business and science) that in return for the speed of calculation and decision of computers we will accept their rigidity, enforced by the process of reducing every step to a two-state condition.

By contrast, a manual system, operated by *people*, can be amended and modified more or less at will. Human beings can adapt themselves in minutes to a new system. But once the computer has been "programmed" to do a job in a certain way (the process of breaking down every step into "yes/no" decisions) that is the way it will do it—albeit at great speed. Change to the system is only possible by reprogramming, and this can be very costly if the alteration is extensive. Computer manufacturers, aware of these limitations, are constantly searching for ways of making computers more flexible: *e.g.* packaged software programmes which can be plugged into the system for special jobs, sub-routines, high-level computer languages which make programming faster and easier. But it is still generally true that computers introduce a rigidity into a system which is not there as a manual operation.

The system which will eventually be used should, therefore, be very carefully thought out. This process of evaluation and alteration will be in three stages. First, the whole system will be reviewed at the time when the decision to have E.D.P. is taken, this review usually being the prime causal factor in making the decision. A second review will be made by the computer or bureau representatives when they make their feasibility study, in which the limitations of cost and computer technology will be taken into account. Third, the (necessarily) outline proposals of the feasibility study will be examined in minute detail by the systems analyst when he comes to write his specification for the programmers. It is likely that at each stage the system will be modified. But at the end of the third stage the specification will be "frozen." Unless time and money are to be wasted, alteration after this point is impossible.

As we have already said, the force which usually motivates the introduction of E.D.P. in a company is absence of sufficient information (at the right time) for effective control. This being the case, it is most important when reviewing the system to ensure that the computer (or bureau) gives that information. It is also important not to go to the other extreme, where so much information is churned out that the wood cannot be seen for the trees. How the right quantity and quality of output can be determined may be seen from an application of E.D.P. to stock control, described in the next chapter.

Summary

The retail trade lends itself to the use of computers because of its high volume of small transactions, which must be individually costed and controlled. Evaluating the data-processing problem requires a complete reappraisal of existing systems and information-flows by the company's own management team, rather than by computer experts or consultants. Size of company is no real criterion for computerisation, only better control and hence profitability.

These benefits should be costed in as much detail as possible, with particular regard to faster stock turnover, better control of margins, improved cash flow and reduced running expenses. Only if a significant increase in efficiency can be confidently anticipated should the large capital outlay of a computer be risked.

For smaller companies or for limited applications computer bureaus can offer many advantages over outright purchase: capital outlay is modest, running costs are not excessive, the space required is small, and experience is gained in E.D.P. which will be most helpful when full computerisation takes place.

Using a computer will necessitate adaptation of systems because of the much greater speed but relative inflexibility of E.D.P. Management at all levels should be fully consulted so that document volumes and changes in procedures can be assessed before the systems specification is finally "frozen."

CHAPTER 13

STOCK CONTROL BY ELECTRONIC
DATA PROCESSING

Introduction

Stock control is by far the most common application of E.D.P. in retail companies. This is not surprising when we consider that retailing is essentially only the purchase of a wide range of merchandise for resale to a widely dispersed population—at least for multiple retailing. For department store retailing the emphasis is shifted: the range of merchandise is wider but the point of sale is more concentrated. In both cases the aim is to obtain as big a turnover as possible from the most economic inventory level. How does E.D.P. help to attain this ideal situation?

Briefly, the computer should tell the management three things:

1. The current stock level per line at each location.
2. What to buy to maintain turnover.
3. What to sell quickly in order not to let stocks accumulate.

Coding

A prerequisite to giving this information is clear and unequivocal identification of each line stocked, *i.e.* coding of merchandise. This is a somewhat tedious operation but it is absolutely vital if the computer is to be successful. A systematic approach is to divide merchandise into major groups, then into sub-groups if necessary, and then to allocate a unique number to each line within sub-group. All the time the present and planned volumes must be borne in mind. For example, in a mail-order house the major selling departments would have the first two digits, the groups of merchandise within each department the second two, and each line in each sub-group the next three or four depending on the number of lines stocked:

Selling department	Sub-group	Item number	Total code
01	01	001	0101001
Camping equipment	Tents	Size, colour, etc.	
27	35	317	2735317
Photographic equipment	Binoculars	Make, type, etc.	

This is a seven-figure code number based on the assumptions that there will never be less than 10 nor more than 99 selling departments and sub-groups within departments, and never more than 999 lines within a sub-group. The company's expansion and diversification plans should be carefully considered before these limitations are accepted. A point of computer practice is that code numbers consisting of a series of similar numbers should be avoided, since a useful check on accuracy of documentation (known as "check-digit verification") may fail in these circumstances. Thus it is possible to have code numbers such as 0000000 or 2222222, but these should not be used. Obviously, code numbers should be as short as possible, not only for speed of input but also so as not to take up expensive room in the computer memory.

Having coded all existing merchandise (or having made a firm and defensible decision not to include certain stocks on the computer, *e.g.* extremely low value items) the next step is to code stock movements. Already by this time a very considerable amount of systems analysis will have been carried out, in the forms of detailed flow-charts showing the movement of paper-work between departments. There should be no excuse for a "new" form of inward or outward booking coming to light, for which provision has not been made. The management will want to know the weekly or monthly (possibly even daily) movement of stock for each major group or sub-group. If these are more than 10 and less than 99 individual movements a two-digit code can be used as follows:

Movement code	Movement	Quantity
00	Opening stock	1,572
01	Purchases	370
02	Purchase returns	−55
03	Part exchange purchases	37
04	Transfers in	15
	Total in	367
10	Sales	412
11	Sales returns	−43
12	Transfers out	27
13	Free replacements	56
14	Stock written off	13
	Total out	465
00	*Closing stock*	1,474

Sometimes this tabulation of stock movement is printed across the paper instead of downwards. At the end of each month (or four-weekly period if a thirteen-period calendar is used) there should be a full print-out of stock movement per line and per branch under the above movement codes. This will be used mainly for stock checking purposes so that the stock auditors can trace all movements through the inward and outward codes and thus reconcile actual with computer stock at each location. The actual stock *balances* (and sales, possibly) may be tabulated per line daily for buying and other purposes, but not usually the whole stock movement of each line.

Having coded stock items and stock movements and settled on the frequency of print-out for management reporting, the rudiments of a stock control system are available. The computer can be programmed to calculate rate of stock turn per line and signal lines that are turning over less than a given number of times per year. It can also signal lines whose stocks are below the re-order level. These "exception reports" can be printed out daily or weekly and give the buying and sales management very valuable control information, which will almost certainly be an improvement on the quality of reporting which previously existed.

Before considering further the input media and computer configuration required for reporting, two more general matters of principle must be resolved. These are the method of stock replenishment to be used and stock valuation.

Stock Replenishment Methods

Much of the inefficiency of retail companies is due to the fact that trying to ensure that each branch has the required amount of the right merchandise presents an enormous physical task. In a sizeable retail company which operates a manual stock control system there are bound to be numerous occasions when some branches are out of stock and others are overstocked, and also occasions when the buying department has failed to keep in touch with selling trends and the company as a whole is understocked. If the computer can help to make more efficient the buying and distribution of stock a very significant increase in profitability may be realised.

There are many techniques in use nowadays for stock replenishment by computer. Some are simple and some extremely complex. Space does not, however, allow us to consider them all in detail, so we must restrict ourselves to a brief review of one of the most popular techniques, which will serve to illustrate the principles which underly them all. This method is known as *exponential smoothing*, a rather awesome title for what is essentially a simple procedure. Briefly, exponential smoothing says that when we are determining what stock to buy for the company as a whole, or for distribution to individual branches, we should weight our estimate by the more recent sales experience, and take less account of earlier experience. This is reasonable since the recent past is more in touch with the present than the distant past. In fact, exponential smoothing simulates the process of calculating moving averages, the smaller the weight used the shorter the moving average simulated. In Chapter 2 we saw how moving averages can be used to smooth out random fluctuations in demand and give a more reliable basis for sales forecasting. The seasonal variation can also be allowed for by taking a moving average which covers the period of the cycle. Thus we should budget for higher sales at Christmas and other Bank holidays, and ensure that stocks are built up in the selling outlets to meet this increased demand.

From the computer point of view exponential smoothing has a particular advantage over moving averages as a means of calculating stock replenishment figures. Moving averages require a considerable amount of storage space in the computer memory: a twelve-month average requires twelve figures. When the number of lines stocked runs into several thousand it will be appreciated how much memory space can be taken up for stock replenishment alone. Exponential smoothing requires only three figures for each line stocked to produce the forecast for the next period: the sales for the current period, the forecast previously made for the current period and the weighting factor. Thus it is far more economic in terms of computer storage and therefore in terms of cost.

The determination of the weights to be used and the precise application of the method to a particular company will require a considerable amount of statistical sophistication. Professional advice from the computer manufacturer or bureau should be sought and, if possible, a "model" should be constructed of the replenishment system so that it can be tested and modified before being programmed. It may be found after all that the company's particular problems simply do not allow for any semi-automatic system of stock replenishment to be effectively used. But, on the other hand, it may turn out that the computer forecasts are very much better (give a higher stock turnover for the same average inventory level) than those made manually or by "intuition," in which case a real increase in productivity will have been achieved.

Stock Valuation

So far we have considered stock control in unit terms only. But to install a computer system to give unit control without at the same time providing financial information is obviously uneconomic. As much financial accounting as possible should be carried out on the computer. A carefully designed system will provide both commercial and financial management with the bulk of the routine control information.

On going over to E.D.P. the opportunity should be taken to value stocks at cost rather than retail price. The latter is the traditional method of book-keeping in retail companies, but, as stated before, where variable gross margins apply, either as a result of different mark-ups or selective price cutting, stock valuation at purchase cost price is the only way of determining the true margin earned on each line sold.

The method generally used to value stocks at cost is to open up a purchase-price file in the computer memory, containing the purchase price of each line stocked. Then, as fresh deliveries are made into stock the purchase price file is up-dated by the new invoice price. Thus, to take a simple example, if 1,000 units of a new line are delivered into stock in period 1 at a purchase price of £1 each, stock value at the end of period 1 will be £1,000. In period 2 if 300 more units are bought at a purchase price of £1 1s. 0d. and 500 are sold, the value of sales and closing stock in period 2 *at cost* will be calculated as follows:

$$1,000 \text{ units at } £1 \text{ } 0s. \text{ } 0d. \text{ each} = £1,000$$
$$300 \text{ units at } £1 \text{ } 1s. \text{ } 0d. \text{ each} = £ \text{ } 315$$

$$1,300 \text{ units} \qquad £1,315$$
$$\text{Average cost} = \frac{£1,315}{1,300} = £1 \text{ } 0s. \text{ } 3d. \text{ approx.}$$

The stock movement for period 2 will therefore be:

	Opening stock	Purchases	Sales	Closing stock
Units	1,000	300	500	800
Cost price	£1 0s. 0d.	£1 1s. 0d.	£1 0s. 3d.	£1 0s. 3d.
Cost value	£1,000	£315	£506	£809

This is known as weighted average cost value of stock, because the cost price used to value stock is being successively weighted by the size and purchase price of each new delivery.

A good deal of calculation is involved if purchase prices fluctuate considerably but this is no problem to the computer. Of all the methods of stock valuation the weighted average seems most suitable for retail companies, because the fast rate of stock turnover inherent in retailing means that stock values will respond quickly to changes in purchase price and thus show management the correct earned margin on sales. Furthermore, the weighted average method is quite acceptable to the tax authorities. It is not proposed to discuss the other bases of stock valuation, such as FIFO (first in, first out) or LIFO (last in, first out), since they tend to distort margins in times of rapidly rising or falling prices, and are for this reason generally unacceptable to the inland revenue.

By building into the computer system the basis of stock valuation, financial control is provided as well as unit control. Table XLVI shows the type of tabulation which the computer can print out for management information. The two lines of figures represent the stock movement in quantities and at cost value for a single merchandise group. Movement codes are shown across the top. It will be seen that opening stock and transfers in are valued at £3 per unit, purchases and purchase returns at £4, and part-exchange purchases at £3 10s. 0d. This gives a weighted average cost price of £3 3s. 5d. which is used to value all outward movements and closing stock. Net selling price per unit is £4 10s. 0d. (*i.e.* a 50% mark-up on the original cost price of £3 0s. 0d.) which gives an earned margin of 29·6%. This compares with a target margin for the group of 30%. In the absence of any other adjustments the column totals for all merchandise groups can be used to make up the company's trading account and balance sheet.

It will be appreciated that the volume of print-out would be very considerable if stock movement *per line* both in units and value were tabulated, say, weekly, for a company with several thousand lines. It would be very expensive (especially on a bureau basis) and would have the great danger that it would not be looked at. On the other hand information about particular lines is obviously extremely relevant. This problem can often be solved by extending the technique of exception reporting to stock control. Thus the computer could be programmed to print out data on lines whose margins were, say, one point or more below target, or whose rates of stock turnover were below a predetermined desirable level. In this way, the management would be given a *manageable* report, highlighting areas which require attention and ignoring those which are under control. This, however, presupposes a fairly sophisticated budgetary control system.

The summary tabulations must necessarily be produced in full for overall statistical and financial control, and regular reports must be produced in full for buying and stock distribution purposes. But, as a principle, only data which require action should be printed out, and programming should as far as possible achieve this objective.

Input Media and Computer Configuration

Having determined the range of the stock control system it is then possible to particularise on the most appropriate input medium and the size and power of the actual computer. Deciding what the computer should do largely defines the amount and frequency of output. We can then work backwards to input to find the best way of providing that output.

TABLE XLVI. COMPUTER TABULATION SHOWING STOCK MOVEMENTS IN UNITS AND AT WEIGHTED AVERAGE COST VALUE, GIVING TRUE EARNED MARGIN

1	2	3	4	5	6	7	8	9	10	11	12	13	14	15	16	17	18	19	20
Merch-andise group	Move-ment code→	Open-ing stock	Pur-chases	Pur-chase returns	Part-ex-change pur-chases	Trans-fers in	Total in	Sales at cost	Sales returns	Net sales	Trans-fers out	Free re-place-ments	Write-offs	Total out	Clos-stock	Sales at retail	Gross profit *	Actual G.P. %	Target G.P. %
		00	01	02	03	04		10	11	10–11	12	13	14		00	10–11			
A Units		1,572	370	55 Cr.	37	15	367	412	43 Cr.	369	27	56	13	465	1·474	—	—	29·6	30·0
£		4,716	1,480	220 Cr.	129	45	1,434	1,306	136 Cr.	1,170	86	177	41	1,474	4,676	1,662	492		
B Units																			
£																			
Total Units																			
£																			

* Col. 17 less col. 11

The choice of input medium will depend on a number of factors. For companies who are already established in E.D.P. and using punched cards there may be much to recommend continuing with that form of input. Punched cards have the great advantage that they can be checked on the verifier before being fed into the computer, thus ensuring error-free input. For companies, however, who are entering E.D.P. for the first time (the great majority) more recently developed forms of input will probably be used.

The determining factors will be the type of trade which the company is engaged in and the content of output required. Many companies in fast-moving, competitive trades (those allied to fashion, for example) want such rapid input, processing and reporting that only virtually instantaneous input at the moment of sale will suffice. For them cardboard tags (Kimball tags, for example) with holes punched to denote the type, style, colour of the item may be the most appropriate form of input. As the item is sold the tag (which is attached to it) is taken off the item and stacked in a container ready for immediate input to the computer. The speed of input is high because the punching operation is already completed at the point of sale, but the disadvantages are that tags may get mislaid (a sale thereby never being recorded) or torn or bent, in which case the reader may jam.

As an alternative to tags optical character recognition (O.C.R.) may be used. This is where the "tally" roll of a cash register machine is printed (as the girl strikes the keys) with characters which can be read by the computer, with no intermediate processing. The tally roll is taken off the cash register at the end of the day and fed straight into the computer.

Both tags and O.C.R. rolls have the disadvantage that the amount of information which can be stored in them is relatively small. The extent of product coding is thus restricted, as well as the amount of data on prices, discounts, and so on. No customer information, of course, can be recorded. So this method of input is limited to very fast-moving, low-value merchandise, sold at a strictly controlled price. The management information required is essentially only rate of stock turnover per line.

For more complex retailing functions where, for example, sales dockets, part-exchange purchase notes and returned approval notes are used, the most common input medium is punched paper tape. All the relevant information can be picked up from any type of documentation, so that output in the form of management reports can be as extensive as required. Paper tape is ideally suited to bureau operations because it is compact and easily transportable. Its speed of input into the computer is also faster than that of punched cards. But it has the disadvantage that checking of input data is not possible, so resort must be made to a fairly elaborate system of check totals, check digit verification, parity checks, and so on. It need not be stressed how vitally important it is to the success of the computer that input is as far as conceivably possible correct.

The computer configuration, *i.e.* the size of memory and number of peripheral units, will depend on the factors which have been considered above: the number of lines stocked, the volume of data handled, the complexity of input and output, the amount of computation required for control reports, the frequency of output, and many more factors. It is not proposed to go into the question of memory storage capacity, size of backing stores, use of buffered or unbuffered line printers, and similar matters, because these are largely technical points which must be resolved in terms of the manufacturer's specification and the company's E.D.P. capital budget. As a general and obvious principle it can be stated that the smaller the configuration the less costly will the computer be but the more restricted will be the potential of the system as a whole.

This point can be exemplified by considering random and sequential access to the computer. When magnetic tapes or discs are used to hold stock balances, finding the balance for any one particular item means that the disc or tape "read head" must search through all balances sequentially until it finds the one required. The time taken to do this is known as "access time," and can be considerable if the item required is right at the extremity of the tape or disc. Therefore, companies which must have the facility of knowing the stock balance of any item on demand must have "random access," the ability to interrogate file storage instantaneously. However, random access devices are more expensive than sequential methods, and the company must decide what loss of efficiency might occur if sequential access is used and stock balances are printed out in total, say, daily, or on some exception principle, to give commercial management the information it requires. This delay time must be set against the extra capital cost of random access and a cost-based decision arrived at.

The complexity and size of the system will also determine the number and skill of the programming staff. But, here again, the company must be very much guided by the manufacturer's recommendations. Some expense in programming may be saved by using "pre-packaged" programmes for certain standard routines. These "software" aids, as they are usually called, not only save programming time but have the additional advantage that they have been fully tested for internal accuracy and logic. An important step in the initial discussions with manufacturers is the available range of relevant software devices.

Summary

Stock replenishment and control are the most common applications of E.D.P. in the retail trade; they offer the biggest scope for improved profitability.

Of the greatest importance in computerised stock control is an informative coding system both for items stocked and for inward and outward bookings. Time spent on this work will be well repaid in the quality of output for management.

Fast stock replenishment from the central warehouse to outlets is the chief aim of E.D.P. Methods vary from the simple to the extremely complex, *viz.* sophisticated exponential smoothing. Here again, much thought must be given to this problem, since so much depends on the solution arrived at. If possible a "model" should be built of the system and the replenishment method tested.

Where possible, financial stock control should be linked to unit control, so that both commercial and financial management enjoy the benefits of E.D.P. Exception reports should be produced rather than an immense volume of paper which management has neither the time nor the inclination to read.

Input media and the computer configuration will be largely determined by the nature of the company's business and the size of the capital budget available. Here it must be borne in mind that the computer must pay for itself, *i.e.* show an increase in profitability over and above the annual running costs. Programming costs can be reduced by using manufacturers' pre-packaged routines for special purposes and these considerations will influence the choice of machine.

CHAPTER 14

CONCLUSION

This book has been concerned to show how techniques of control can be used to increase profitability. It may be worth while summarising the main conclusions arrived at.

First, having control implies having a reasonably good idea of what the future is likely to bring. This is easier to achieve than might appear possible at first sight. Fortunately, business transactions do not generally have too erratic a pattern, and by eliminating random variations and so discovering trends, the future can be predicted accurately enough to enable rational decisions to be made. Sales forecasting is therefore of paramount importance in achieving and maintaining control.

Second, control implies analysis. To control a business necessitates understanding how each part of the profit-earning organism reacts on the others and how the business as a whole affects and is affected by external influences. This requires analysis in depth of margins, merchandise groups, expense categories, rates of stock turnover, speed of cash flow and so on. And not only must management know *where* to look to check falling profitability (or to improve further increasing profitability) but it must also be able to look *in time* to take corrective action. Analysed trading results must therefore be produced quickly, succinctly and accurately. Hence, the rapid computer developments in retailing which are now taking place.

Third, control presupposes a sustained campaign for higher efficiency, *i.e.* optimal use of available resources, in the current jargon. A degree of control is of course exercised if actual results conform to a budget, but this means little unless the budget is based on efficient standards. Budgeting must therefore contain task-setting elements to ensure that systems and methods are efficient and that labour is employed as productively as possible. That is why a large part of this book concentrates on techniques of reducing costs in the major expense categories: distribution, staff and administration.

Control therefore contains prediction, analysis and a continuous review of performance. (It doubtless implies other attributes too, such as human and behavioural qualities: leadership, tenacity, capacity for hard work, and so on. These, however, fall outside the scope of this book and must in any event be assumed in dynamic business management.) Control in this sense, of course, applies to all types of business. What are the special problems of control in retail companies?

At least three aspects of control must be emphasised for retailers trading in today's conditions. First is the absolute necessity of controlling the gross margin. Although, with the break-down of R.P.M., retailers are on equal terms with manufacturers in so far as they can set their own prices, the inherently more competitive nature of retailing means that its margins will always be under a downward pressure, whereas this is not necessarily true for manufacturing. The retailer can certainly share in manufacturers' lower unit costs which result from increasing production, but to do this he must increase his own sales volume, which will almost certainly necessitate a price cut and probably require more capital tied up in stock and in an enlarged sales area. The concept of elasticity of demand is therefore fundamental to retailing: precisely what extra volume of sales can be expected from a given reduction in price. Trial and error will alone give a measure, but each experiment must be rigidly controlled.

Closely linked with margins is the recovery of expenses so that *net* profit is increased. If the break-down of R.P.M. gives flexibility to price policy, it also makes that much more urgent the tight control of expenses and the installation of an accounting system which ensures that selling prices recover all departmental and central expenses and yield an acceptable net return on capital invested. Marginal costing methods can profitably be employed to achieve these aims for short-term trading policies, but in the long term price policy must be based on the full absorption of both fixed and variable costs. Fully developed budgetary control will be of inestimable value in deriving a profitable yet flexible price policy.

The third aspect of control which must be particularly stressed for retail companies is capital investment appraisal and cash flow. Traditionally unaccustomed to much sophistication in this field, the retail trade now finds capital expenditure evaluation of the utmost importance. The crumbling of R.P.M., higher overheads, S.E.T., the move towards bigger units and self-service, all these mean that the justification for heavy capital outlay must be scientifically based, and the area of doubt reduced to a minimum. Techniques such as discounted cash flow should be used to assess competing investment possibilities. Apart from long-range financial planning, the nature of retailing demands that close attention is given to the day-to-day cash position: stocks must be moved quickly to pay for incoming merchandise, bills payable must be met, tax and dividend payments made. A detailed short-period cash forecast is therefore essential.

Finally, apart from techniques, there is the question of the attitude taken to budgetary control. It is very easy for forecasting and budgeting to become just an accountancy exercise which gives the management some feeling of security but in which they play no active part at all. This is a situation which must be strenuously avoided. If budgeting is to make a real contribution to profitability (and there can be no other reason for its existence) it must have the full and active participation of management at all levels. The marketing and commercial directors must at least approve the sales forecast even if they do not actually initiate it. Likewise, the Board generally should understand and approve the financial implications of the budget as a whole. Further down the line, departmental managers should be set realistic but task-setting budgets for capital and revenue expenditure, and top management should call them to account for deviations from the estimates.

There is no need for this attitude to "formalise" the running of the company unnecessarily. The writer has deliberately avoided drawing up an ideal management "tree," which purports to show where the financial/budget controller fits into the management structure, to whom he reports and who are responsible to him. There is much to be said for informality in business, where initiative and enthusiasm are not choked by the weight of the hierarchy. No conflict should exist between effective budgetary control and flexible, informal management. It will be found that the most successful companies are precisely those where the reins of management are held lightly and firmly, but with a complete control over direction.

INDEX

Figures in italics indicate page nos. of illustrations